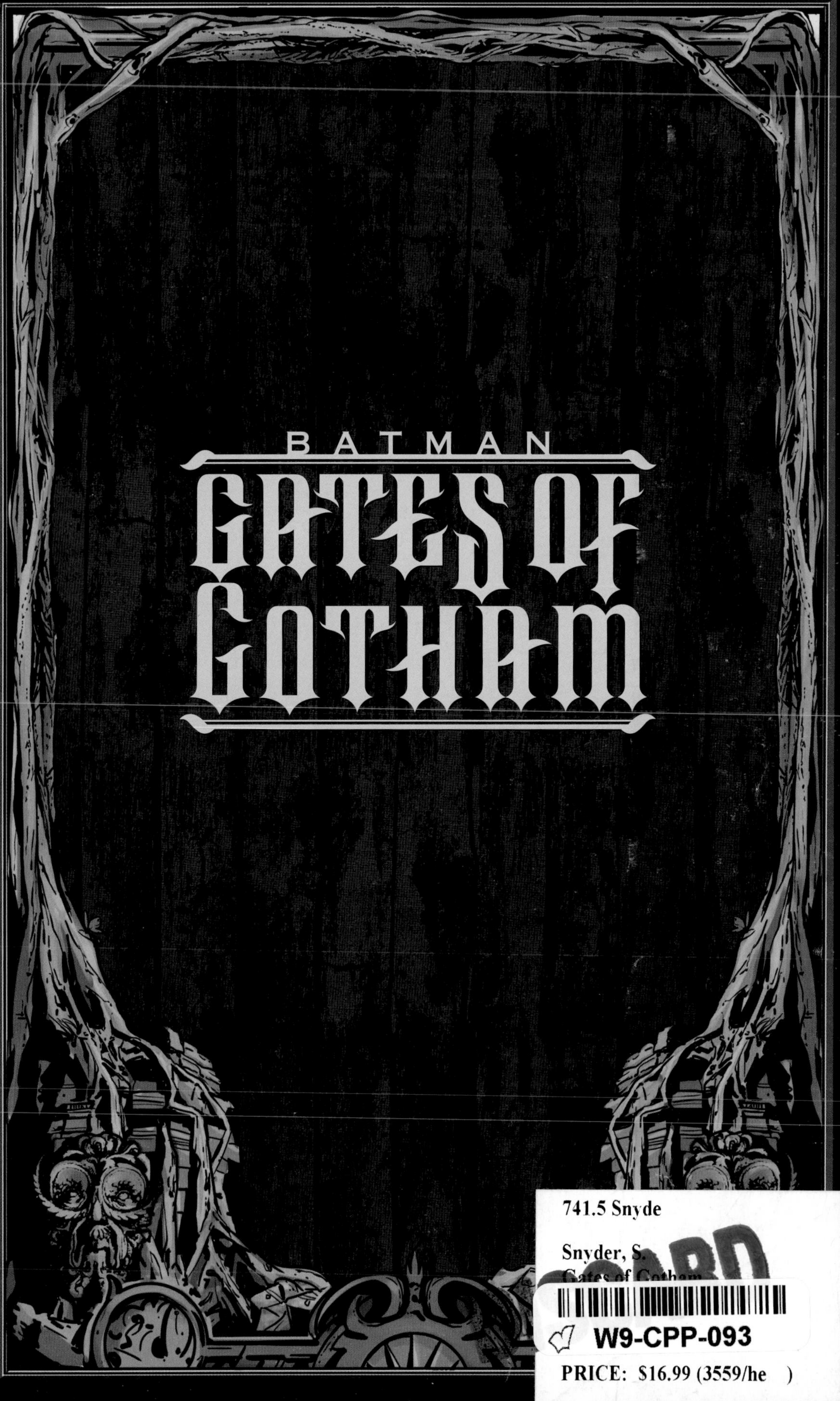
BATMAN
GATES OF GOTHAM

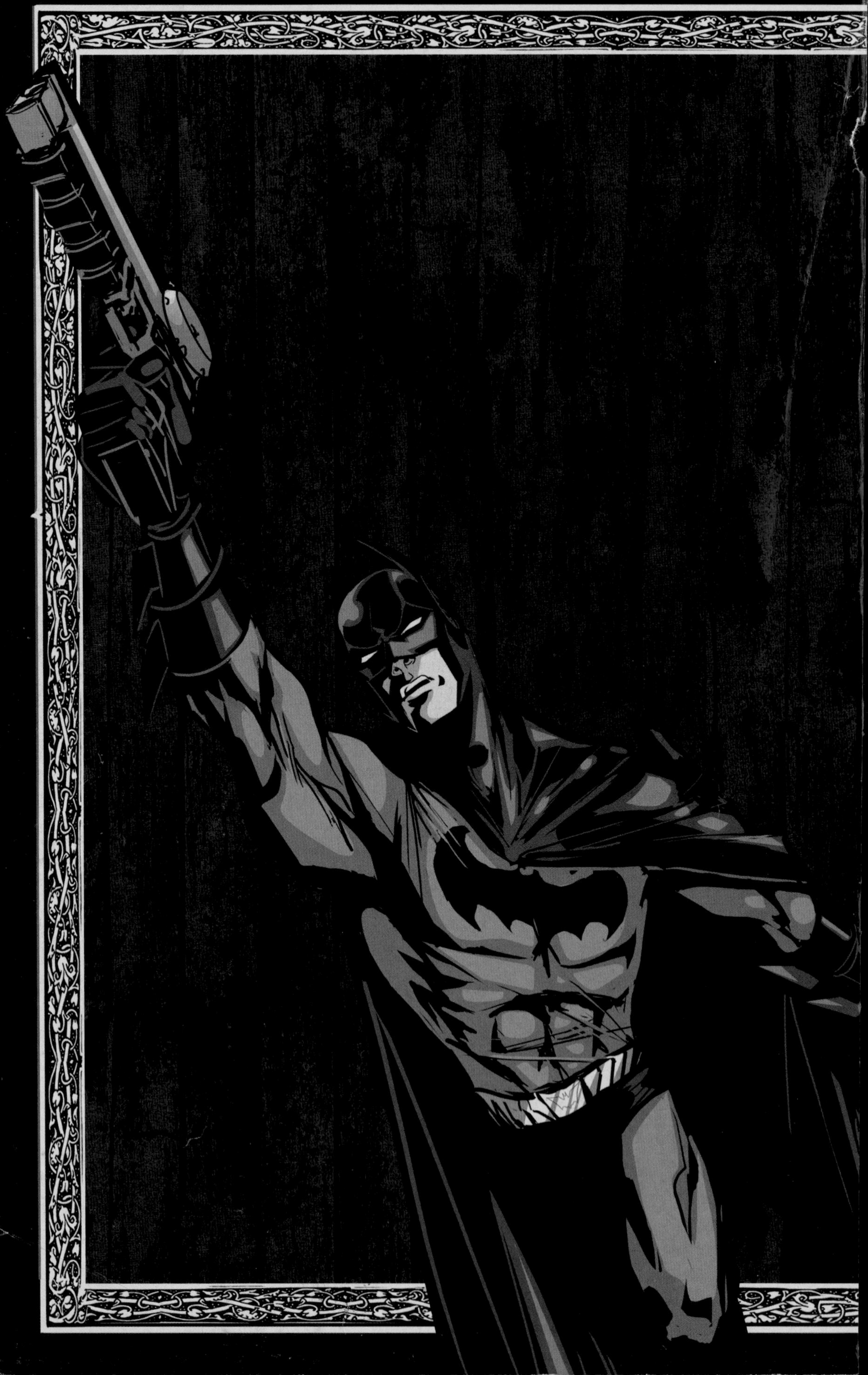

BATMAN

GATES OF GOTHAM

Scott Snyder & **Kyle Higgins**
story

Kyle Higgins & **Ryan Parrott**
dialogue

Trevor McCarthy

Graham **Nolan**

Dustin **Nguyen**

Derec **Donovan**
art

Guy Major
colors

Jared K. Fletcher
letters

Trevor McCarthy
collection cover

Batman created by
Bob Kane

Mike Marts Editor – Original Series
Janelle Asselin **Harvey Richards** Associate Editors – Original Series
Katie Kubert Assistant Editor – Original Series
Ian Sattler Director – Editorial, Special Projects and Archival Editions
Robin Wildman Editor
Robbin Brosterman Design Director – Books
Robbie Biederman Publication Design

Eddie Berganza Executive Editor
Bob Harras VP – Editor-in-Chief

Diane Nelson President
Dan DiDio and **Jim Lee** Co-Publishers
Geoff Johns Chief Creative Officer
John Rood Executive VP – Sales, Marketing and Business Development
Amy Genkins Senior VP – Business and Legal Affairs
Nairi Gardiner Senior VP – Finance
Jeff Boison VP – Publishing Operations
Mark Chiarello VP – Art Direction and Design
John Cunningham VP – Marketing
Terri Cunningham VP – Talent Relations and Services
Alison Gill Senior VP – Manufacturing and Operations
David Hyde VP – Publicity
Hank Kanalz Senior VP – Digital
Jay Kogan VP – Business and Legal Affairs, Publishing
Jack Mahan VP – Business Affairs, Talent
Nick Napolitano VP – Manufacturing Administration
Sue Pohja VP – Book Sales
Courtney Simmons Senior VP – Publicity
Bob Wayne Senior VP – Sales

BATMAN: GATES OF GOTHAM

DC Comics, 1700 Broadway, New York, NY 10019
A Warner Bros. Entertainment Company.
Printed by RR Donnelley, Salem, VA, USA. 12/30/11. First Printing.
ISBN: 978-1-4012-3341-9

SUSTAINABLE FORESTRY INITIATIVE
Certified Chain of Custody
Promoting Sustainable Forest Management
www.sfiprogram.org

Fiber used in this product line meets the sourcing requirements of the SFI program.
www.sfiprogram.org SGS-SFI/COC-US10/81072

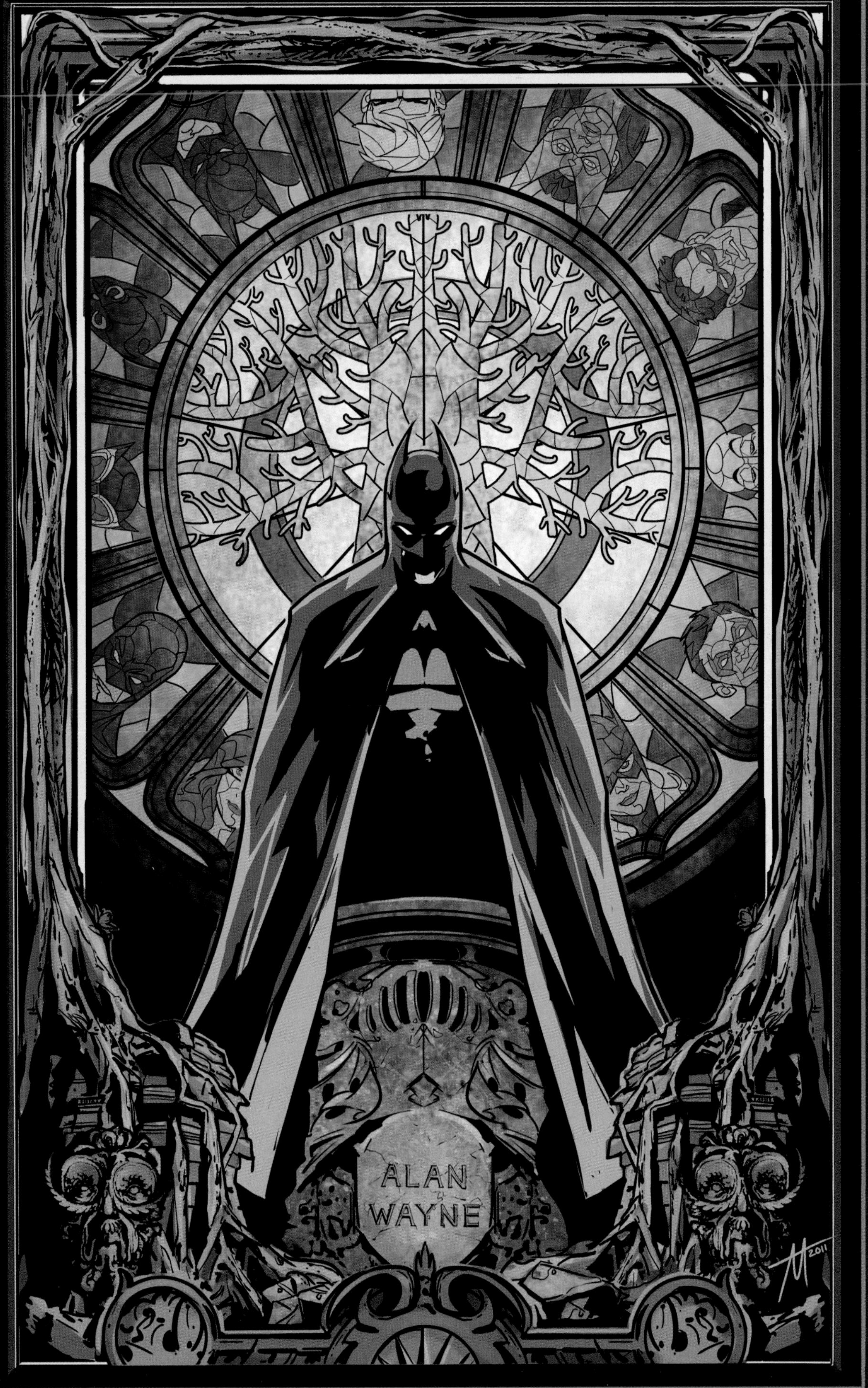
ALAN
WAYNE

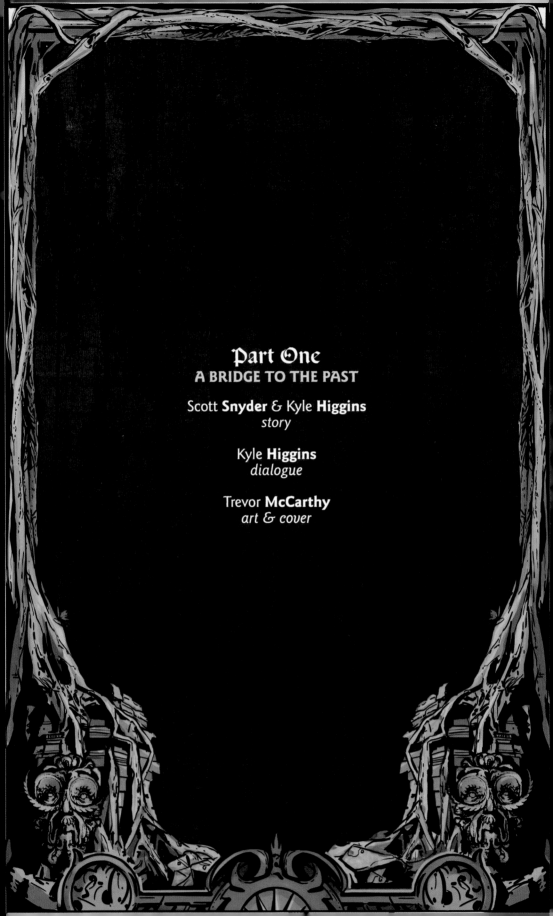

Part One
A BRIDGE TO THE PAST

Scott **Snyder** & Kyle **Higgins**
story

Kyle **Higgins**
dialogue

Trevor **McCarthy**
art & cover

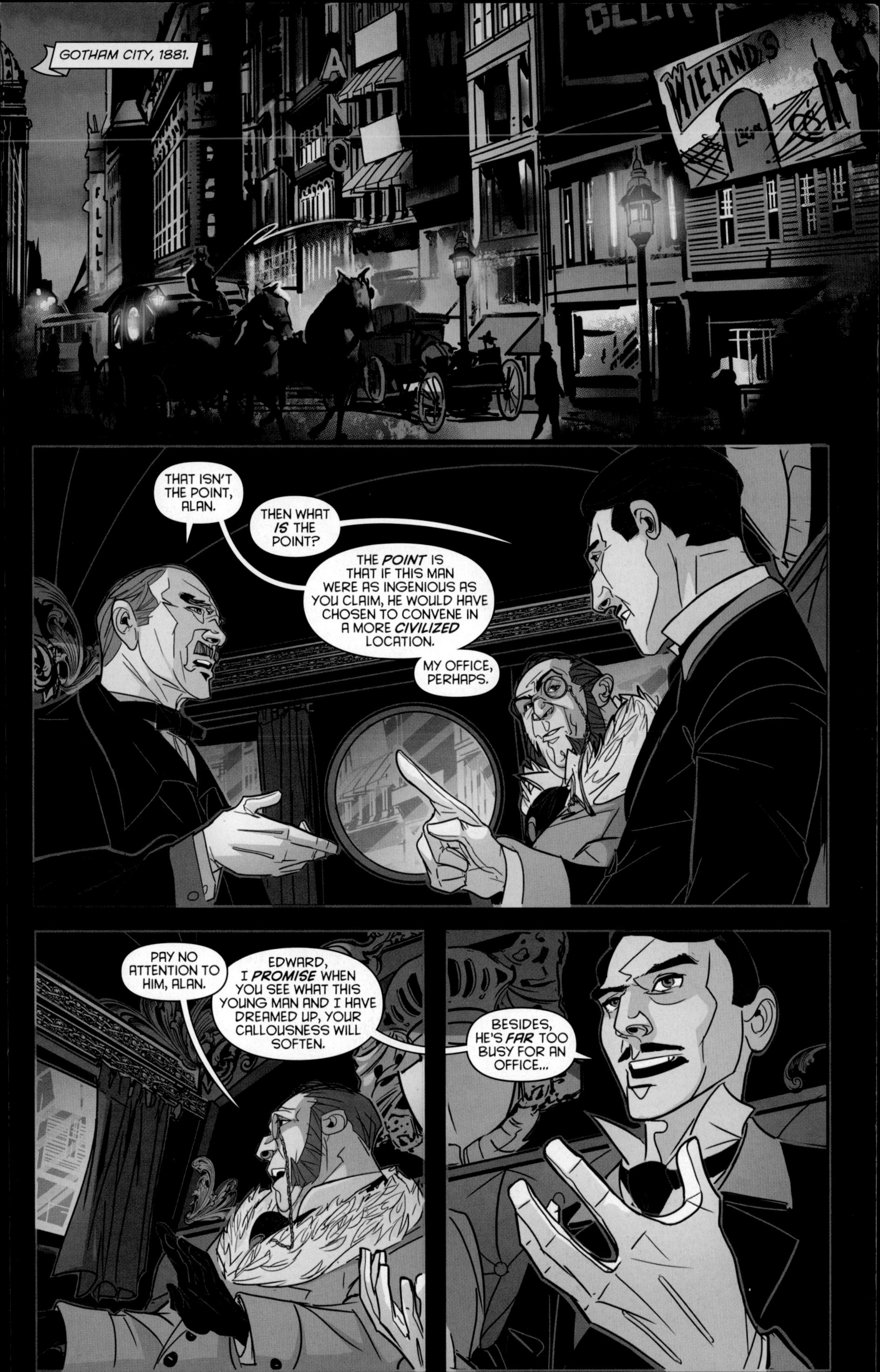
GOTHAM CITY, 1881.
THAT ISN'T THE POINT, ALAN.
THEN WHAT IS THE POINT?
THE POINT IS THAT IF THIS MAN WERE AS INGENIOUS AS YOU CLAIM, HE WOULD HAVE CHOSEN TO CONVENE IN A MORE CIVILIZED LOCATION.
MY OFFICE, PERHAPS.
PAY NO ATTENTION TO HIM, ALAN.
EDWARD, I PROMISE WHEN YOU SEE WHAT THIS YOUNG MAN AND I HAVE DREAMED UP, YOUR CALLOUSNESS WILL SOFTEN.
BESIDES, HE'S FAR TOO BUSY FOR AN OFFICE...

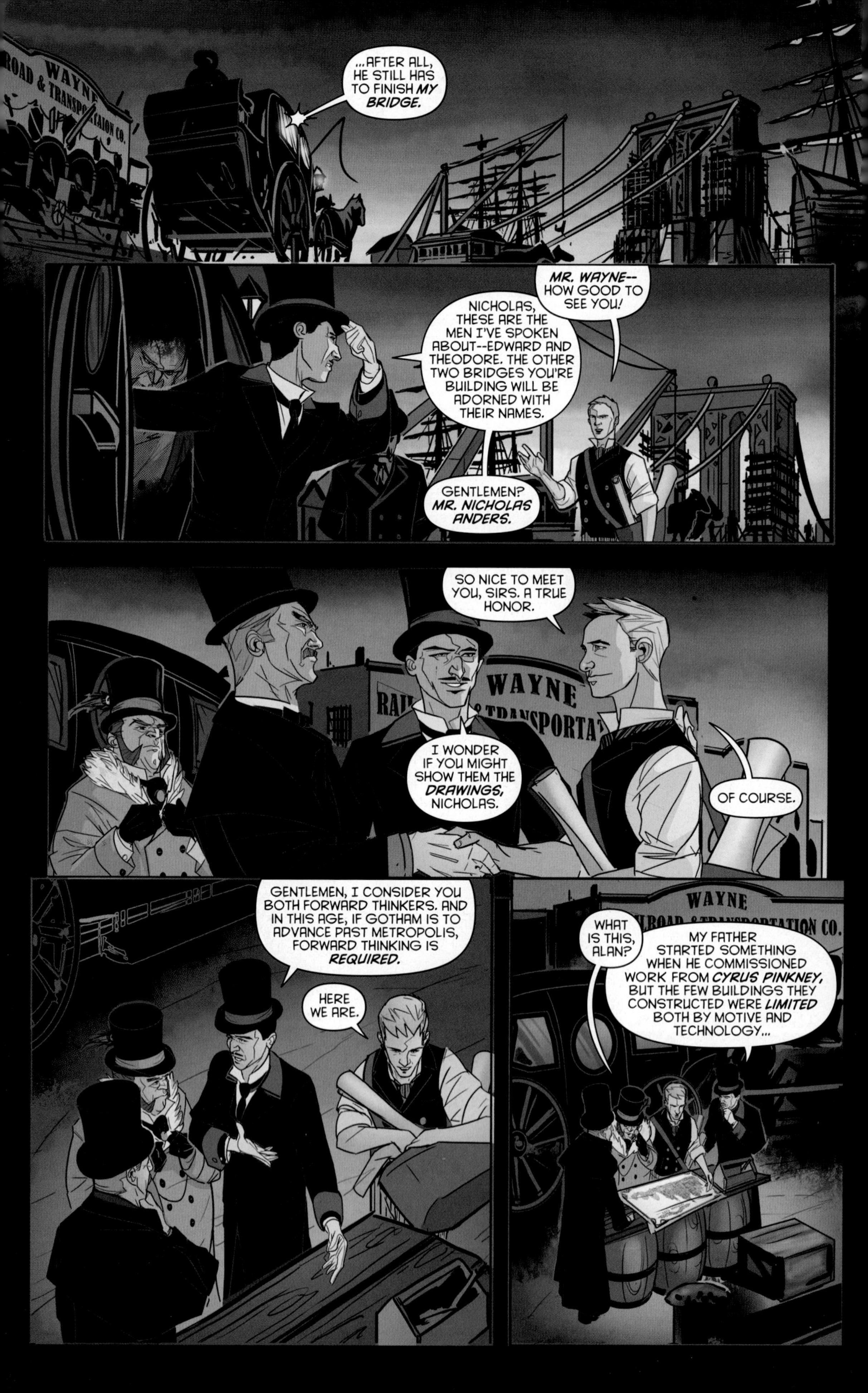
...AFTER ALL, HE STILL HAS TO FINISH *MY BRIDGE.*
MR. WAYNE-- HOW GOOD TO SEE YOU!
NICHOLAS, THESE ARE THE MEN I'VE SPOKEN ABOUT--EDWARD AND THEODORE. THE OTHER TWO BRIDGES YOU'RE BUILDING WILL BE ADORNED WITH THEIR NAMES.
GENTLEMEN? *MR. NICHOLAS ANDERS.*
SO NICE TO MEET YOU, SIRS. A TRUE HONOR.
I WONDER IF YOU MIGHT SHOW THEM THE *DRAWINGS,* NICHOLAS.
OF COURSE.
GENTLEMEN, I CONSIDER YOU BOTH FORWARD THINKERS. AND IN THIS AGE, IF GOTHAM IS TO ADVANCE PAST METROPOLIS, FORWARD THINKING IS *REQUIRED.*
HERE WE ARE.
WHAT IS THIS, ALAN?
MY FATHER STARTED SOMETHING WHEN HE COMMISSIONED WORK FROM *CYRUS PINKNEY,* BUT THE FEW BUILDINGS THEY CONSTRUCTED WERE *LIMITED* BOTH BY MOTIVE AND TECHNOLOGY...

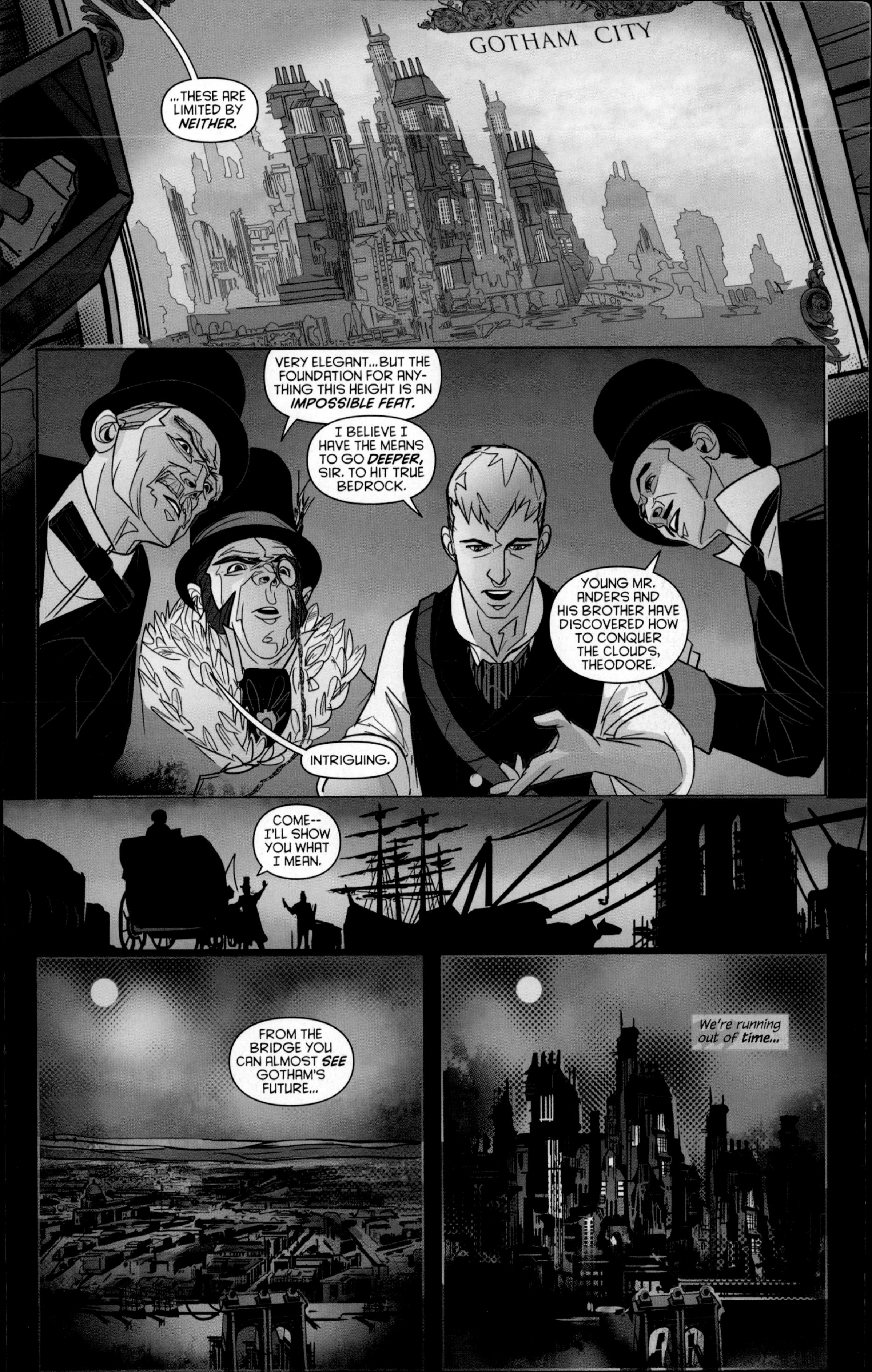
GOTHAM CITY
...THESE ARE LIMITED BY NEITHER.
VERY ELEGANT...BUT THE FOUNDATION FOR ANY-THING THIS HEIGHT IS AN IMPOSSIBLE FEAT.
I BELIEVE I HAVE THE MEANS TO GO DEEPER, SIR. TO HIT TRUE BEDROCK.
YOUNG MR. ANDERS AND HIS BROTHER HAVE DISCOVERED HOW TO CONQUER THE CLOUDS, THEODORE.
INTRIGUING.
COME-- I'LL SHOW YOU WHAT I MEAN.
FROM THE BRIDGE YOU CAN ALMOST SEE GOTHAM'S FUTURE...
We're running out of time...

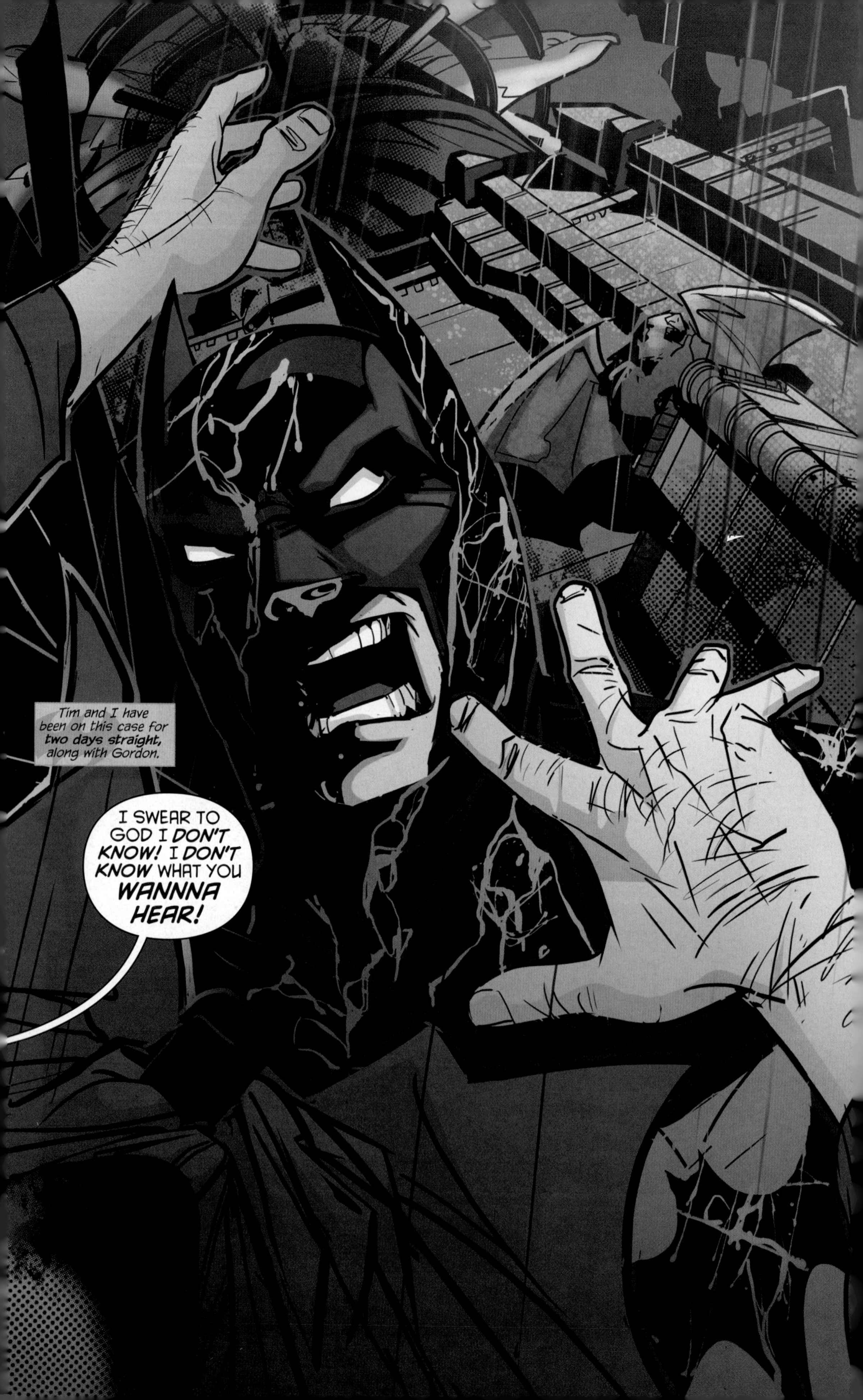
Tim and I have been on this case for two days straight, along with Gordon.
I SWEAR TO GOD I DON'T KNOW! I DON'T KNOW WHAT YOU WANNA HEAR!

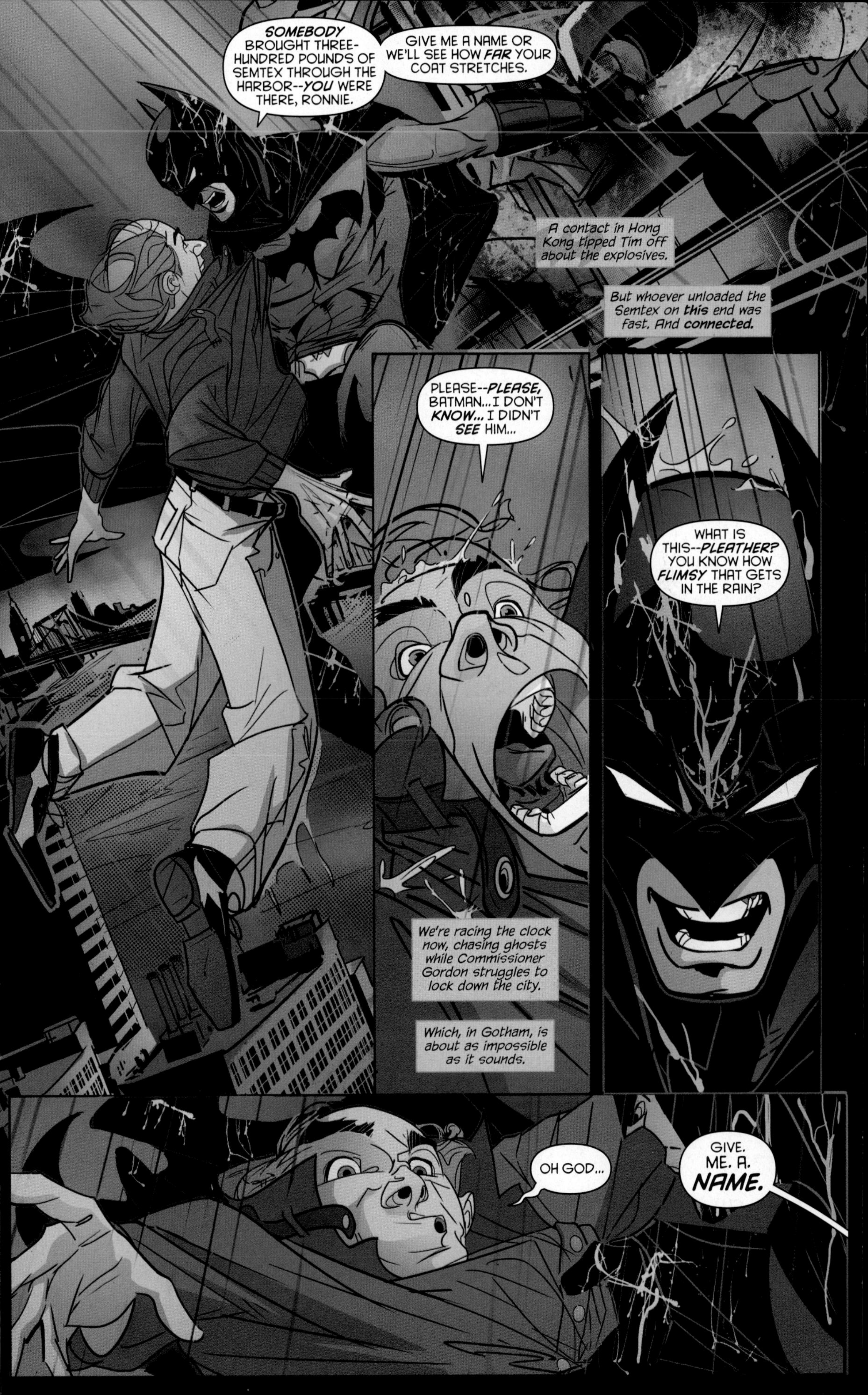
SOMEBODY BROUGHT THREE-HUNDRED POUNDS OF SEMTEX THROUGH THE HARBOR--YOU WERE THERE, RONNIE.
GIVE ME A NAME OR WE'LL SEE HOW FAR YOUR COAT STRETCHES.
A contact in Hong Kong tipped Tim off about the explosives.
But whoever unloaded the Semtex on this end was fast. And connected.
PLEASE--PLEASE, BATMAN... I DON'T KNOW... I DIDN'T SEE HIM...
We're racing the clock now, chasing ghosts while Commissioner Gordon struggles to lock down the city.
Which, in Gotham, is about as impossible as it sounds.
WHAT IS THIS--PLEATHER? YOU KNOW HOW FLIMSY THAT GETS IN THE RAIN?
OH GOD...
GIVE. ME. A. NAME.

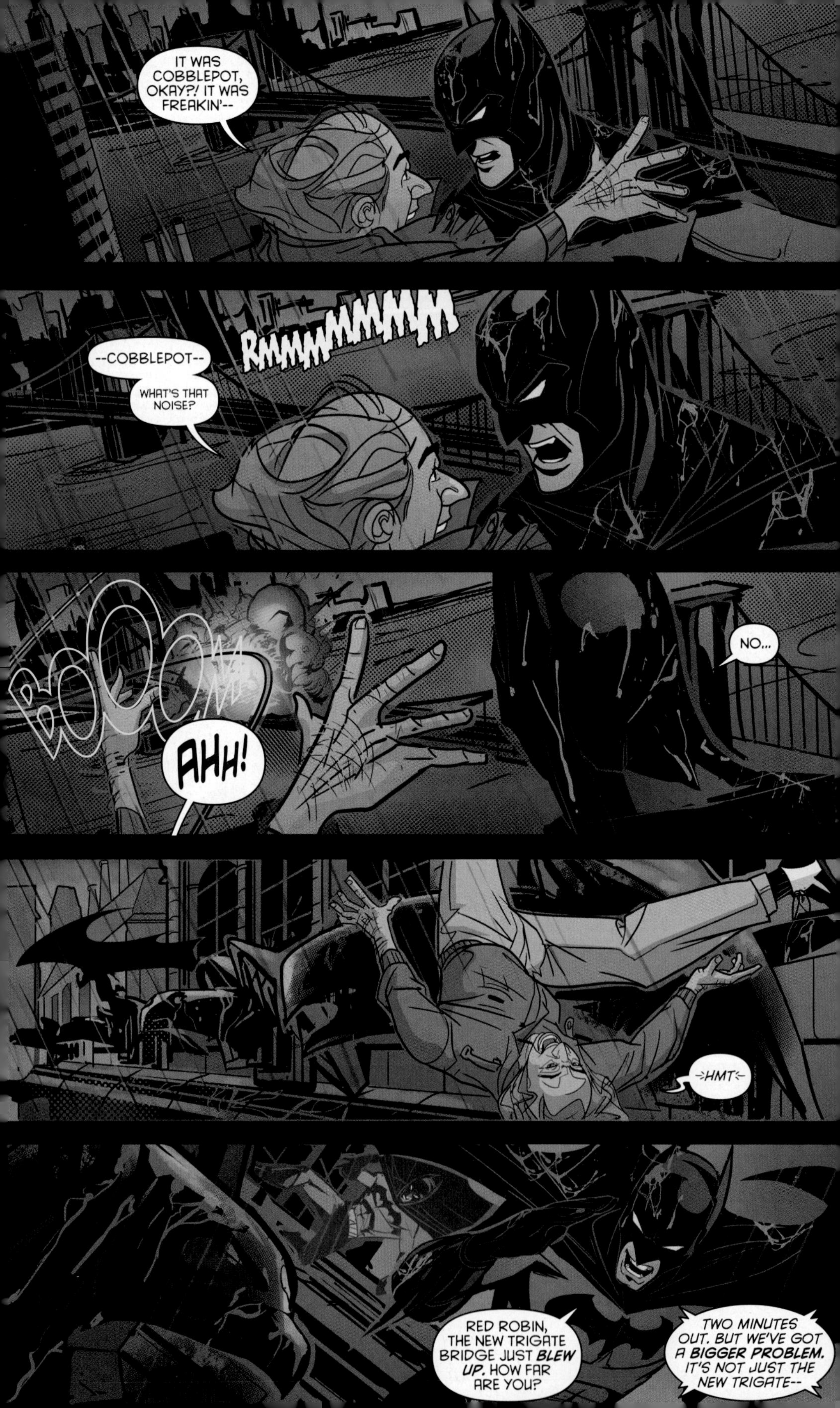
IT WAS COBBLEPOT, OKAY?! IT WAS FREAKIN'--
RMMMMMMMM
--COBBLEPOT--
WHAT'S THAT NOISE?
BOOOM
NO...
AHH!
HMT
RED ROBIN, THE NEW TRIGATE BRIDGE JUST BLEW UP. HOW FAR ARE YOU?
TWO MINUTES OUT. BUT WE'VE GOT A BIGGER PROBLEM. IT'S NOT JUST THE NEW TRIGATE--

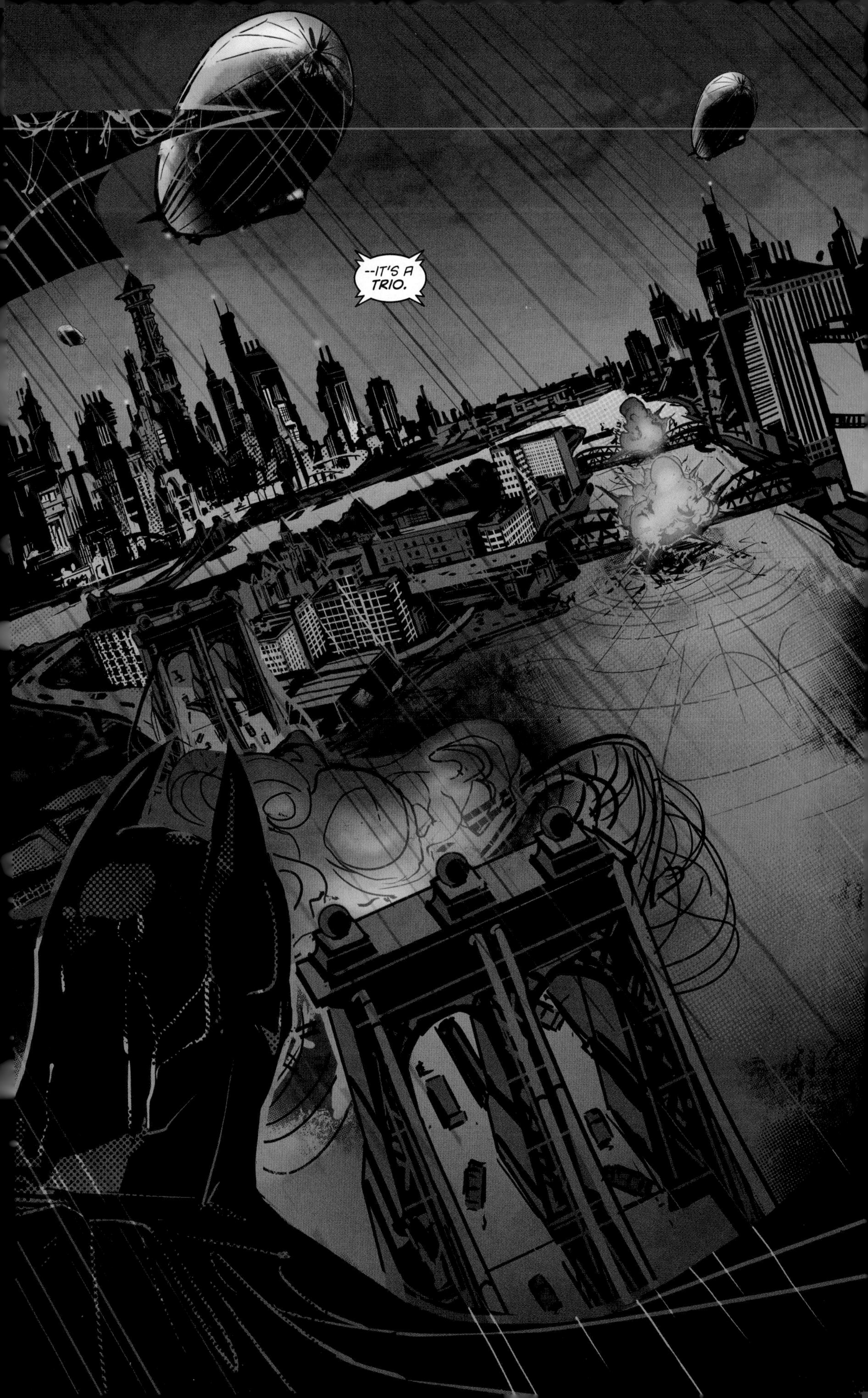
--IT'S A TRIO.

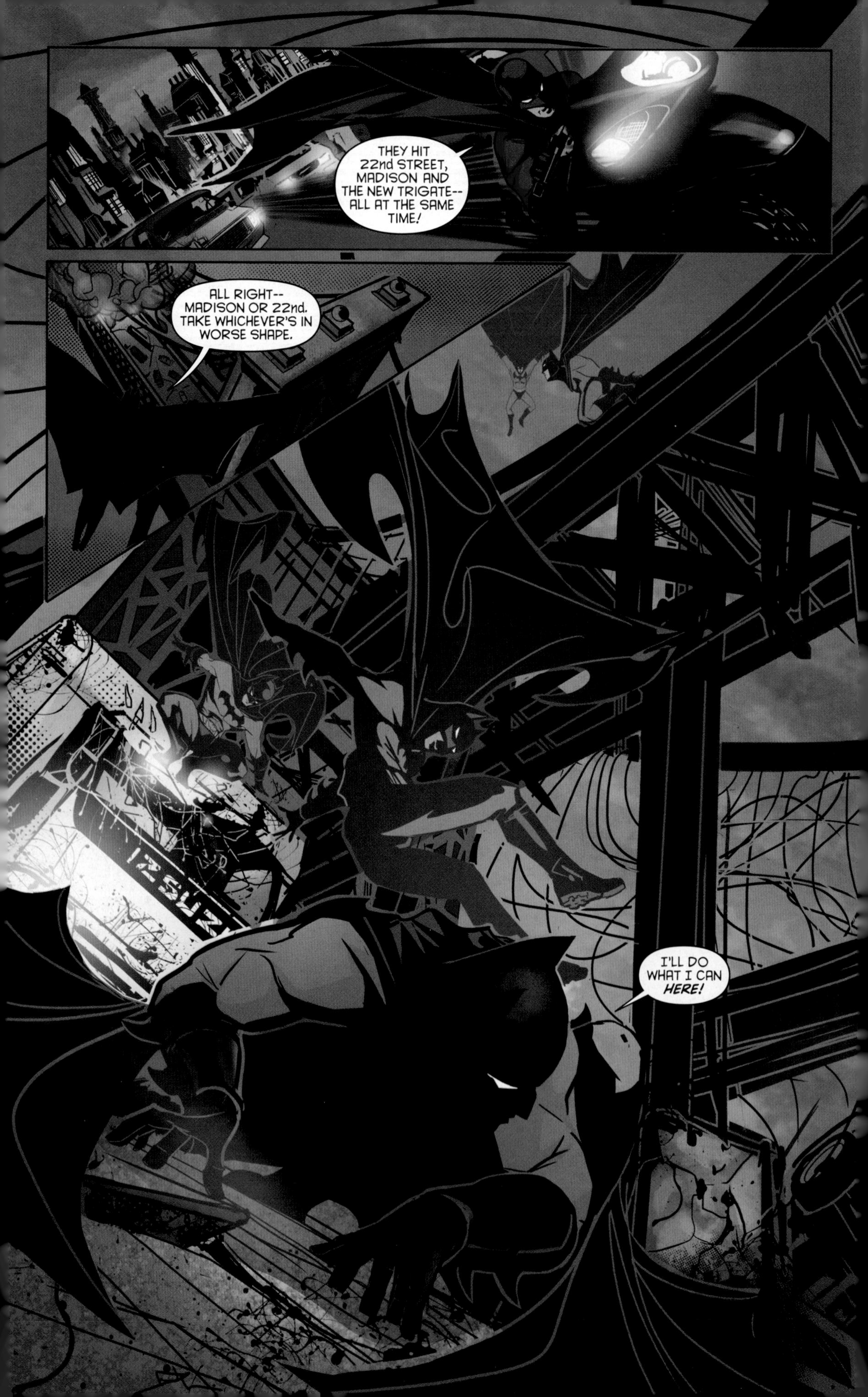
THEY HIT 22nd STREET, MADISON AND THE NEW TRIGATE-- ALL AT THE SAME TIME!
ALL RIGHT-- MADISON OR 22nd. TAKE WHICHEVER'S IN WORSE SHAPE.
I'LL DO WHAT I CAN HERE!

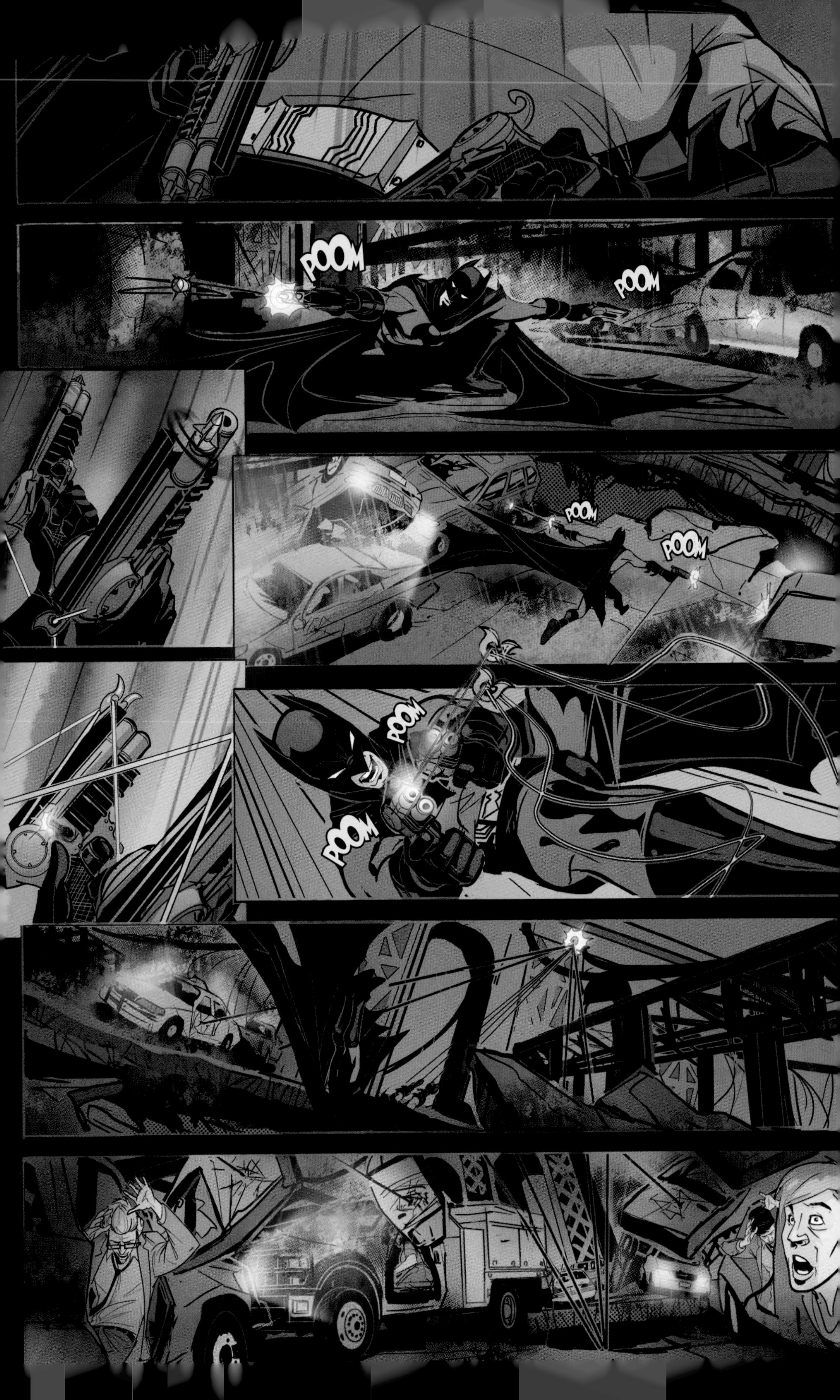

POOM
POOM
POOM
POOM
POOM
POOM

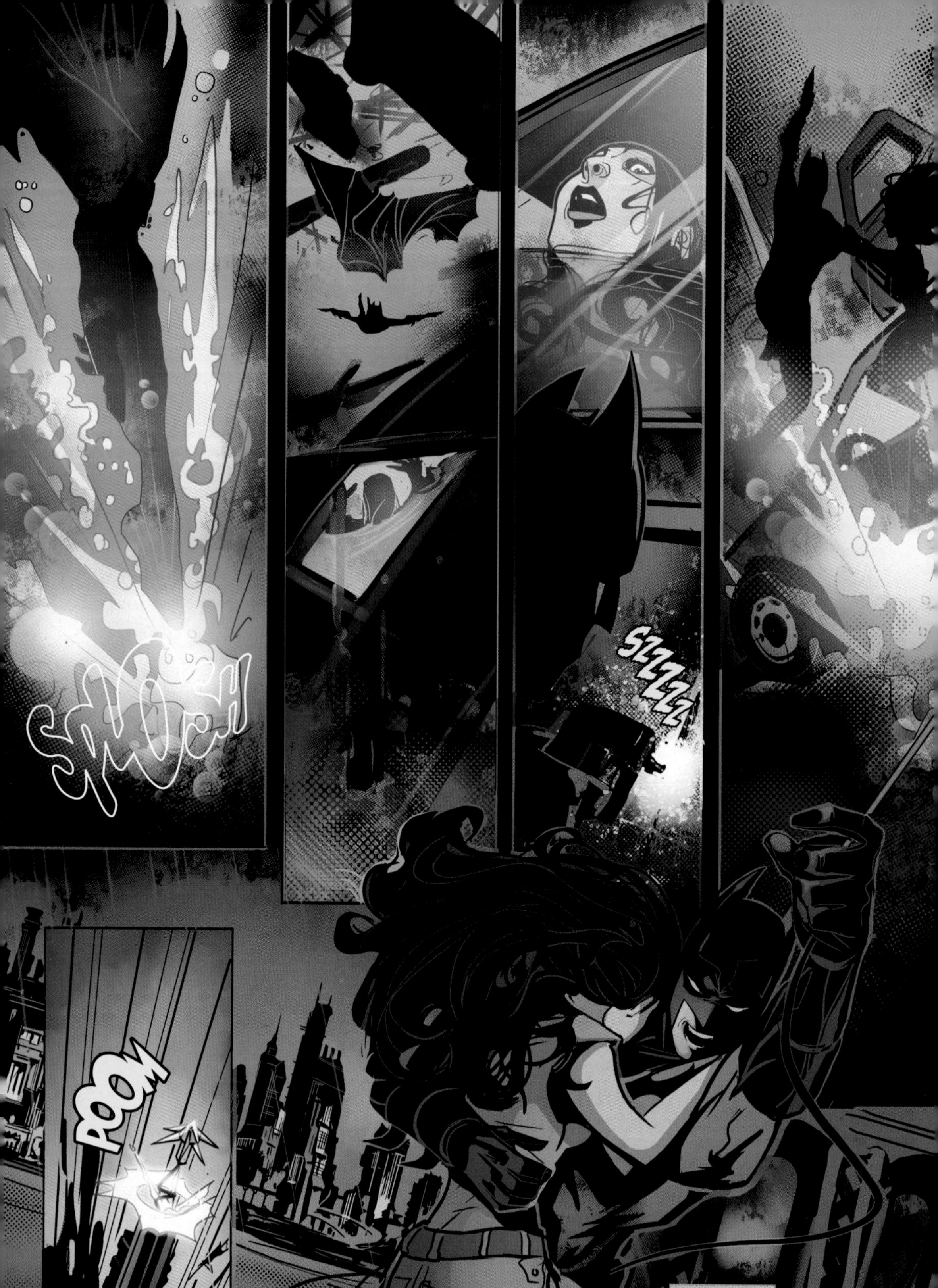
SZZZZZ
POOM
"HOW BAD IS IT SO FAR?"
"BAD. THIRTY-ONE DEAD, WITH ANOTHER TWENTY-FIVE GOING TO THE HOSPITAL--MOSTLY BURNS AND CONCUSSIONS."

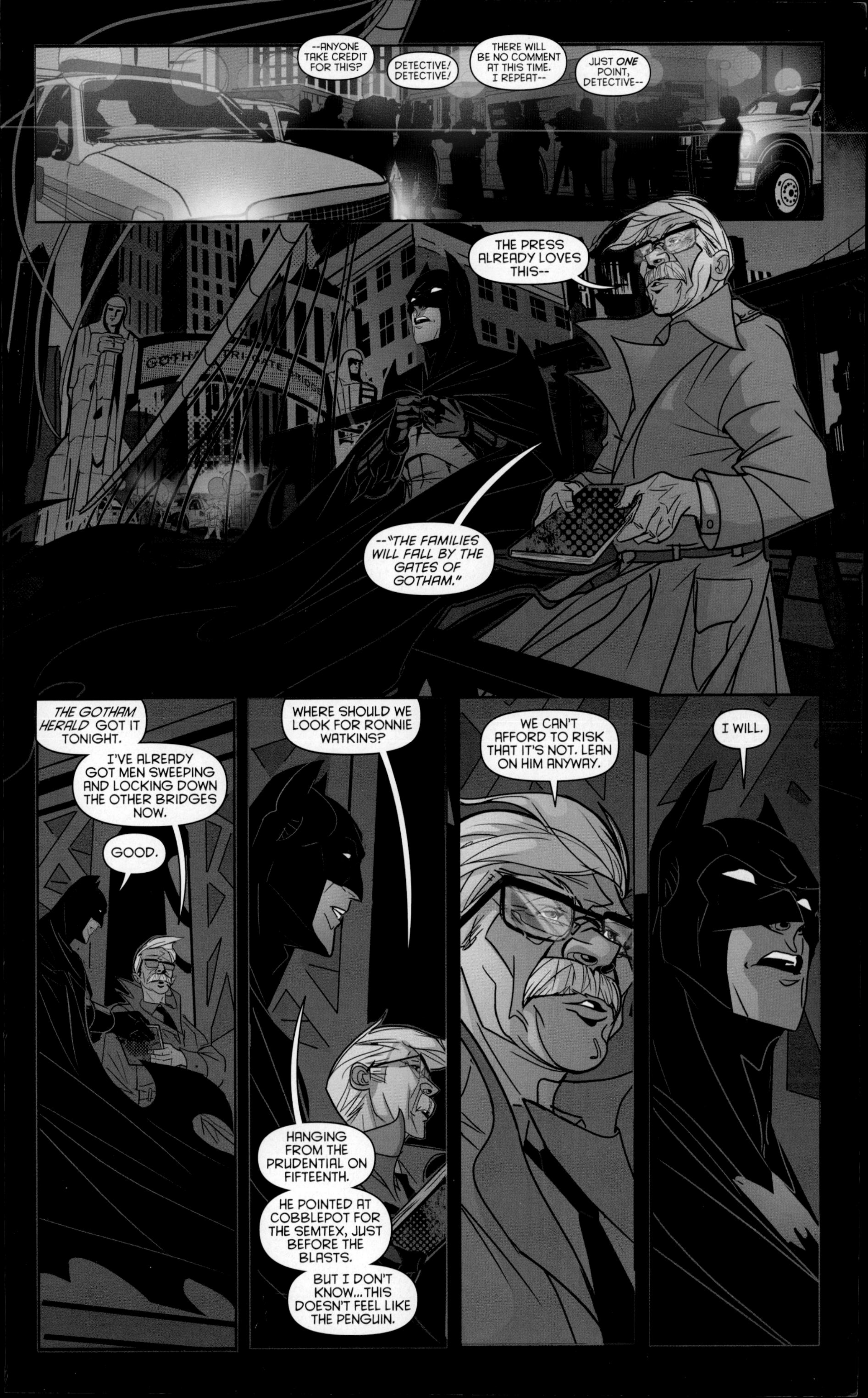
--ANYONE TAKE CREDIT FOR THIS?
DETECTIVE! DETECTIVE!
THERE WILL BE NO COMMENT AT THIS TIME. I REPEAT--
JUST *ONE* POINT, DETECTIVE--
THE PRESS ALREADY LOVES THIS--
--*"THE FAMILIES WILL FALL BY THE GATES OF GOTHAM."*
THE GOTHAM HERALD GOT IT TONIGHT.
I'VE ALREADY GOT MEN SWEEPING AND LOCKING DOWN THE OTHER BRIDGES NOW.
GOOD.
WHERE SHOULD WE LOOK FOR RONNIE WATKINS?
HANGING FROM THE PRUDENTIAL ON FIFTEENTH.
HE POINTED AT COBBLEPOT FOR THE SEMTEX, JUST BEFORE THE BLASTS.
BUT I DON'T KNOW...THIS DOESN'T FEEL LIKE THE PENGUIN.
WE CAN'T AFFORD TO RISK THAT IT'S NOT. LEAN ON HIM ANYWAY.
I WILL.

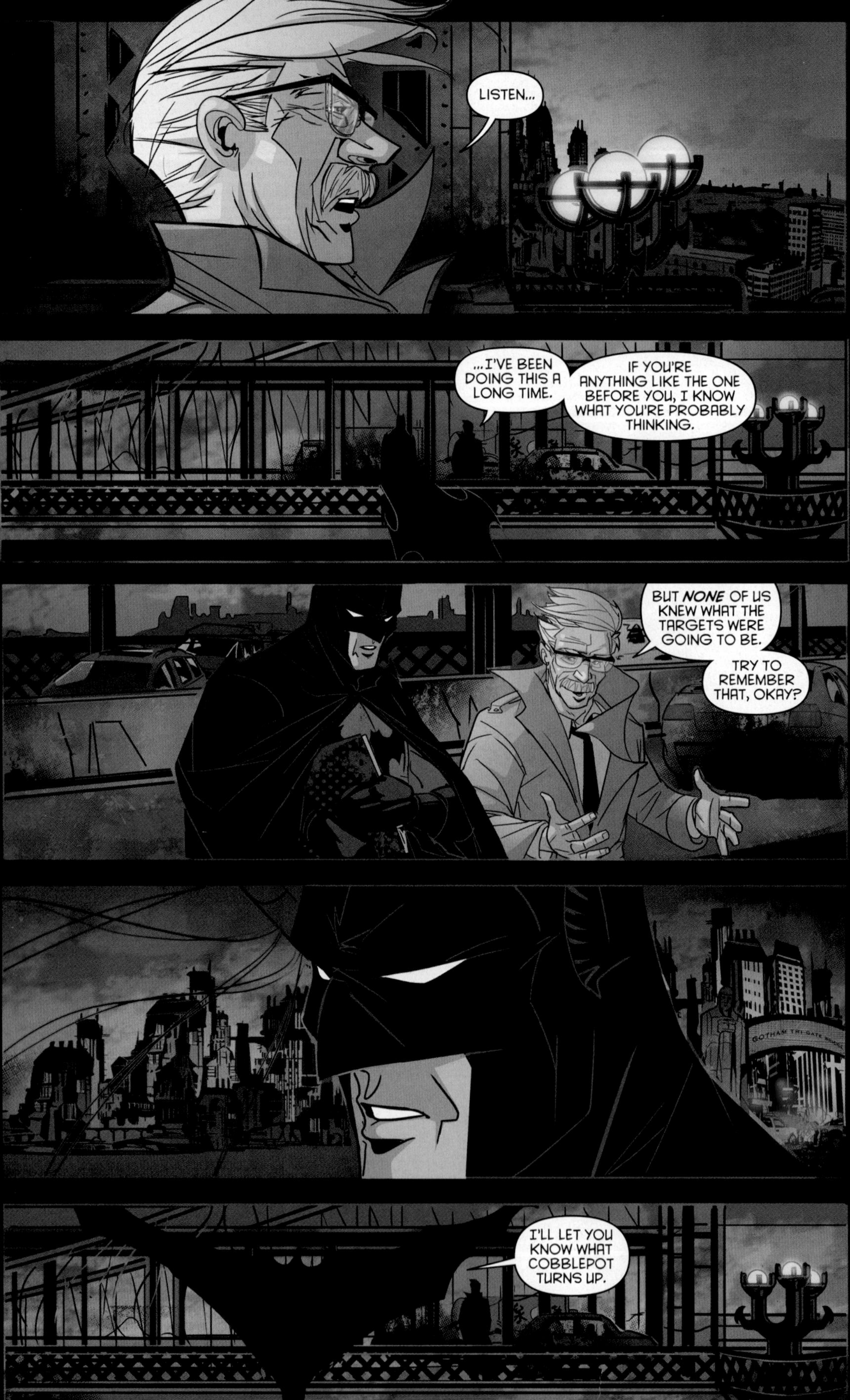
LISTEN...
...I'VE BEEN DOING THIS A LONG TIME.
IF YOU'RE ANYTHING LIKE THE ONE BEFORE YOU, I KNOW WHAT YOU'RE PROBABLY THINKING.
BUT *NONE* OF US KNEW WHAT THE TARGETS WERE GOING TO BE.
TRY TO REMEMBER THAT, OKAY?
GOTHAM TRI-GATE
I'LL LET YOU KNOW WHAT COBBLEPOT TURNS UP.

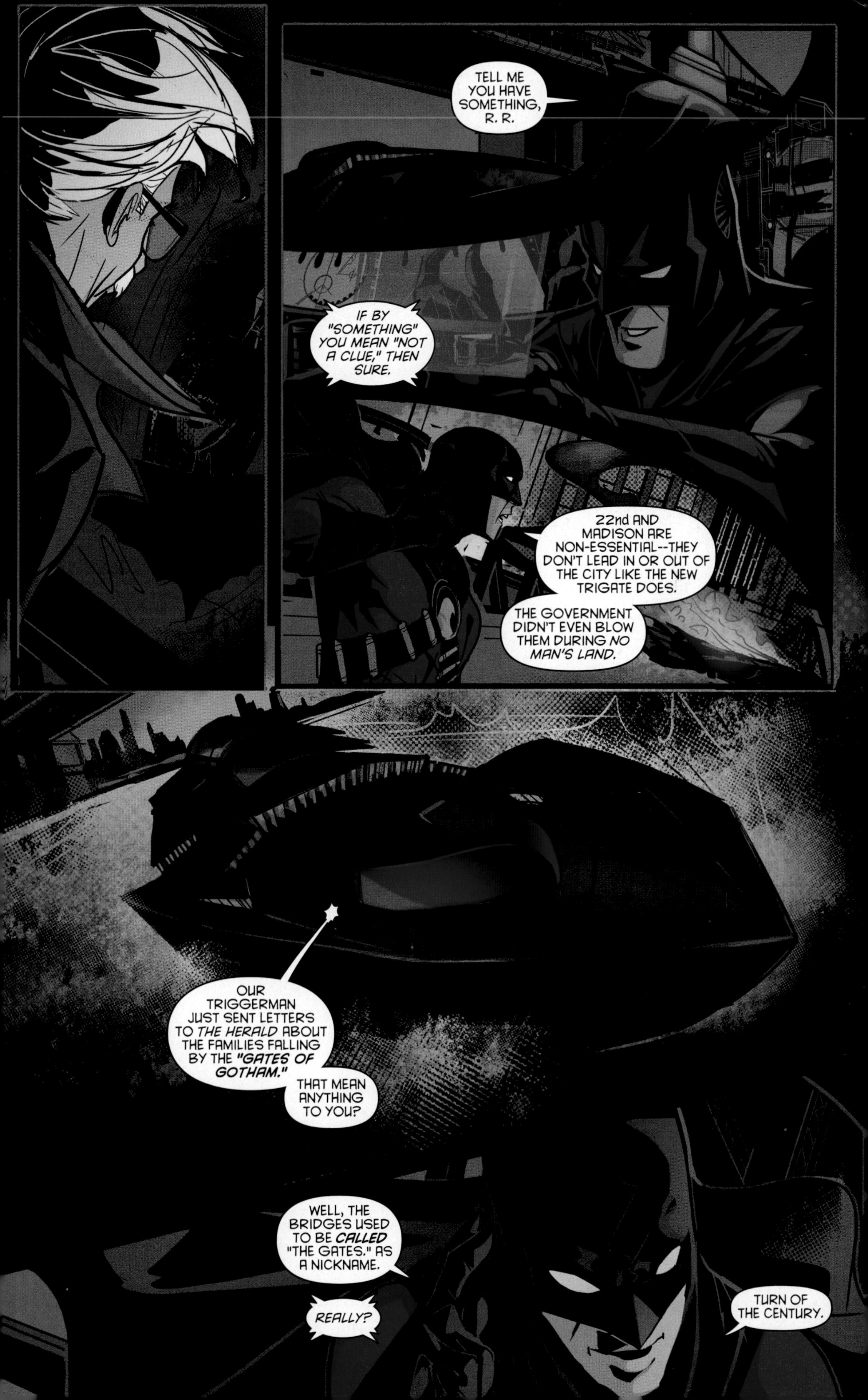
TELL ME YOU HAVE SOMETHING, R. R.
IF BY "SOMETHING" YOU MEAN "NOT A CLUE," THEN SURE.
22nd AND MADISON ARE NON-ESSENTIAL--THEY DON'T LEAD IN OR OUT OF THE CITY LIKE THE NEW TRIGATE DOES.
THE GOVERNMENT DIDN'T EVEN BLOW THEM DURING NO MAN'S LAND.
OUR TRIGGERMAN JUST SENT LETTERS TO THE HERALD ABOUT THE FAMILIES FALLING BY THE "GATES OF GOTHAM."
THAT MEAN ANYTHING TO YOU?
WELL, THE BRIDGES USED TO BE CALLED "THE GATES." AS A NICKNAME.
REALLY?
TURN OF THE CENTURY.

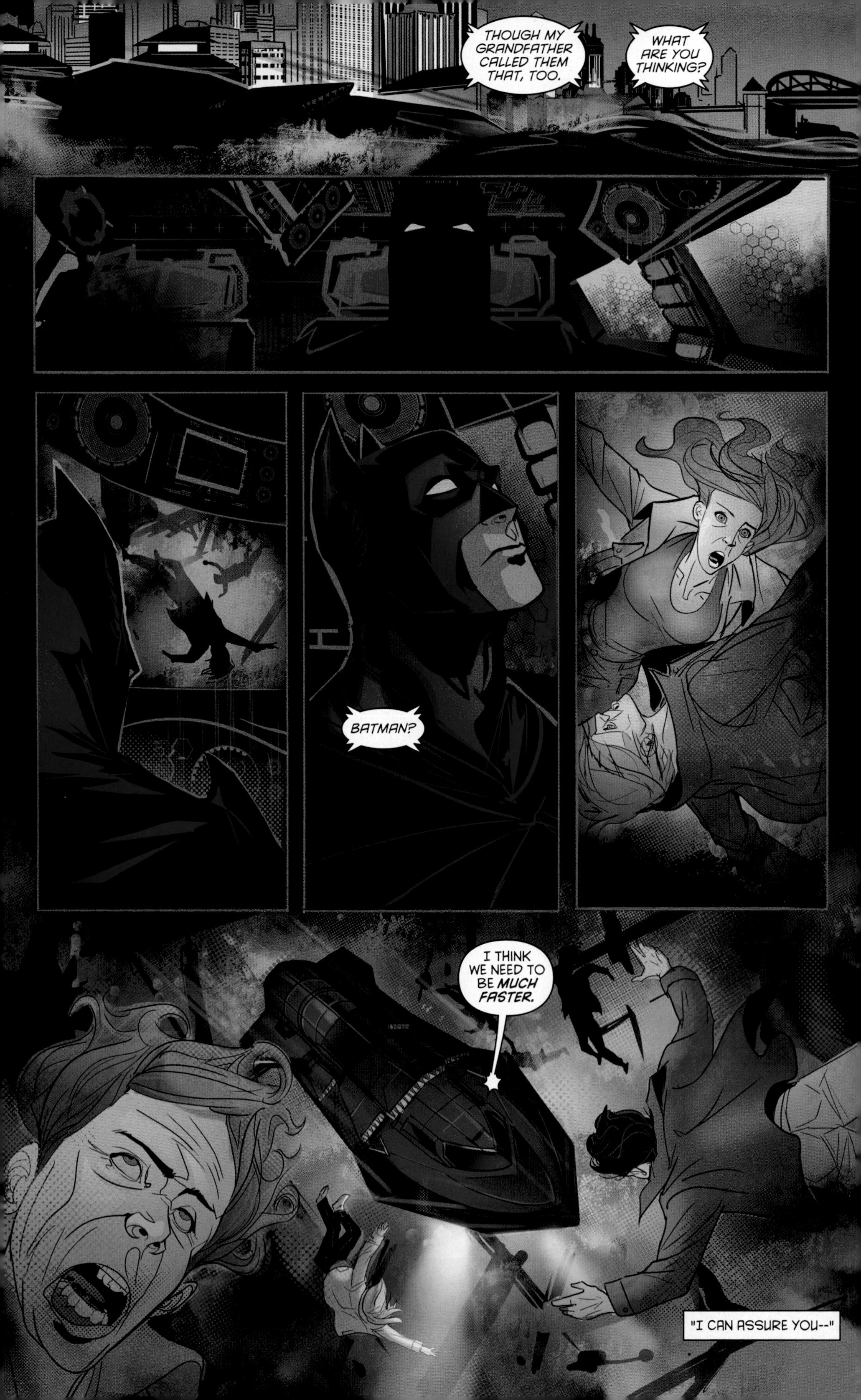
THOUGH MY GRANDFATHER CALLED THEM THAT, TOO.
WHAT ARE YOU THINKING?
BATMAN?
I THINK WE NEED TO BE *MUCH FASTER.*
"I CAN ASSURE YOU--"

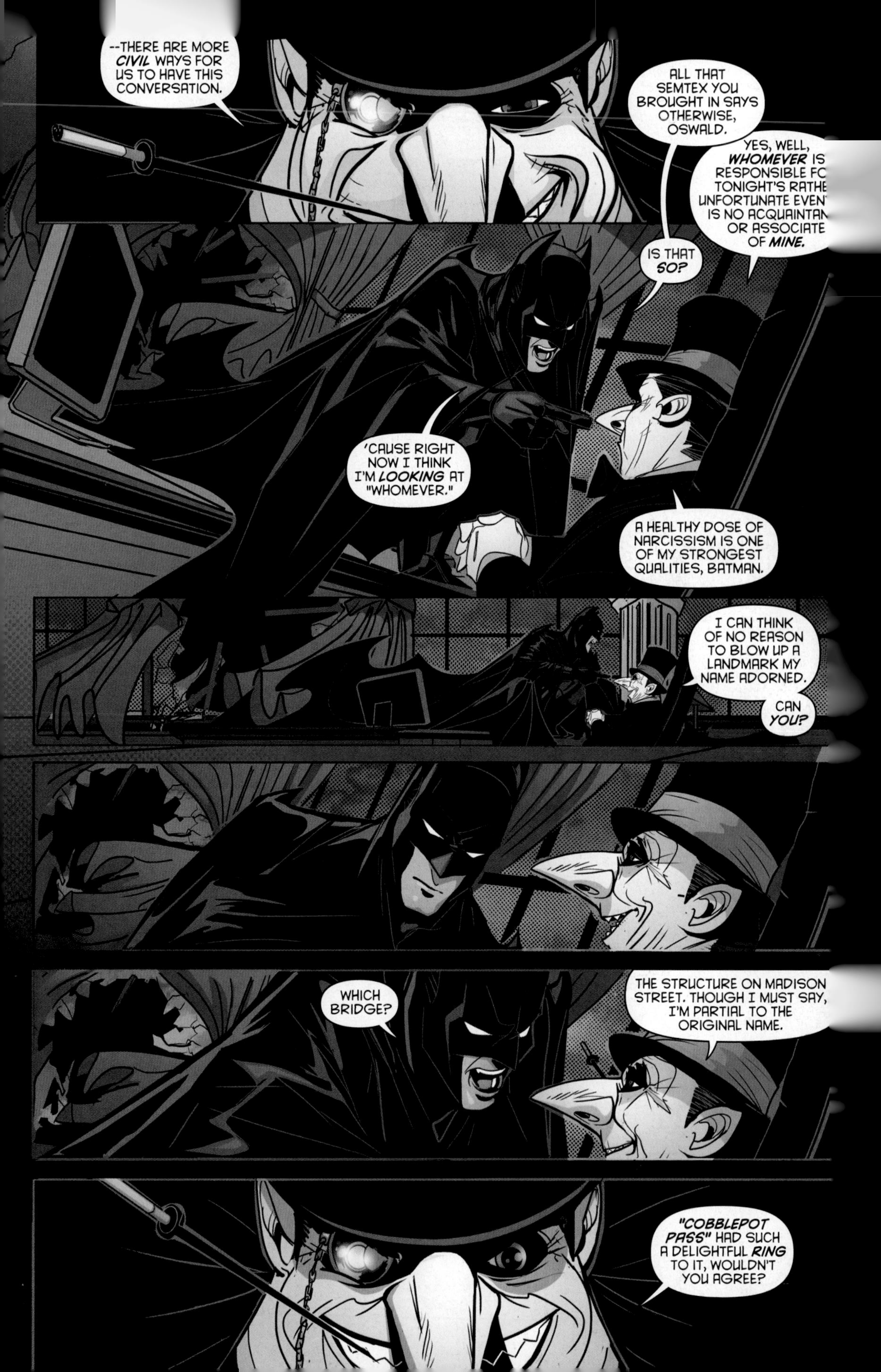
--THERE ARE MORE CIVIL WAYS FOR US TO HAVE THIS CONVERSATION.
ALL THAT SEMTEX YOU BROUGHT IN SAYS OTHERWISE, OSWALD.
YES, WELL, WHOMEVER IS RESPONSIBLE FO TONIGHT'S RATHE UNFORTUNATE EVENT IS NO ACQUAINTAN OR ASSOCIATE OF MINE.
IS THAT SO?
'CAUSE RIGHT NOW I THINK I'M LOOKING AT "WHOMEVER."
A HEALTHY DOSE OF NARCISSISM IS ONE OF MY STRONGEST QUALITIES, BATMAN.
I CAN THINK OF NO REASON TO BLOW UP A LANDMARK MY NAME ADORNED.
CAN YOU?
WHICH BRIDGE?
THE STRUCTURE ON MADISON STREET. THOUGH I MUST SAY, I'M PARTIAL TO THE ORIGINAL NAME.
"COBBLEPOT PASS" HAD SUCH A DELIGHTFUL RING TO IT, WOULDN'T YOU AGREE?

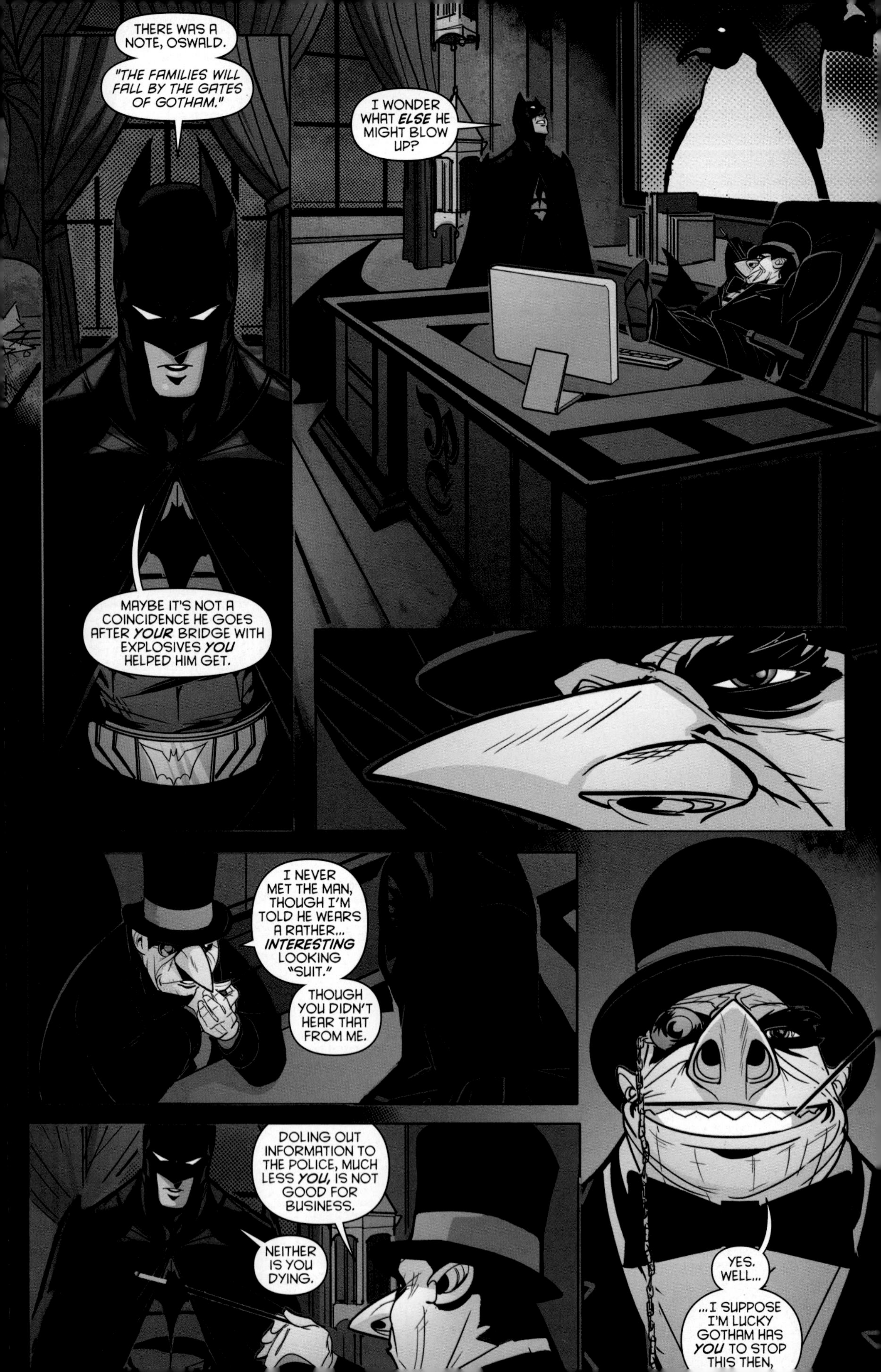
THERE WAS A NOTE, OSWALD.
"THE FAMILIES WILL FALL BY THE GATES OF GOTHAM."
I WONDER WHAT ELSE HE MIGHT BLOW UP?
MAYBE IT'S NOT A COINCIDENCE HE GOES AFTER YOUR BRIDGE WITH EXPLOSIVES YOU HELPED HIM GET.
I NEVER MET THE MAN, THOUGH I'M TOLD HE WEARS A RATHER... INTERESTING LOOKING "SUIT."
THOUGH YOU DIDN'T HEAR THAT FROM ME.
DOLING OUT INFORMATION TO THE POLICE, MUCH LESS YOU, IS NOT GOOD FOR BUSINESS.
NEITHER IS YOU DYING.
YES. WELL...
...I SUPPOSE I'M LUCKY GOTHAM HAS YOU TO STOP THIS THEN,

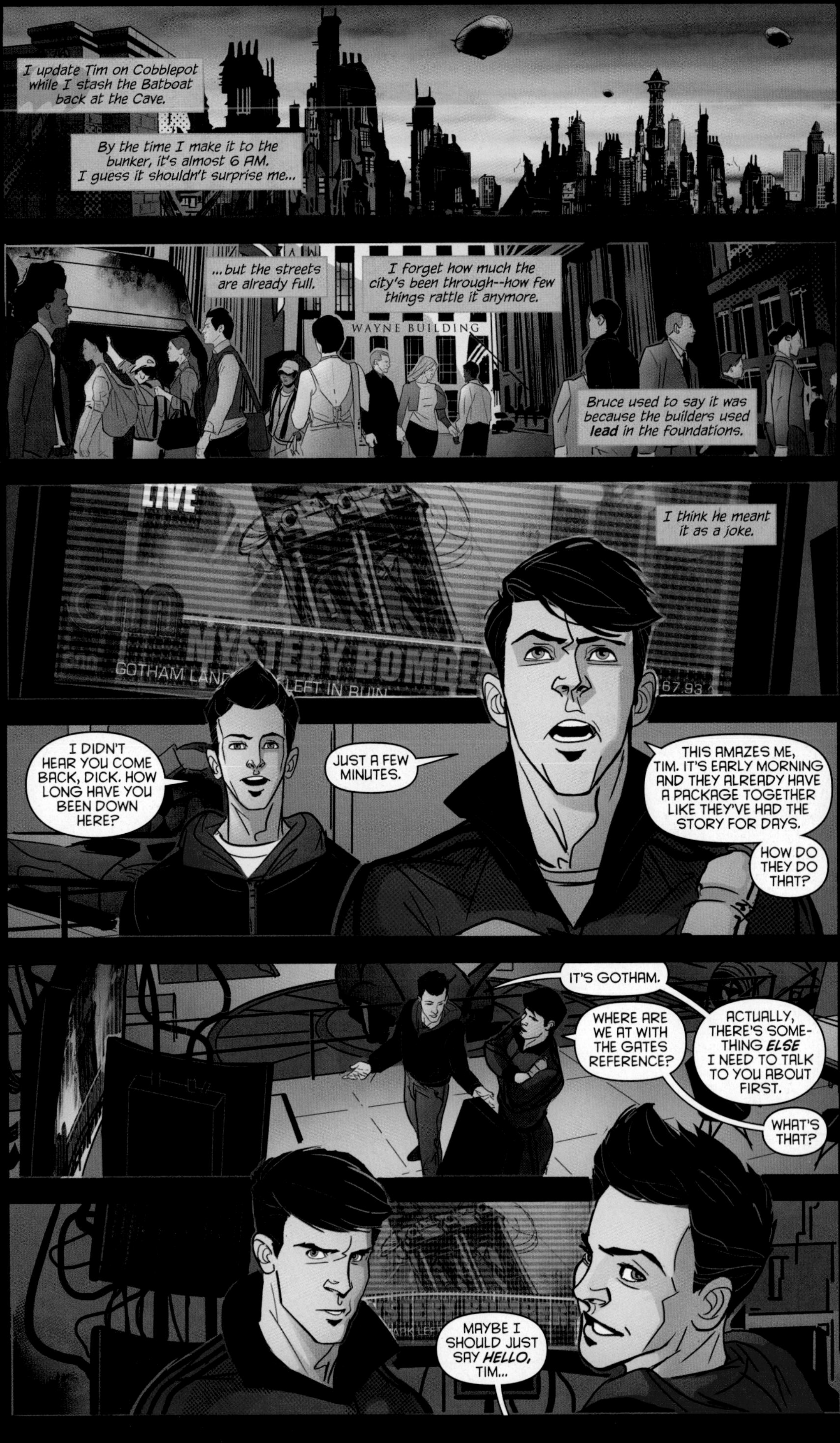

I update Tim on Cobblepot while I stash the Batboat back at the Cave.
By the time I make it to the bunker, it's almost 6 AM. I guess it shouldn't surprise me...
...but the streets are already full.
I forget how much the city's been through--how few things rattle it anymore.
WAYNE BUILDING
Bruce used to say it was because the builders used **lead** in the foundations.
LIVE
I think he meant it as a joke.
MYSTERY BOMB
I DIDN'T HEAR YOU COME BACK, DICK. HOW LONG HAVE YOU BEEN DOWN HERE?
JUST A FEW MINUTES.
THIS AMAZES ME, TIM. IT'S EARLY MORNING AND THEY ALREADY HAVE A PACKAGE TOGETHER LIKE THEY'VE HAD THE STORY FOR DAYS.
HOW DO THEY DO THAT?
IT'S GOTHAM.
WHERE ARE WE AT WITH THE GATES REFERENCE?
ACTUALLY, THERE'S SOMETHING *ELSE* I NEED TO TALK TO YOU ABOUT FIRST.
WHAT'S THAT?
MAYBE I SHOULD JUST SAY *HELLO,* TIM...

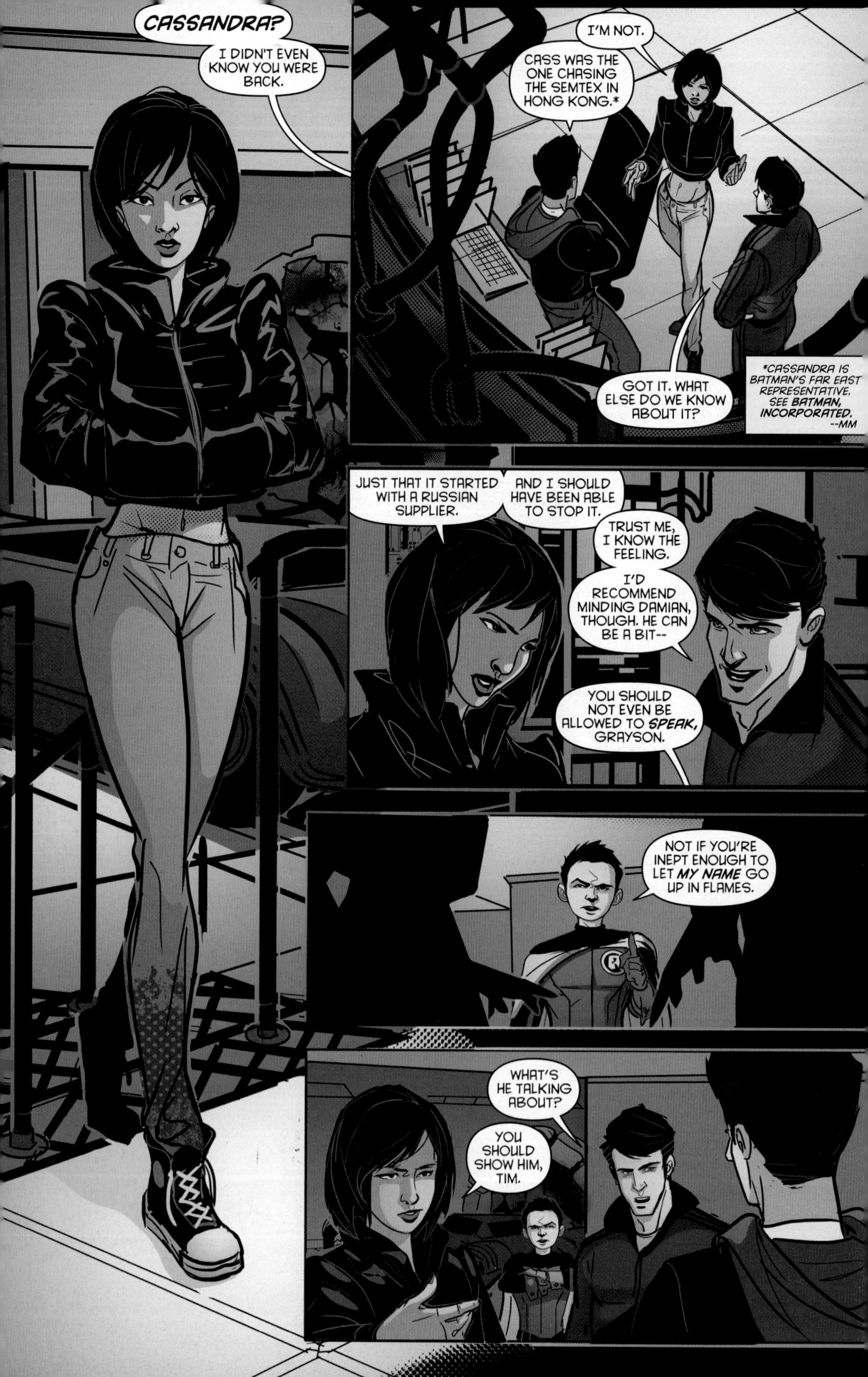
CASSANDRA?
I DIDN'T EVEN KNOW YOU WERE BACK.
I'M NOT.
CASS WAS THE ONE CHASING THE SEMTEX IN HONG KONG.*
GOT IT. WHAT ELSE DO WE KNOW ABOUT IT?
*CASSANDRA IS BATMAN'S FAR EAST REPRESENTATIVE. SEE BATMAN, INCORPORATED. --MM
JUST THAT IT STARTED WITH A RUSSIAN SUPPLIER.
AND I SHOULD HAVE BEEN ABLE TO STOP IT.
TRUST ME, I KNOW THE FEELING.
I'D RECOMMEND MINDING DAMIAN, THOUGH. HE CAN BE A BIT--
YOU SHOULD NOT EVEN BE ALLOWED TO SPEAK, GRAYSON.
NOT IF YOU'RE INEPT ENOUGH TO LET MY NAME GO UP IN FLAMES.
WHAT'S HE TALKING ABOUT?
YOU SHOULD SHOW HIM, TIM.

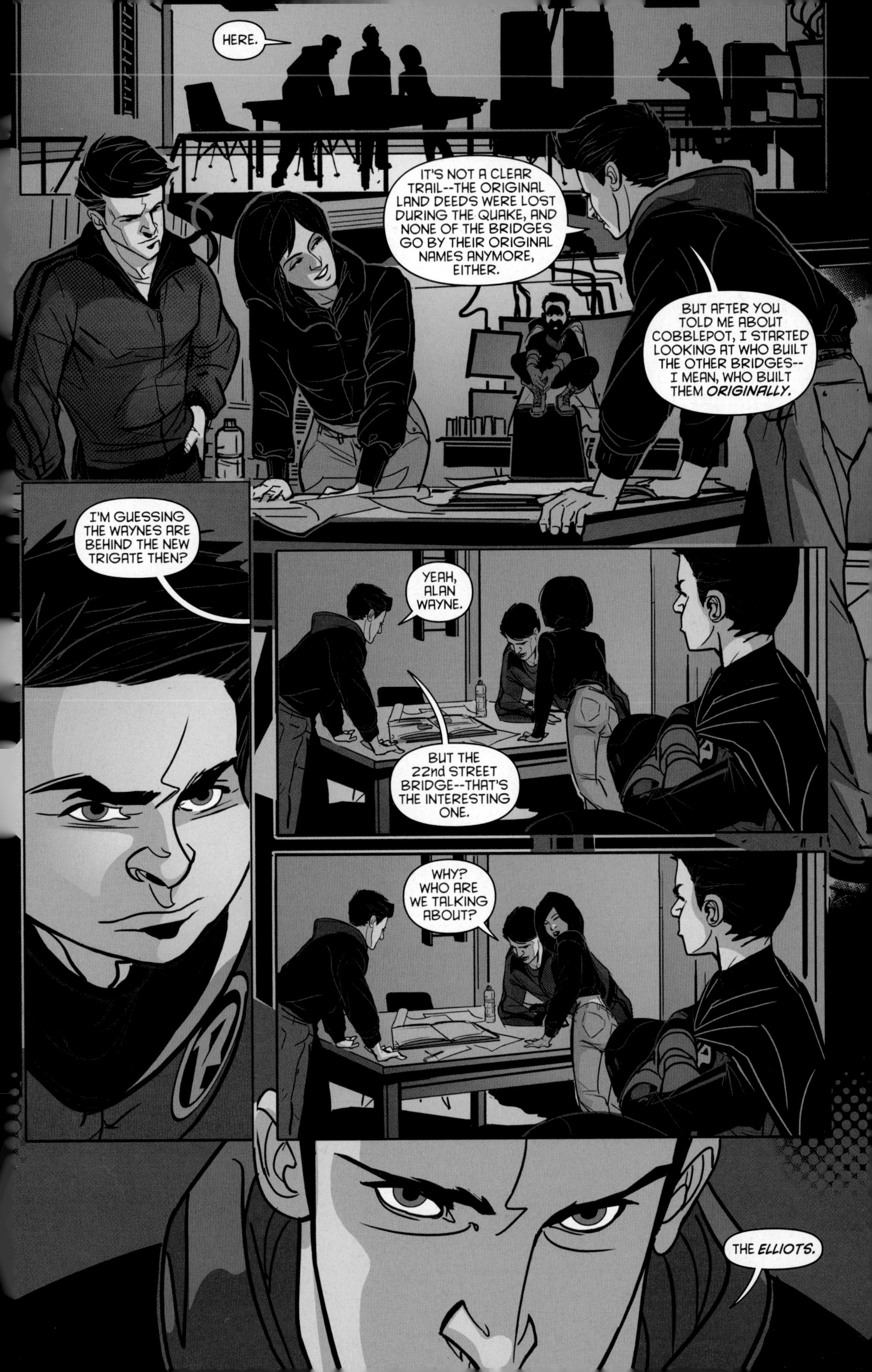
HERE.
IT'S NOT A CLEAR TRAIL--THE ORIGINAL LAND DEEDS WERE LOST DURING THE QUAKE, AND NONE OF THE BRIDGES GO BY THEIR ORIGINAL NAMES ANYMORE, EITHER.
BUT AFTER YOU TOLD ME ABOUT COBBLEPOT, I STARTED LOOKING AT WHO BUILT THE OTHER BRIDGES-- I MEAN, WHO BUILT THEM *ORIGINALLY.*
I'M GUESSING THE WAYNES ARE BEHIND THE NEW TRIGATE THEN?
YEAH, ALAN WAYNE.
BUT THE 22nd STREET BRIDGE--THAT'S THE INTERESTING ONE.
WHY? WHO ARE WE TALKING ABOUT?
THE *ELLIOTS.*

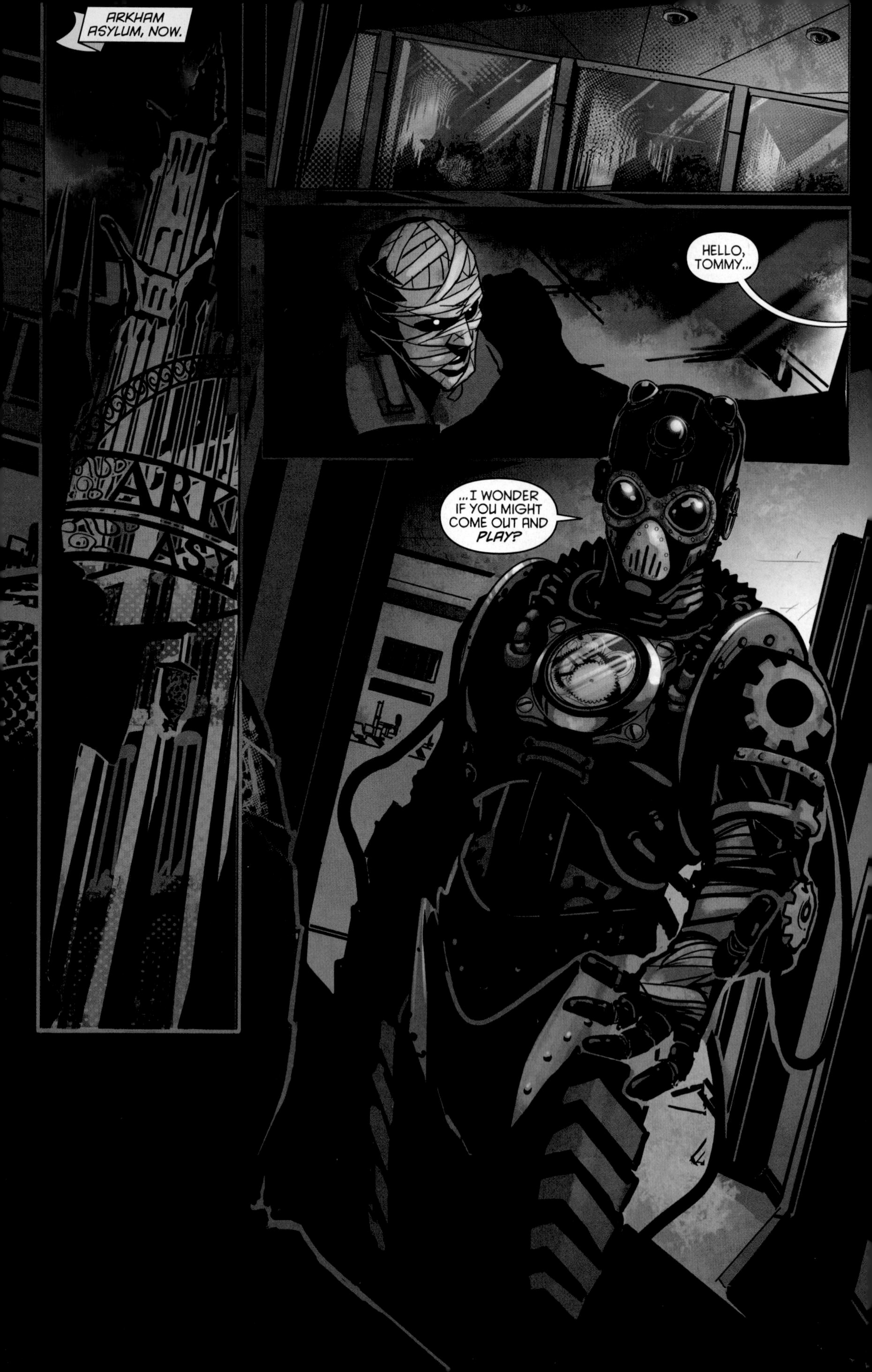
ARKHAM ASYLUM, NOW.
HELLO, TOMMY...
...I WONDER IF YOU MIGHT COME OUT AND PLAY?

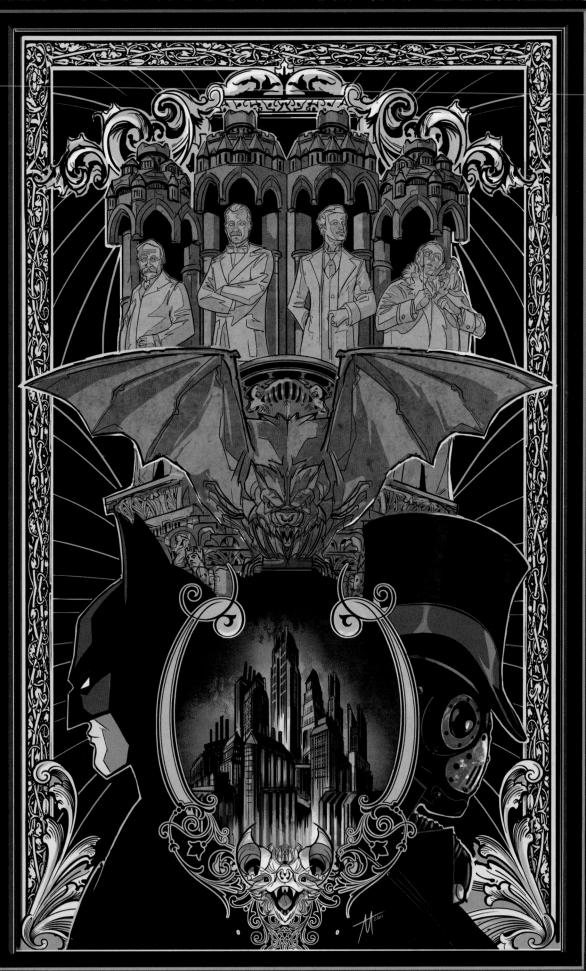

Part Two
THE FOUR FAMILIES OF GOTHAM

Scott **Snyder** & Kyle **Higgins**
story

Kyle **Higgins**
dialogue

Trevor **McCarthy**
art & cover

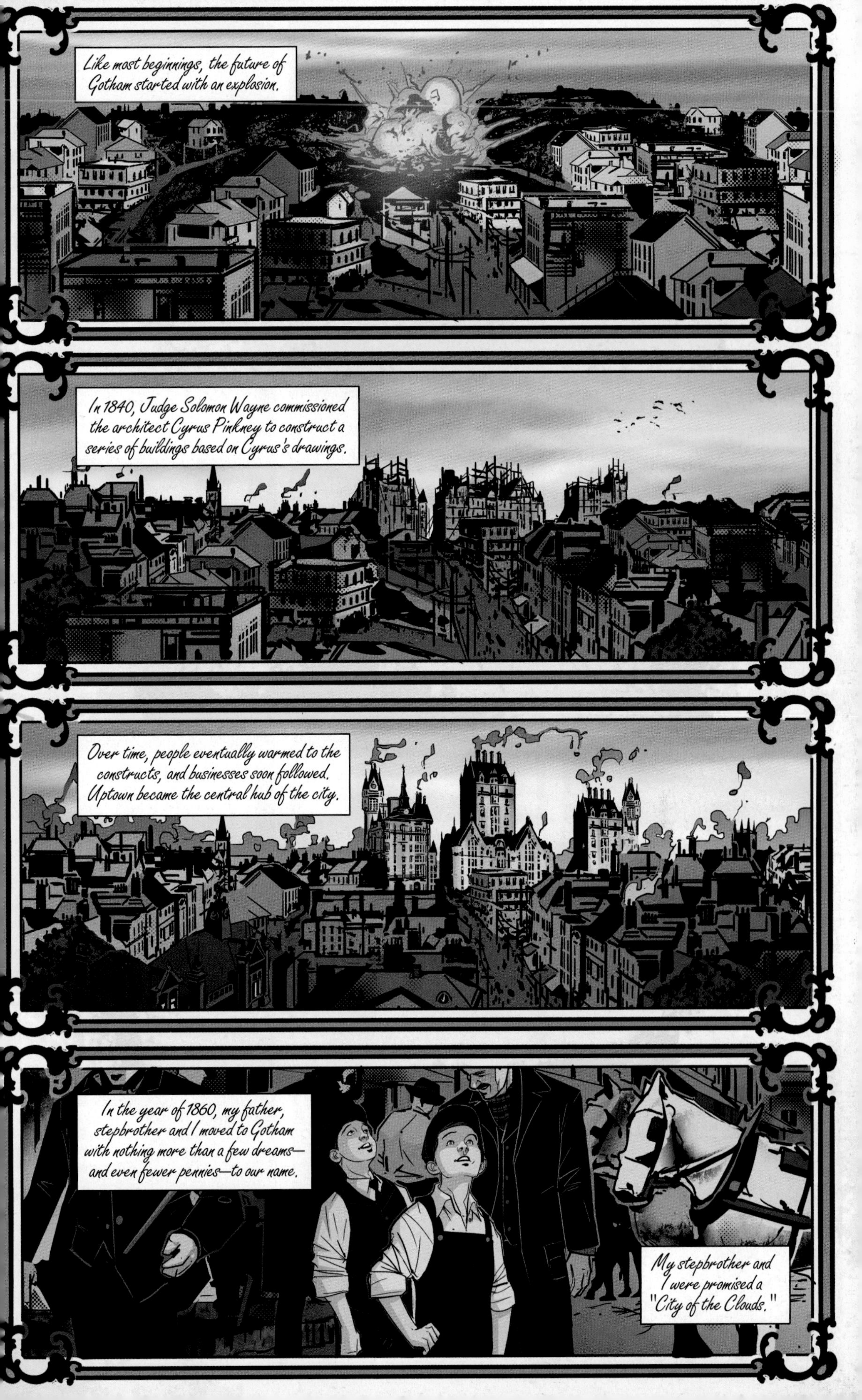
Like most beginnings, the future of Gotham started with an explosion.
In 1840, Judge Solomon Wayne commissioned the architect Cyrus Pinkney to construct a series of buildings based on Cyrus's drawings.
Over time, people eventually warmed to the constructs, and businesses soon followed. Uptown became the central hub of the city.
In the year of 1860, my father, stepbrother and I moved to Gotham with nothing more than a few dreams—and even fewer pennies—to our name.
My stepbrother and I were promised a "City of the Clouds."

However, on viewing the buildings for the first time, there was a feeling of disappointment.

The spires were taller than we'd ever seen, but not even close to piercing the sky.

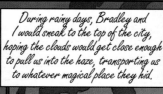

During rainy days, Bradley and I would sneak to the top of the city, hoping the clouds would get close enough to pull us into the haze, transporting us to whatever magical place they hid.

To where we thought our mother must be.

It was a game for children, nothing more than impossible dreams and fantasies.

And yet, isn't that often how the future is created? In the minds of children and dreamers?

As we grew older, we often spoke of a city above the clouds. It became an obsession for us, but not out of sentimentality.

It became an obsession because no one said it was possible.

We worked our way from the streets to the art boards, eventually procuring jobs as draftsmen in a small architecture firm just outside the hub of the city.

Our days were spent refining bridge and aqueduct designs around the country.

We were a good partnership from the beginning, my strengths as an idea man complementing Bradley's as a technician.

And then in 1877, after nearly two dozen bridges and a few small buildings, everything changed.

I HEAR YOU GENTLEMEN LIKE TO **BUILD**.

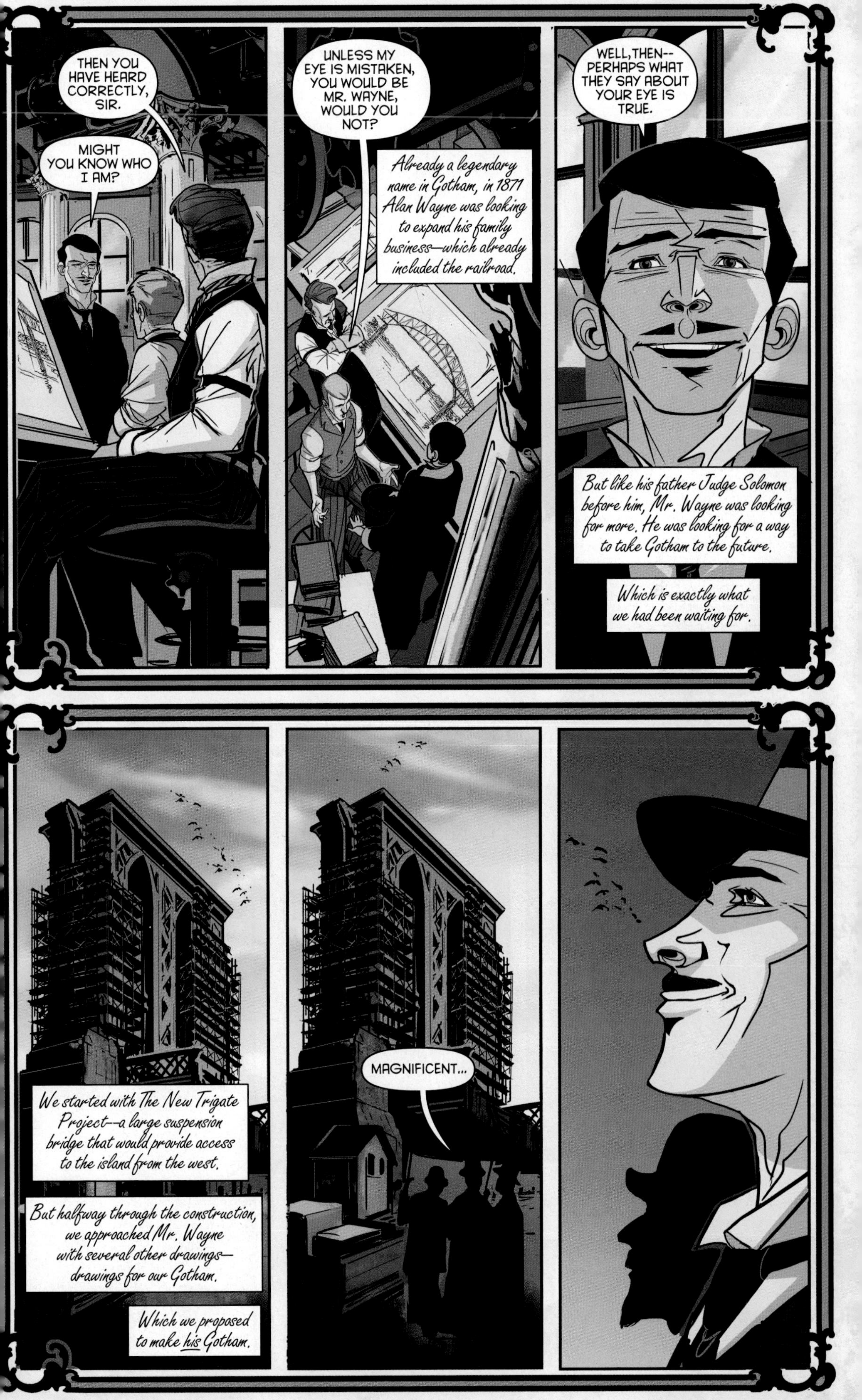
THEN YOU HAVE HEARD CORRECTLY, SIR.
MIGHT YOU KNOW WHO I AM?
UNLESS MY EYE IS MISTAKEN, YOU WOULD BE MR. WAYNE, WOULD YOU NOT?
Already a legendary name in Gotham, in 1871 Alan Wayne was looking to expand his family business—which already included the railroad.
WELL, THEN-- PERHAPS WHAT THEY SAY ABOUT YOUR EYE IS TRUE.
But like his father Judge Solomon before him, Mr. Wayne was looking for more. He was looking for a way to take Gotham to the future.
Which is exactly what we had been waiting for.
We started with The New Trigate Project—a large suspension bridge that would provide access to the island from the west.
But halfway through the construction, we approached Mr. Wayne with several other drawings—drawings for our Gotham.
Which we proposed to make his Gotham.
MAGNIFICENT...

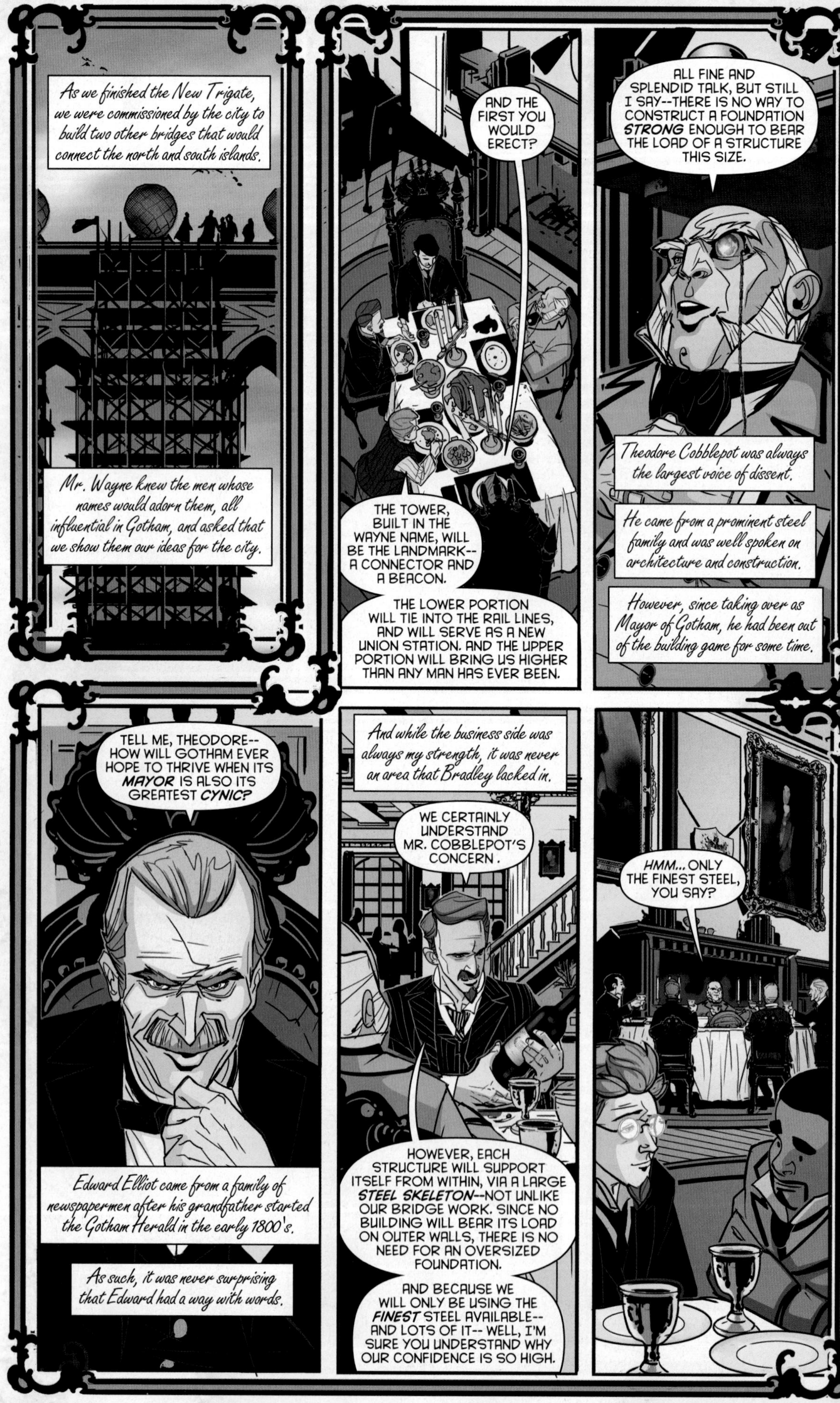

As we finished the New Trigate, we were commissioned by the city to build two other bridges that would connect the north and south islands.
Mr. Wayne knew the men whose names would adorn them, all influential in Gotham, and asked that we show them our ideas for the city.
AND THE FIRST YOU WOULD ERECT?
THE TOWER, BUILT IN THE WAYNE NAME, WILL BE THE LANDMARK-- A CONNECTOR AND A BEACON.
THE LOWER PORTION WILL TIE INTO THE RAIL LINES, AND WILL SERVE AS A NEW UNION STATION. AND THE UPPER PORTION WILL BRING US HIGHER THAN ANY MAN HAS EVER BEEN.
ALL FINE AND SPLENDID TALK, BUT STILL I SAY--THERE IS NO WAY TO CONSTRUCT A FOUNDATION STRONG ENOUGH TO BEAR THE LOAD OF A STRUCTURE THIS SIZE.
Theodore Cobblepot was always the largest voice of dissent.
He came from a prominent steel family and was well spoken on architecture and construction.
However, since taking over as Mayor of Gotham, he had been out of the building game for some time.
TELL ME, THEODORE-- HOW WILL GOTHAM EVER HOPE TO THRIVE WHEN ITS MAYOR IS ALSO ITS GREATEST CYNIC?
Edward Elliot came from a family of newspapermen after his grandfather started the Gotham Herald in the early 1800's.
As such, it was never surprising that Edward had a way with words.
And while the business side was always my strength, it was never an area that Bradley lacked in.
WE CERTAINLY UNDERSTAND MR. COBBLEPOT'S CONCERN.
HOWEVER, EACH STRUCTURE WILL SUPPORT ITSELF FROM WITHIN, VIA A LARGE STEEL SKELETON--NOT UNLIKE OUR BRIDGE WORK. SINCE NO BUILDING WILL BEAR ITS LOAD ON OUTER WALLS, THERE IS NO NEED FOR AN OVERSIZED FOUNDATION.
AND BECAUSE WE WILL ONLY BE USING THE FINEST STEEL AVAILABLE-- AND LOTS OF IT-- WELL, I'M SURE YOU UNDERSTAND WHY OUR CONFIDENCE IS SO HIGH.
HMM... ONLY THE FINEST STEEL, YOU SAY?

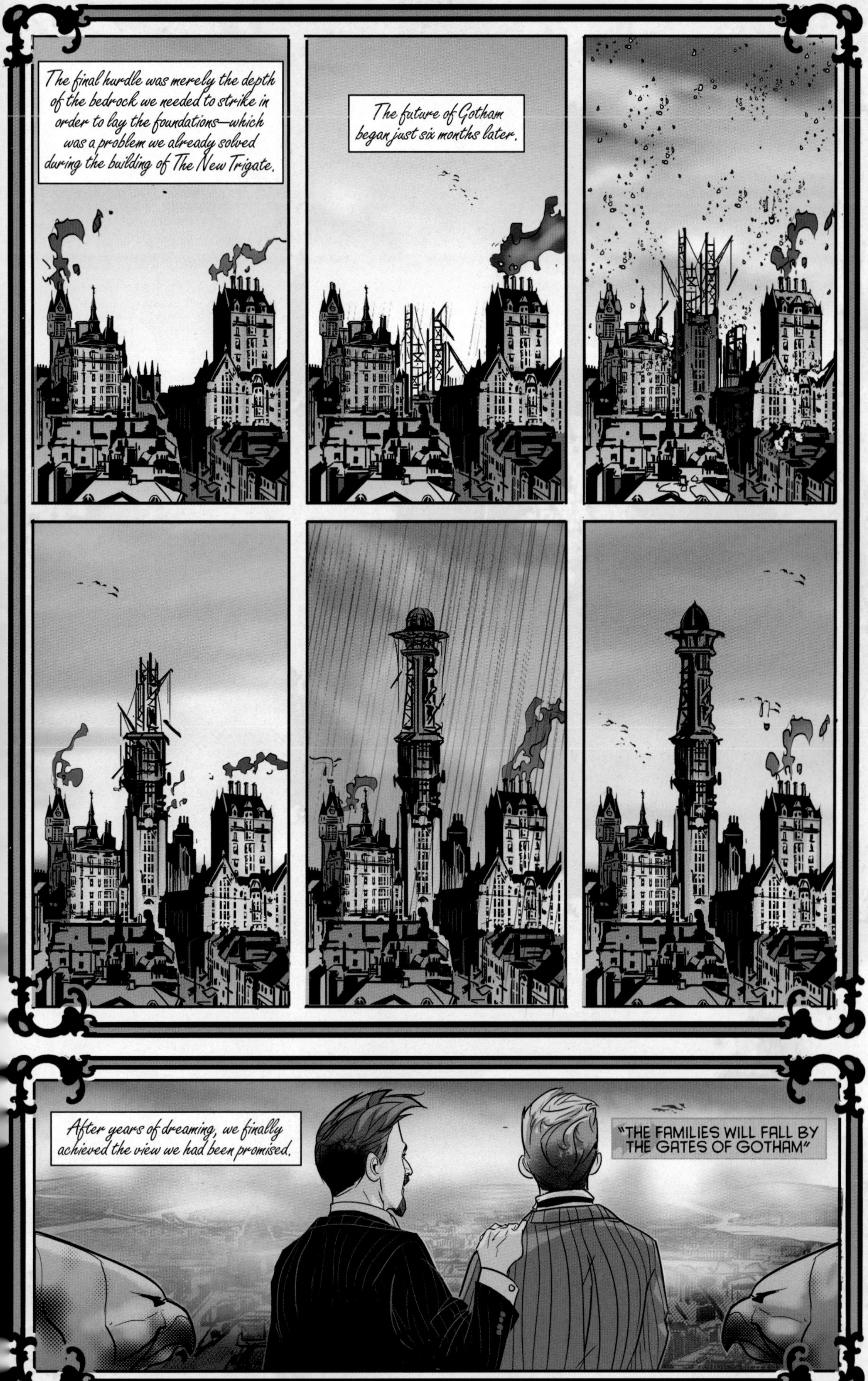
The final hurdle was merely the depth of the bedrock we needed to strike in order to lay the foundations—which was a problem we already solved during the building of The New Trigate.
The future of Gotham began just six months later.
After years of dreaming, we finally achieved the view we had been promised.
"THE FAMILIES WILL FALL BY THE GATES OF GOTHAM"

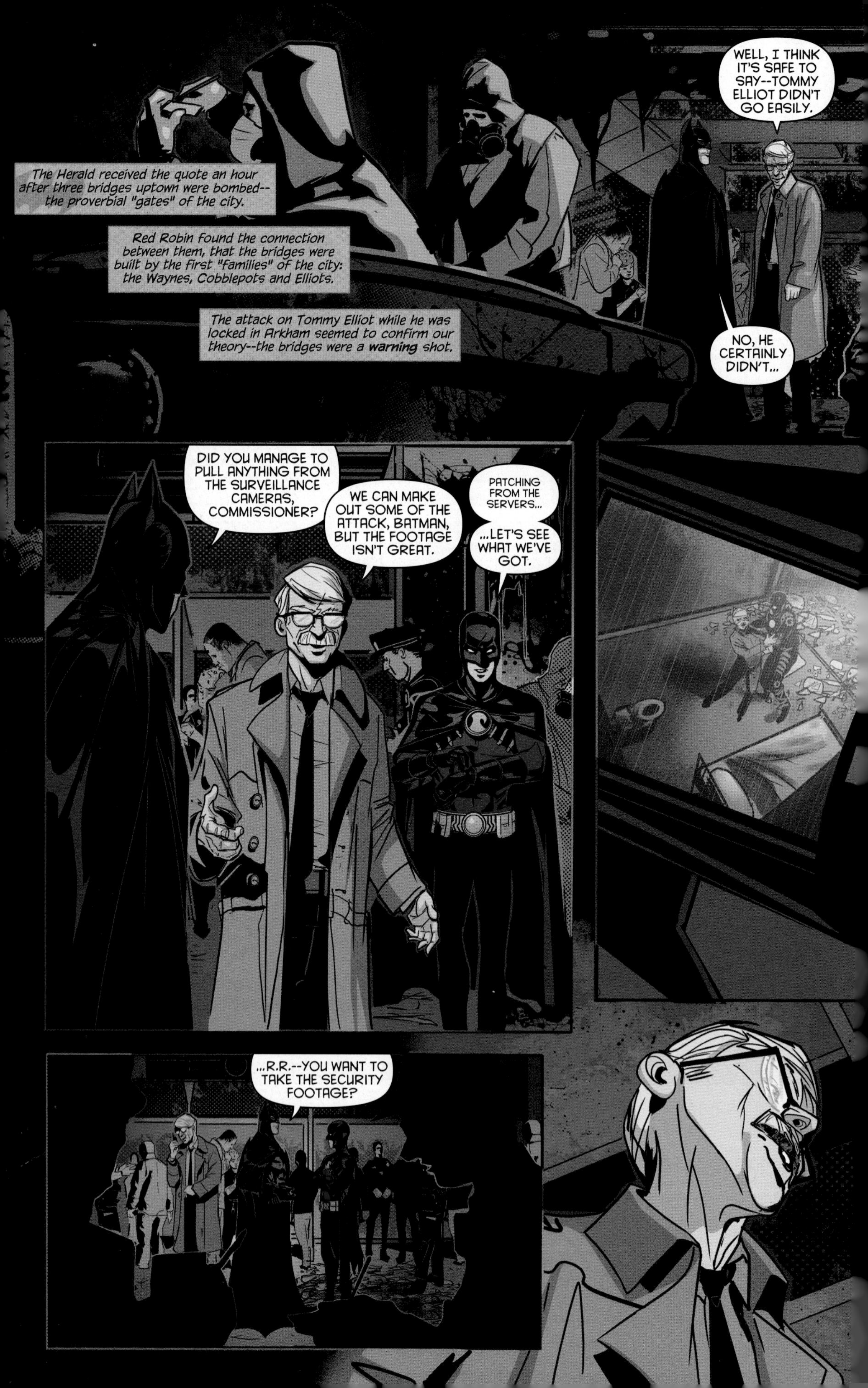
The Herald received the quote an hour after three bridges uptown were bombed--the proverbial "gates" of the city.
Red Robin found the connection between them, that the bridges were built by the first "families" of the city: the Waynes, Cobblepots and Elliots.
The attack on Tommy Elliot while he was locked in Arkham seemed to confirm our theory--the bridges were a warning shot.
WELL, I THINK IT'S SAFE TO SAY--TOMMY ELLIOT DIDN'T GO EASILY.
NO, HE CERTAINLY DIDN'T...
DID YOU MANAGE TO PULL ANYTHING FROM THE SURVEILLANCE CAMERAS, COMMISSIONER?
WE CAN MAKE OUT SOME OF THE ATTACK, BATMAN, BUT THE FOOTAGE ISN'T GREAT.
PATCHING FROM THE SERVERS...
...LET'S SEE WHAT WE'VE GOT.
...R.R.--YOU WANT TO TAKE THE SECURITY FOOTAGE?

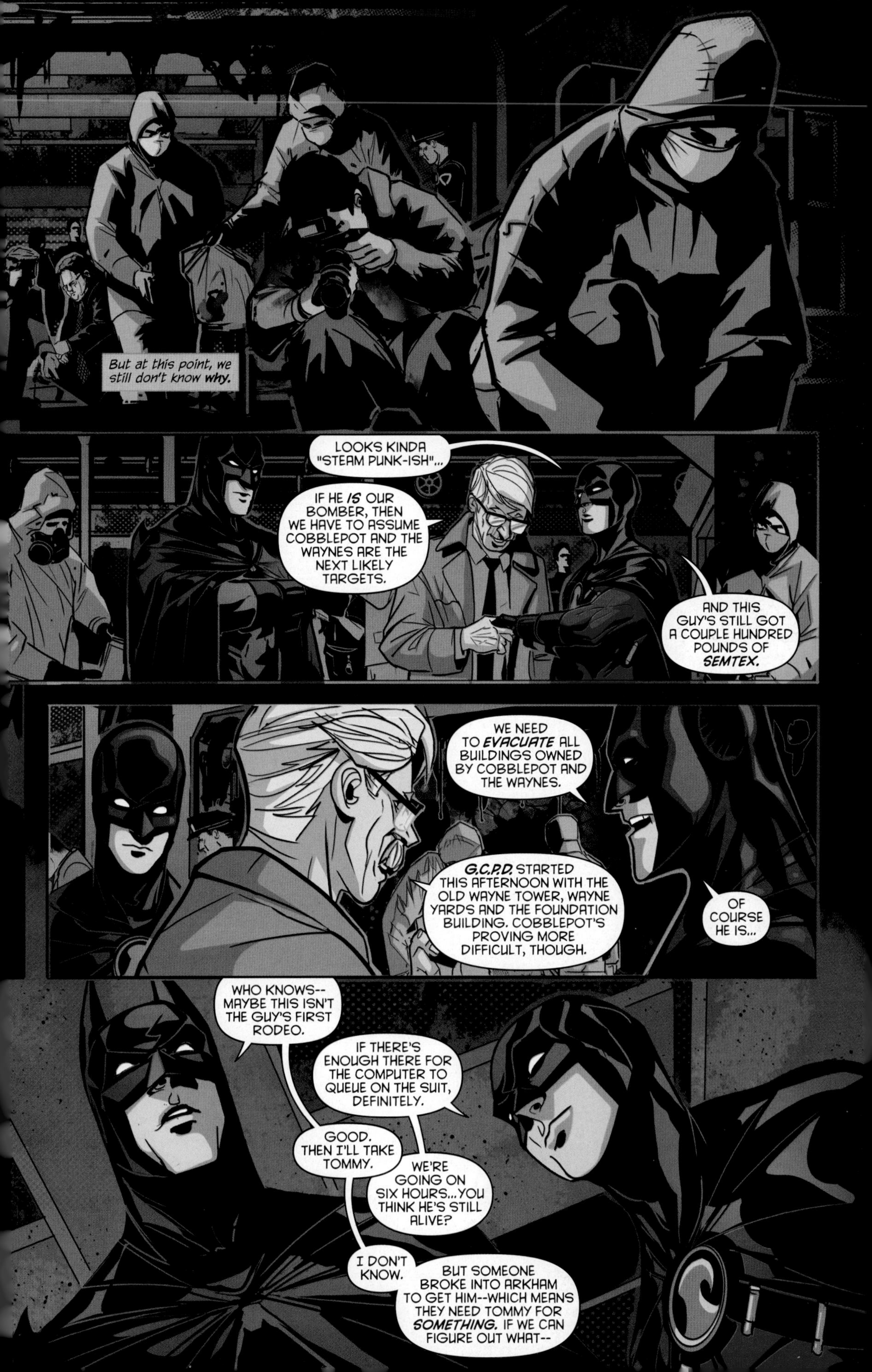
But at this point, we still don't know **why.**
LOOKS KINDA "STEAM PUNK-ISH"...
IF HE *IS* OUR BOMBER, THEN WE HAVE TO ASSUME COBBLEPOT AND THE WAYNES ARE THE NEXT LIKELY TARGETS.
AND THIS GUY'S STILL GOT A COUPLE HUNDRED POUNDS OF *SEMTEX.*
WE NEED TO *EVACUATE* ALL BUILDINGS OWNED BY COBBLEPOT AND THE WAYNES.
G.C.P.D. STARTED THIS AFTERNOON WITH THE OLD WAYNE TOWER, WAYNE YARDS AND THE FOUNDATION BUILDING. COBBLEPOT'S PROVING MORE DIFFICULT, THOUGH.
OF COURSE HE IS...
WHO KNOWS--MAYBE THIS ISN'T THE GUY'S FIRST RODEO.
IF THERE'S ENOUGH THERE FOR THE COMPUTER TO QUEUE ON THE SUIT, DEFINITELY.
GOOD. THEN I'LL TAKE TOMMY.
WE'RE GOING ON SIX HOURS...YOU THINK HE'S STILL ALIVE?
I DON'T KNOW.
BUT SOMEONE BROKE INTO ARKHAM TO GET HIM--WHICH MEANS THEY NEED TOMMY FOR *SOMETHING.* IF WE CAN FIGURE OUT WHAT--

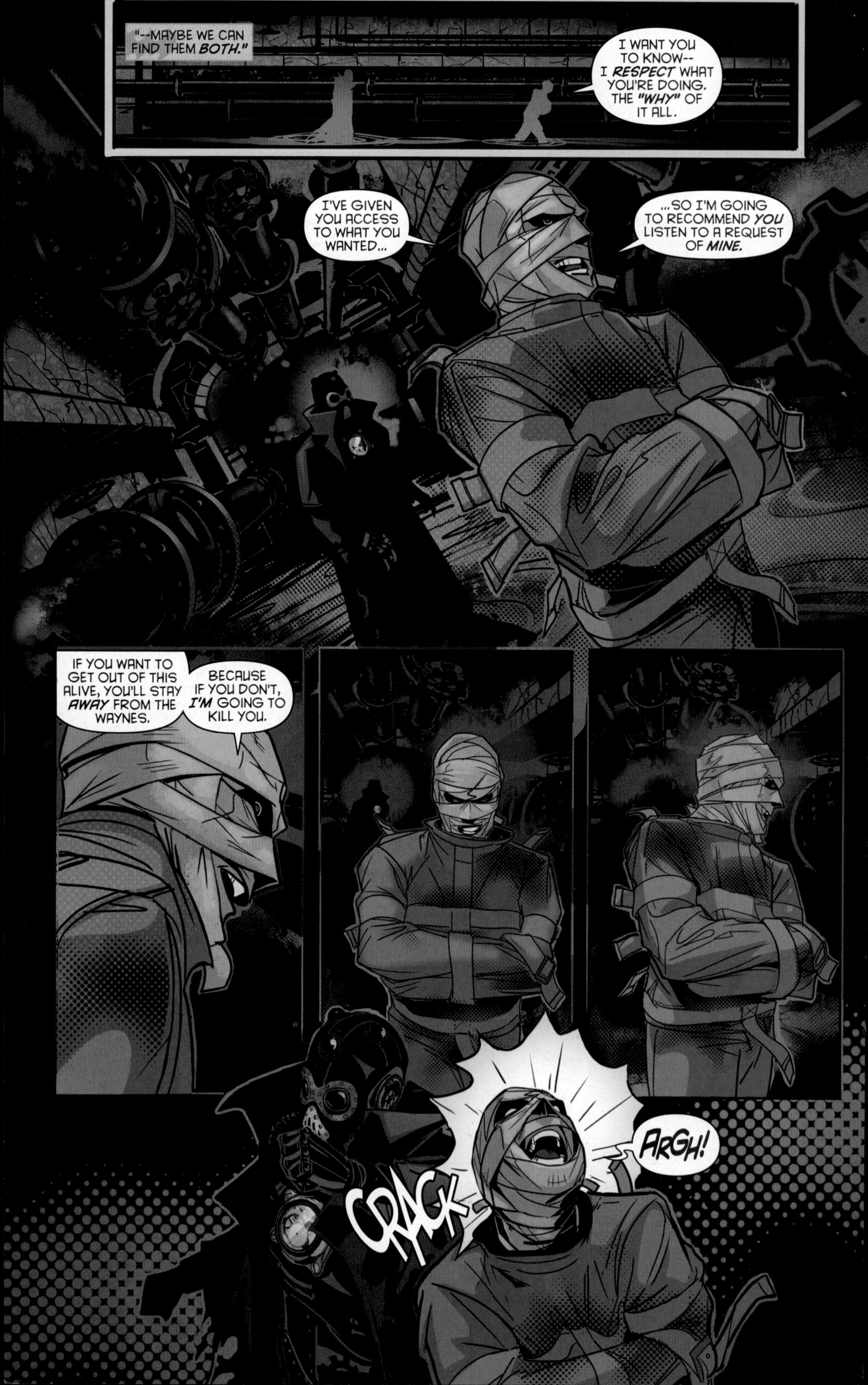
"--MAYBE WE CAN FIND THEM *BOTH.*"
I WANT YOU TO KNOW-- I *RESPECT* WHAT YOU'RE DOING. THE *"WHY"* OF IT ALL.
I'VE GIVEN YOU ACCESS TO WHAT YOU WANTED...
...SO I'M GOING TO RECOMMEND *YOU* LISTEN TO A REQUEST OF *MINE.*
IF YOU WANT TO GET OUT OF THIS ALIVE, YOU'LL STAY *AWAY* FROM THE WAYNES.
BECAUSE IF YOU DON'T, *I'M* GOING TO KILL YOU.
CRACK
ARGH!

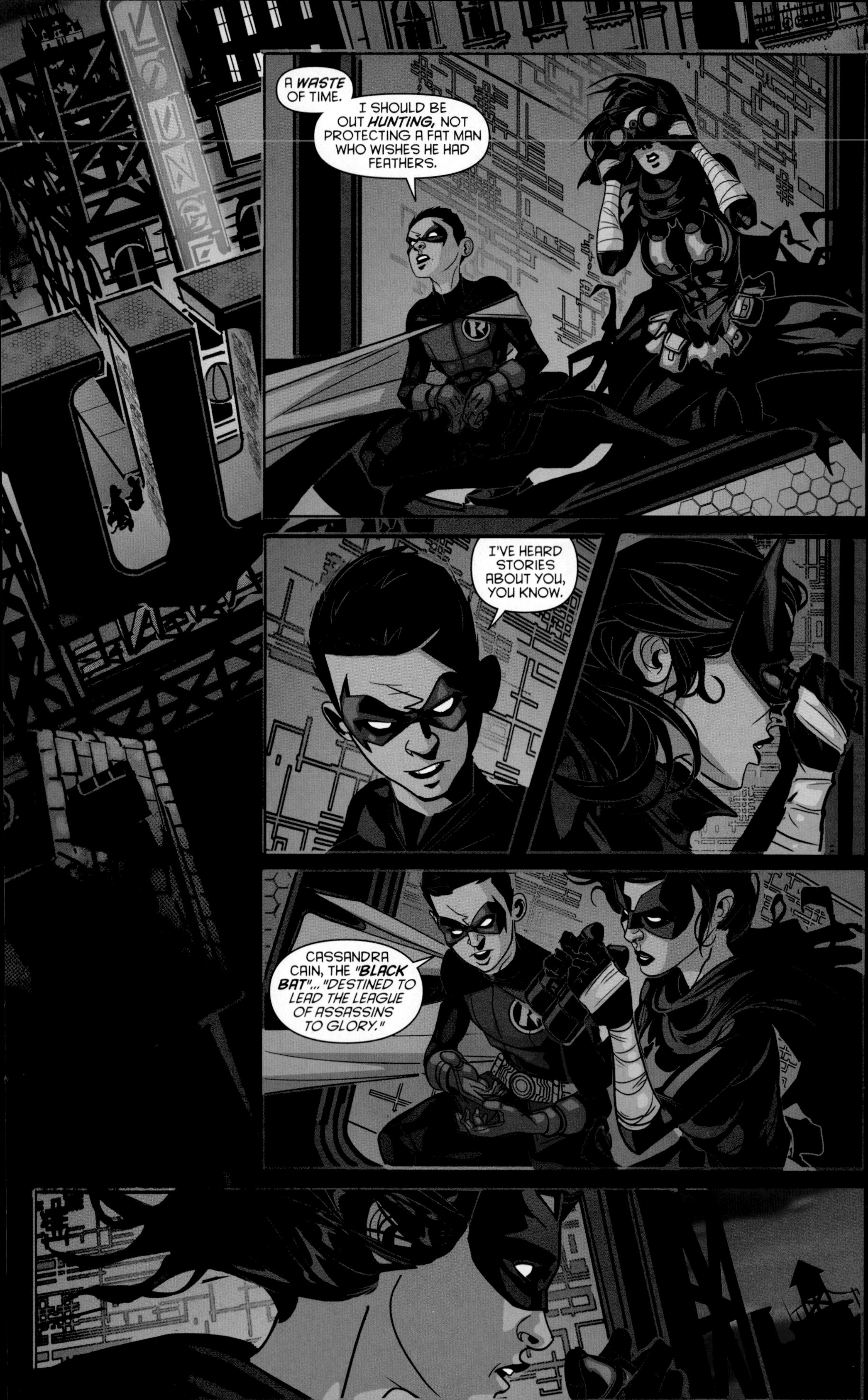

A WASTE OF TIME.
I SHOULD BE OUT HUNTING, NOT PROTECTING A FAT MAN WHO WISHES HE HAD FEATHERS.
I'VE HEARD STORIES ABOUT YOU, YOU KNOW.
CASSANDRA CAIN, THE "BLACK BAT"... "DESTINED TO LEAD THE LEAGUE OF ASSASSINS TO GLORY."

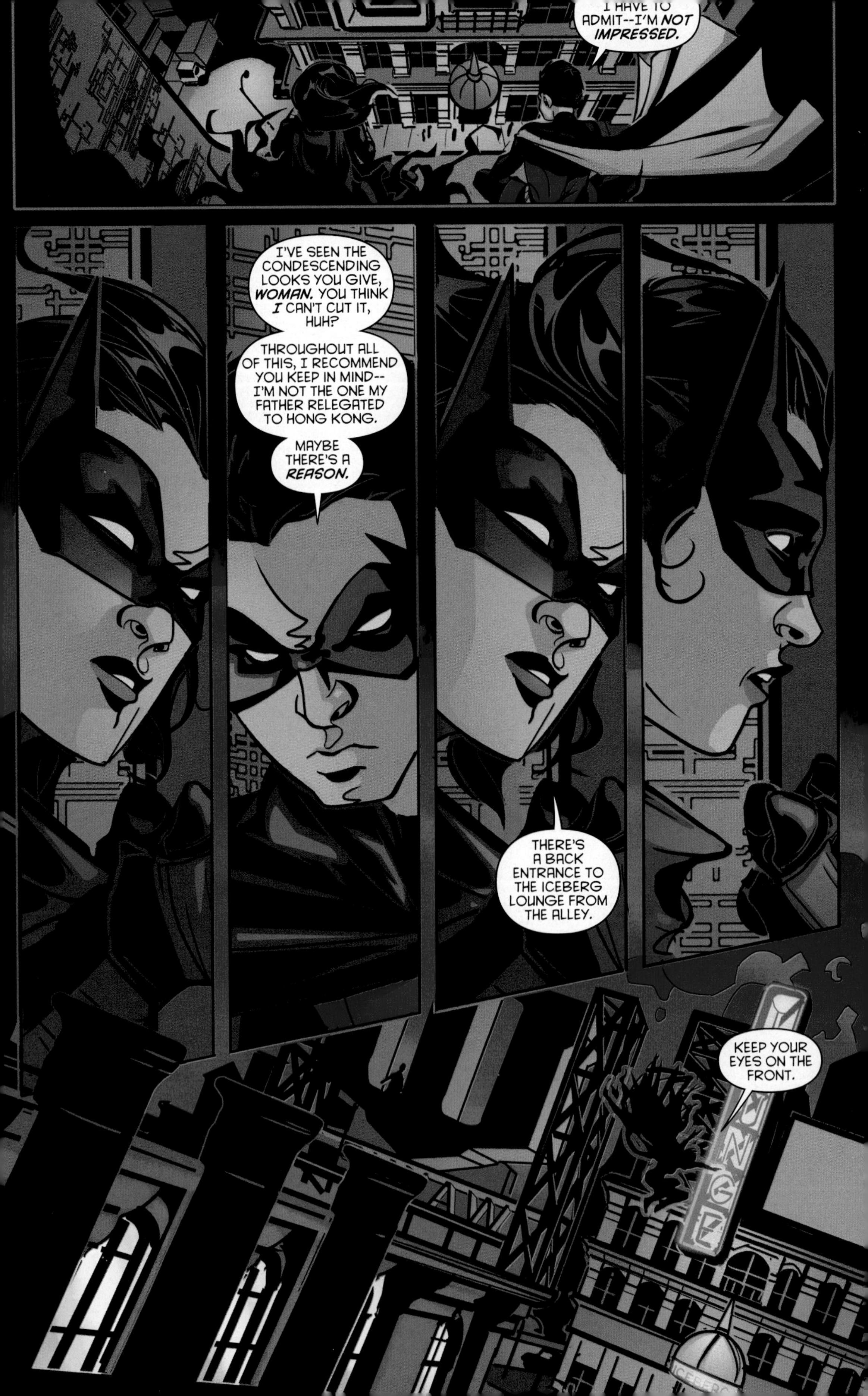
I HAVE TO ADMIT--I'M NOT IMPRESSED.
I'VE SEEN THE CONDESCENDING LOOKS YOU GIVE, WOMAN. YOU THINK I CAN'T CUT IT, HUH?
THROUGHOUT ALL OF THIS, I RECOMMEND YOU KEEP IN MIND-- I'M NOT THE ONE MY FATHER RELEGATED TO HONG KONG.
MAYBE THERE'S A REASON.
THERE'S A BACK ENTRANCE TO THE ICEBERG LOUNGE FROM THE ALLEY.
KEEP YOUR EYES ON THE FRONT.
LOUNGE

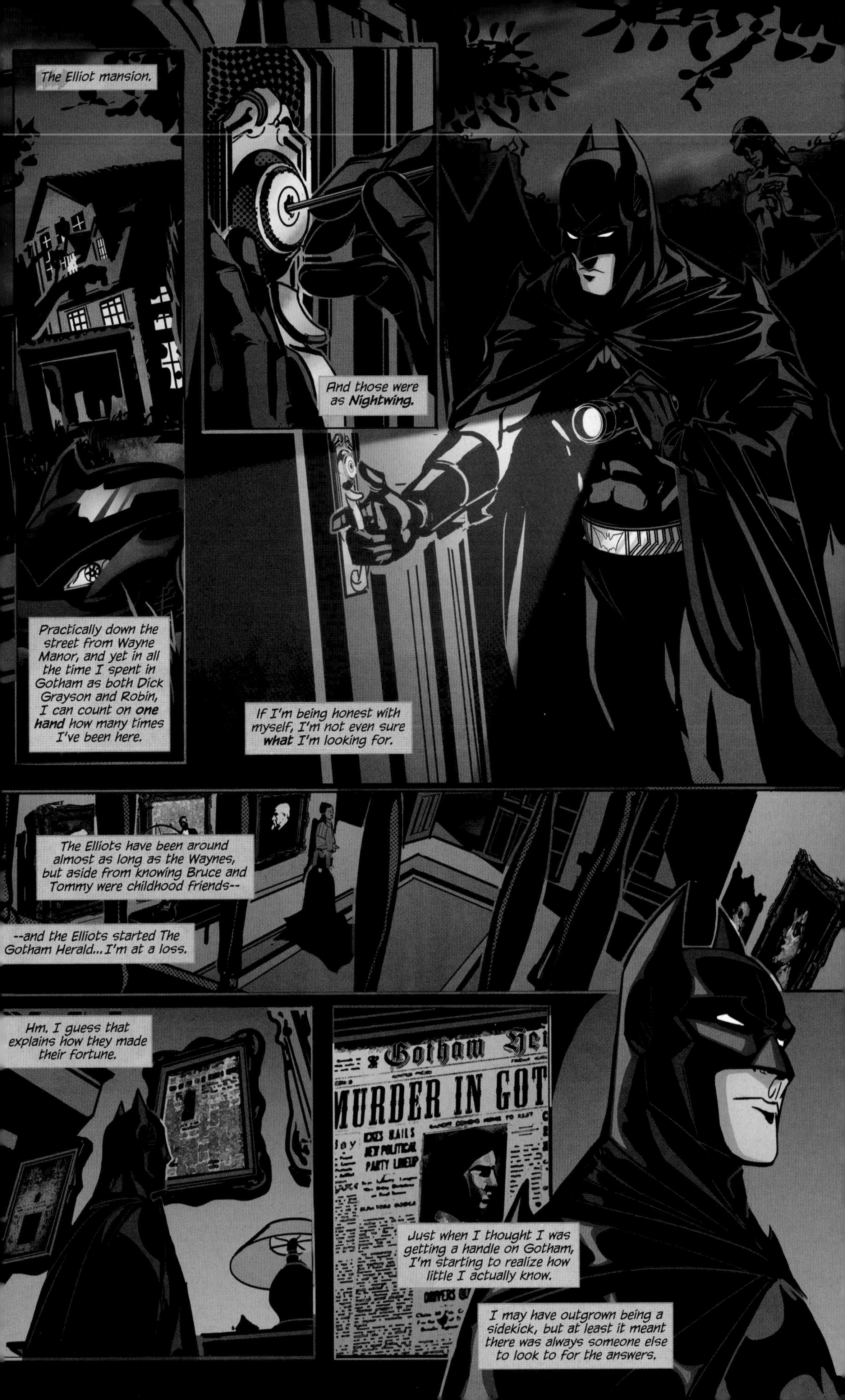

The Elliot mansion.
And those were as **Nightwing.**
Practically down the street from Wayne Manor, and yet in all the time I spent in Gotham as both Dick Grayson and Robin, I can count on **one hand** how many times I've been here.
If I'm being honest with myself, I'm not even sure **what** I'm looking for.
The Elliots have been around almost as long as the Waynes, but aside from knowing Bruce and Tommy were childhood friends--
--and the Elliots started The Gotham Herald... I'm at a loss.
Hm. I guess that explains how they made their fortune.
Gotham
MURDER IN GOT
Just when I thought I was getting a handle on Gotham, I'm starting to realize how little I actually know.
I may have outgrown being a sidekick, but at least it meant there was always someone else to look to for the answers.

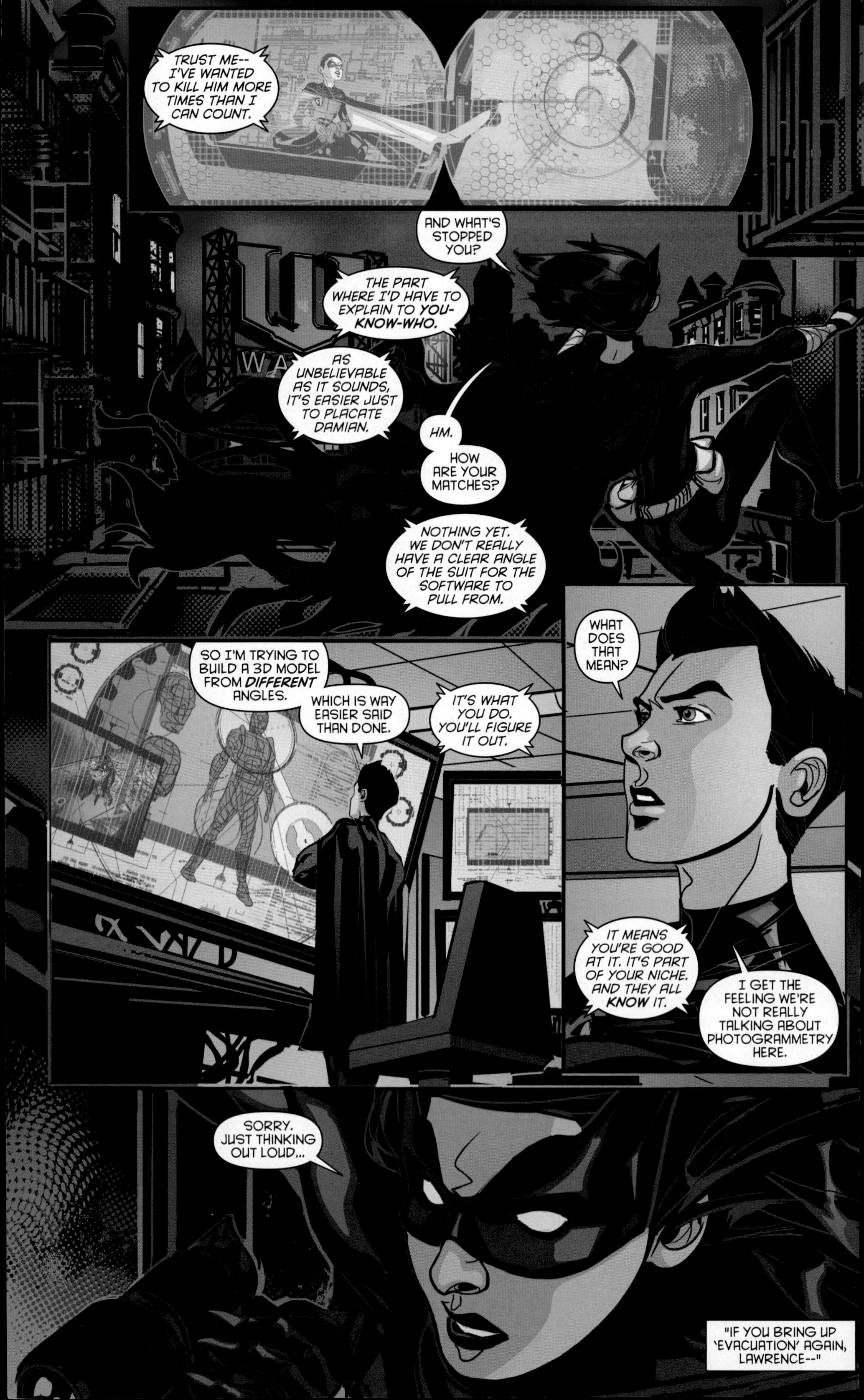

TRUST ME-- I'VE WANTED TO KILL HIM MORE TIMES THAN I CAN COUNT.
AND WHAT'S STOPPED YOU?
THE PART WHERE I'D HAVE TO EXPLAIN TO YOU-KNOW-WHO.
AS UNBELIEVABLE AS IT SOUNDS, IT'S EASIER JUST TO PLACATE DAMIAN.
HM.
HOW ARE YOUR MATCHES?
NOTHING YET. WE DON'T REALLY HAVE A CLEAR ANGLE OF THE SUIT FOR THE SOFTWARE TO PULL FROM.
SO I'M TRYING TO BUILD A 3D MODEL FROM DIFFERENT ANGLES.
WHICH IS WAY EASIER SAID THAN DONE.
IT'S WHAT YOU DO. YOU'LL FIGURE IT OUT.
WHAT DOES THAT MEAN?
IT MEANS YOU'RE GOOD AT IT. IT'S PART OF YOUR NICHE. AND THEY ALL KNOW IT.
I GET THE FEELING WE'RE NOT REALLY TALKING ABOUT PHOTOGRAMMETRY HERE.
SORRY. JUST THINKING OUT LOUD...
"IF YOU BRING UP 'EVACUATION' AGAIN, LAWRENCE--"

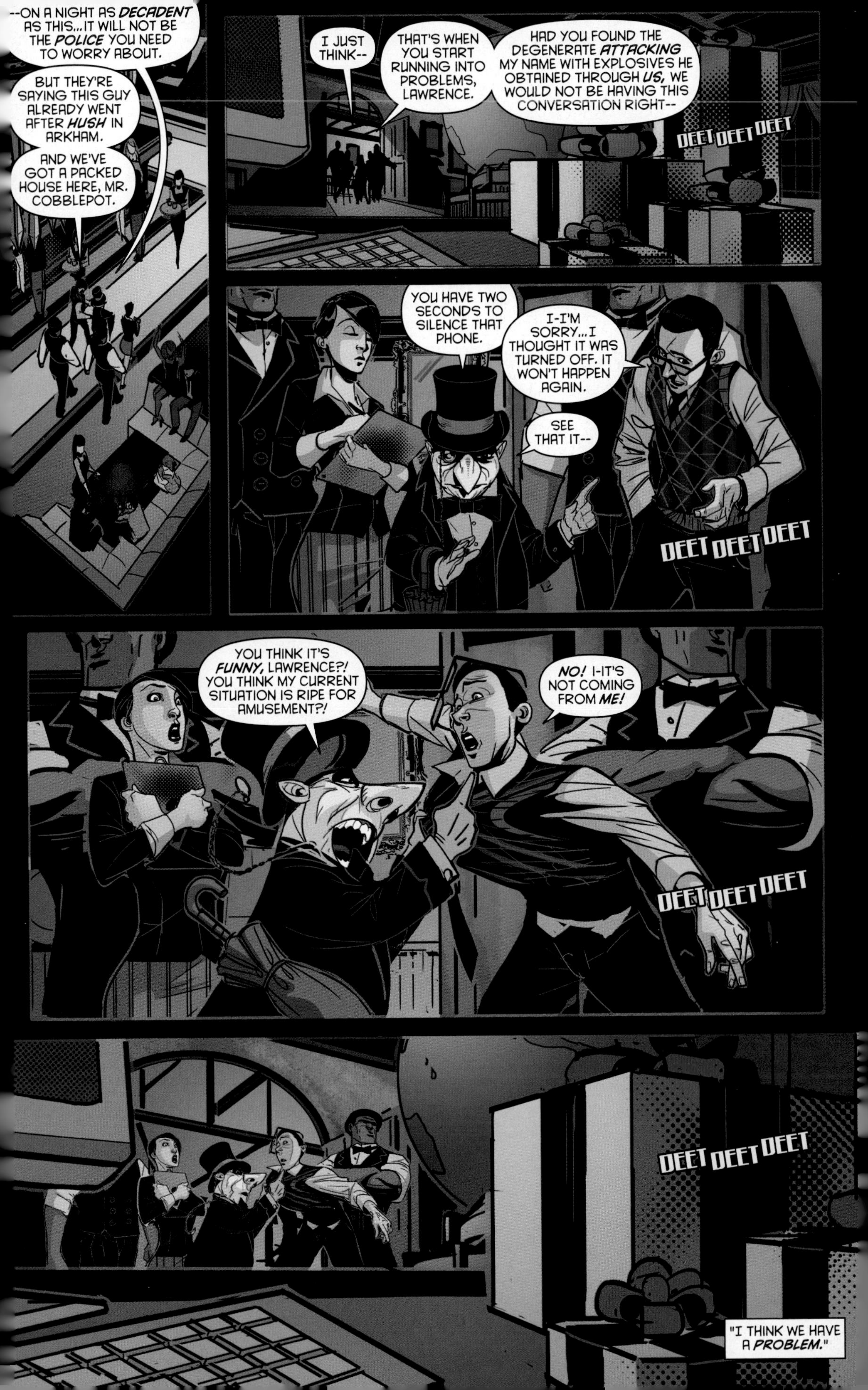
--ON A NIGHT AS *DECADENT* AS THIS...IT WILL NOT BE THE *POLICE* YOU NEED TO WORRY ABOUT.
BUT THEY'RE SAYING THIS GUY ALREADY WENT AFTER *HUSH* IN ARKHAM.
AND WE'VE GOT A PACKED HOUSE HERE, MR. COBBLEPOT.
I JUST THINK--
THAT'S WHEN YOU START RUNNING INTO PROBLEMS, LAWRENCE.
HAD YOU FOUND THE DEGENERATE *ATTACKING* MY NAME WITH EXPLOSIVES HE OBTAINED THROUGH *US,* WE WOULD NOT BE HAVING THIS CONVERSATION RIGHT--
DEET DEET DEET
YOU HAVE TWO SECONDS TO SILENCE THAT PHONE.
I-I'M SORRY...I THOUGHT IT WAS TURNED OFF. IT WON'T HAPPEN AGAIN.
SEE THAT IT--
DEET DEET DEET
YOU THINK IT'S *FUNNY,* LAWRENCE?! YOU THINK MY CURRENT SITUATION IS RIPE FOR AMUSEMENT?!
NO! I-IT'S NOT COMING FROM *ME!*
DEET DEET DEET
DEET DEET DEET
"I THINK WE HAVE A *PROBLEM.*"

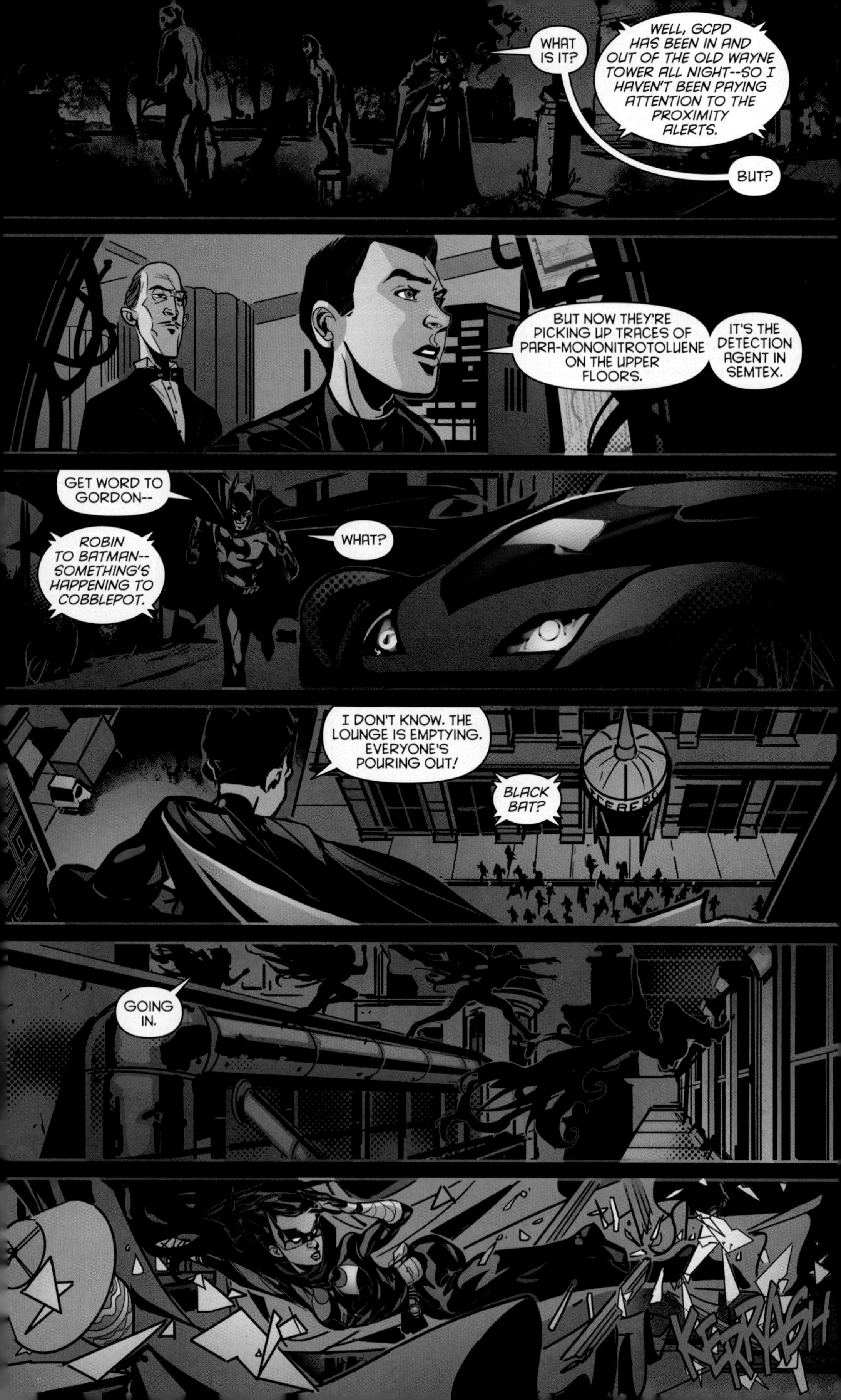
WHAT IS IT?
WELL, GCPD HAS BEEN IN AND OUT OF THE OLD WAYNE TOWER ALL NIGHT--SO I HAVEN'T BEEN PAYING ATTENTION TO THE PROXIMITY ALERTS.
BUT?
BUT NOW THEY'RE PICKING UP TRACES OF PARA-MONONITROTOLUENE ON THE UPPER FLOORS.
IT'S THE DETECTION AGENT IN SEMTEX.
GET WORD TO GORDON--
ROBIN TO BATMAN--SOMETHING'S HAPPENING TO COBBLEPOT.
WHAT?
I DON'T KNOW. THE LOUNGE IS EMPTYING. EVERYONE'S POURING OUT!
BLACK BAT?
GOING IN.
KERRASH

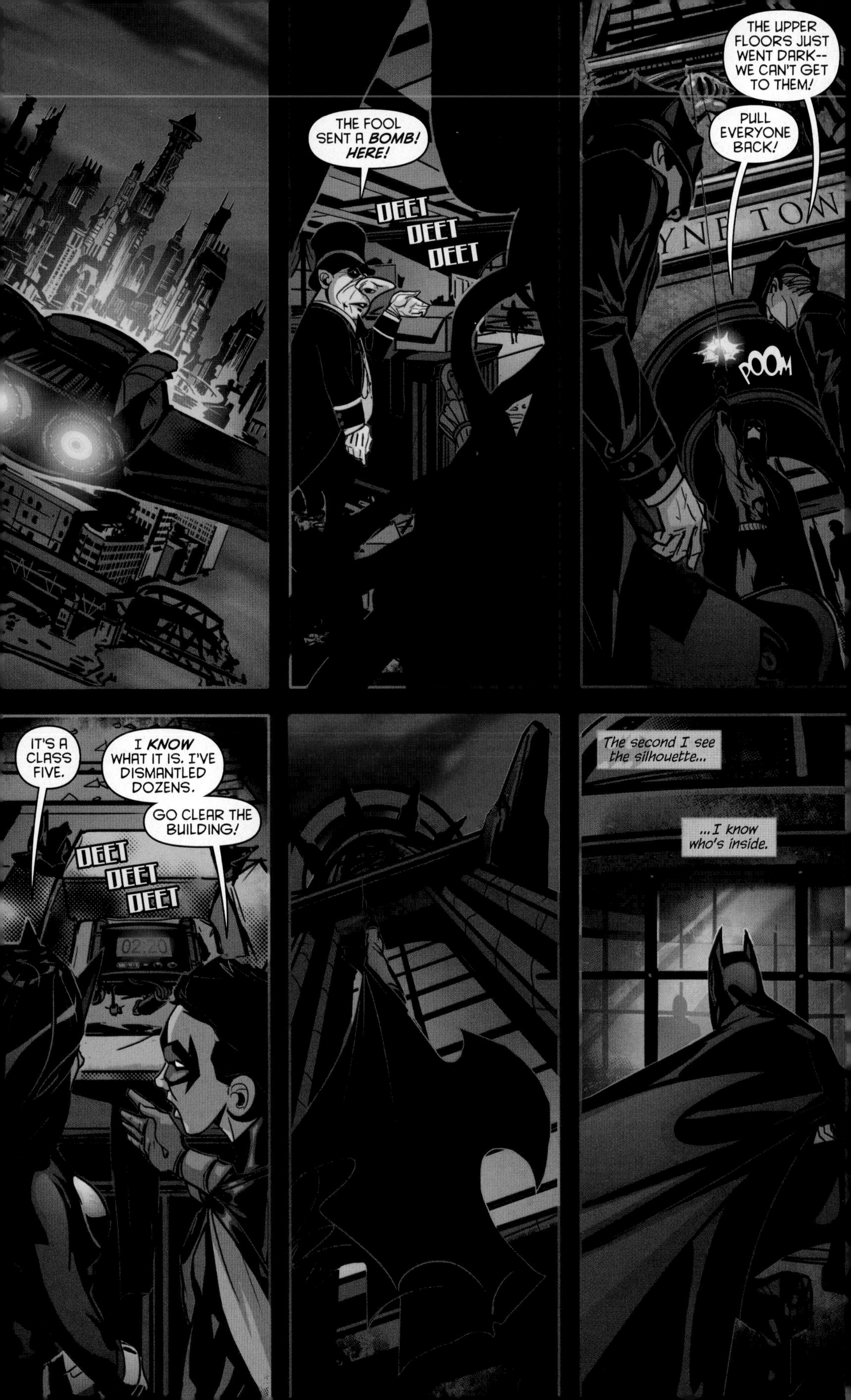
THE FOOL SENT A BOMB! HERE!
DEET DEET DEET
THE UPPER FLOORS JUST WENT DARK-- WE CAN'T GET TO THEM!
PULL EVERYONE BACK!
YNE TOW
POOM
IT'S A CLASS FIVE.
I KNOW WHAT IT IS. I'VE DISMANTLED DOZENS.
GO CLEAR THE BUILDING!
DEET DEET DEET
02:20
The second I see the silhouette...
...I know who's inside.

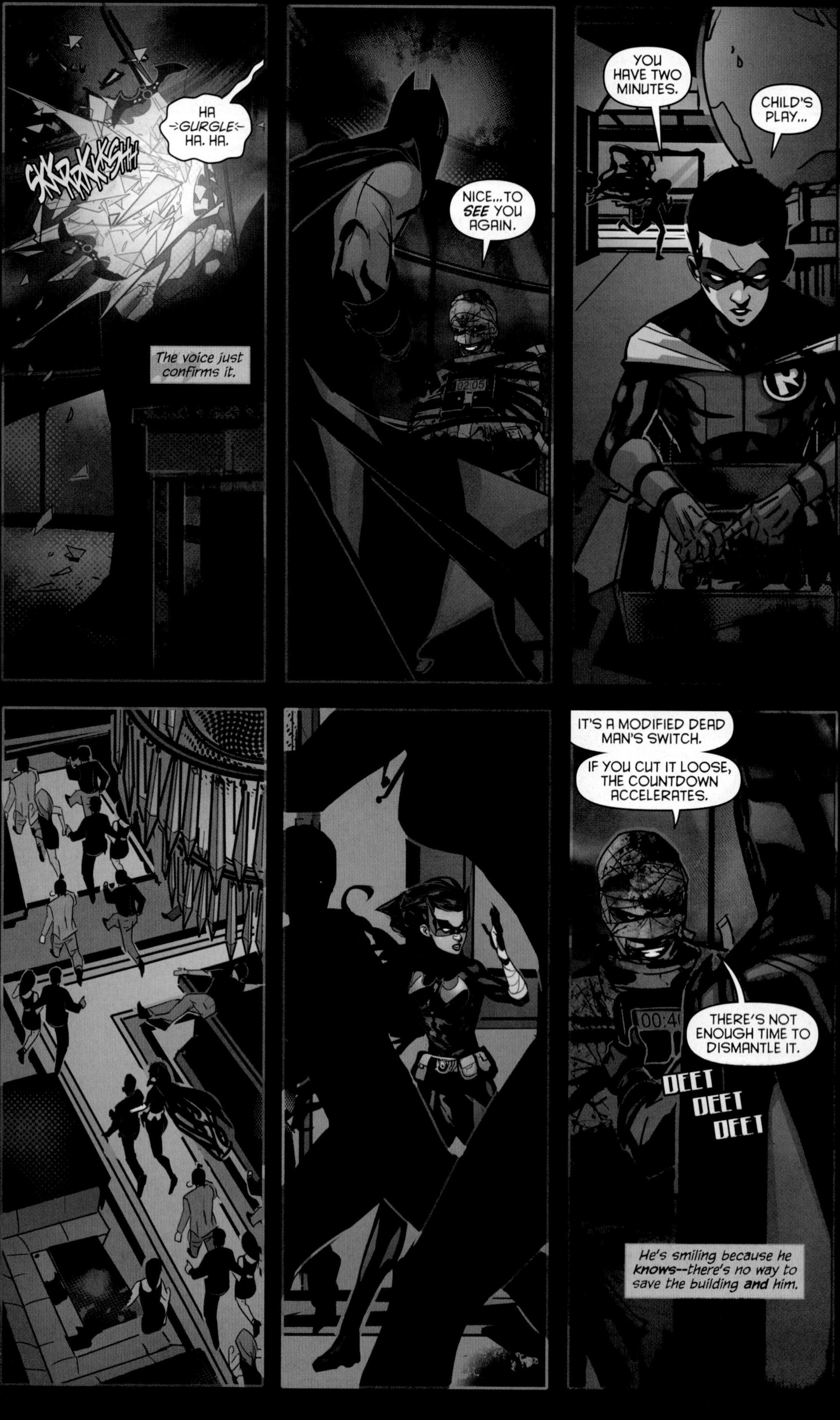
SKKRKKKSHH
HA
-GURGLE-
HA. HA.
The voice just confirms it.
NICE...TO SEE YOU AGAIN.
02:05
YOU HAVE TWO MINUTES.
CHILD'S PLAY...
IT'S A MODIFIED DEAD MAN'S SWITCH.
IF YOU CUT IT LOOSE, THE COUNTDOWN ACCELERATES.
THERE'S NOT ENOUGH TIME TO DISMANTLE IT.
DEET
DEET
DEET
He's smiling because he knows--there's no way to save the building and him.

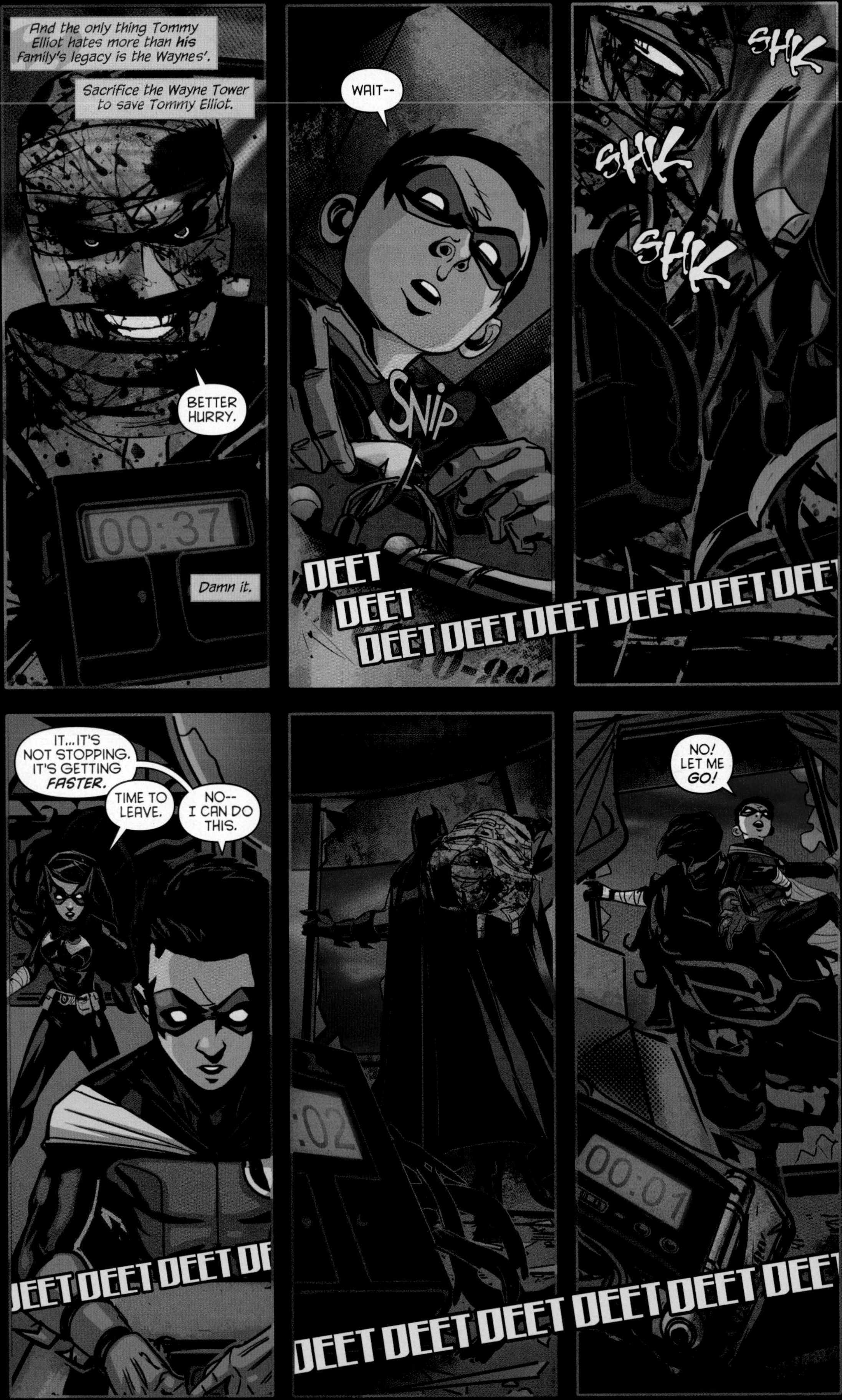

And the only thing Tommy Elliot hates more than his family's legacy is the Waynes'.
Sacrifice the Wayne Tower to save Tommy Elliot.
BETTER HURRY.
00:37
Damn it.
WAIT--
SNIP
DEET DEET DEET DEET DEET DEET DEET DEE
SHK
SHK
SHK
IT...IT'S NOT STOPPING. IT'S GETTING FASTER.
TIME TO LEAVE.
NO-- I CAN DO THIS.
DEET DEET DEET
:02
DEET DEET DEET DEET DEET DEET
NO! LET ME GO!
00:01

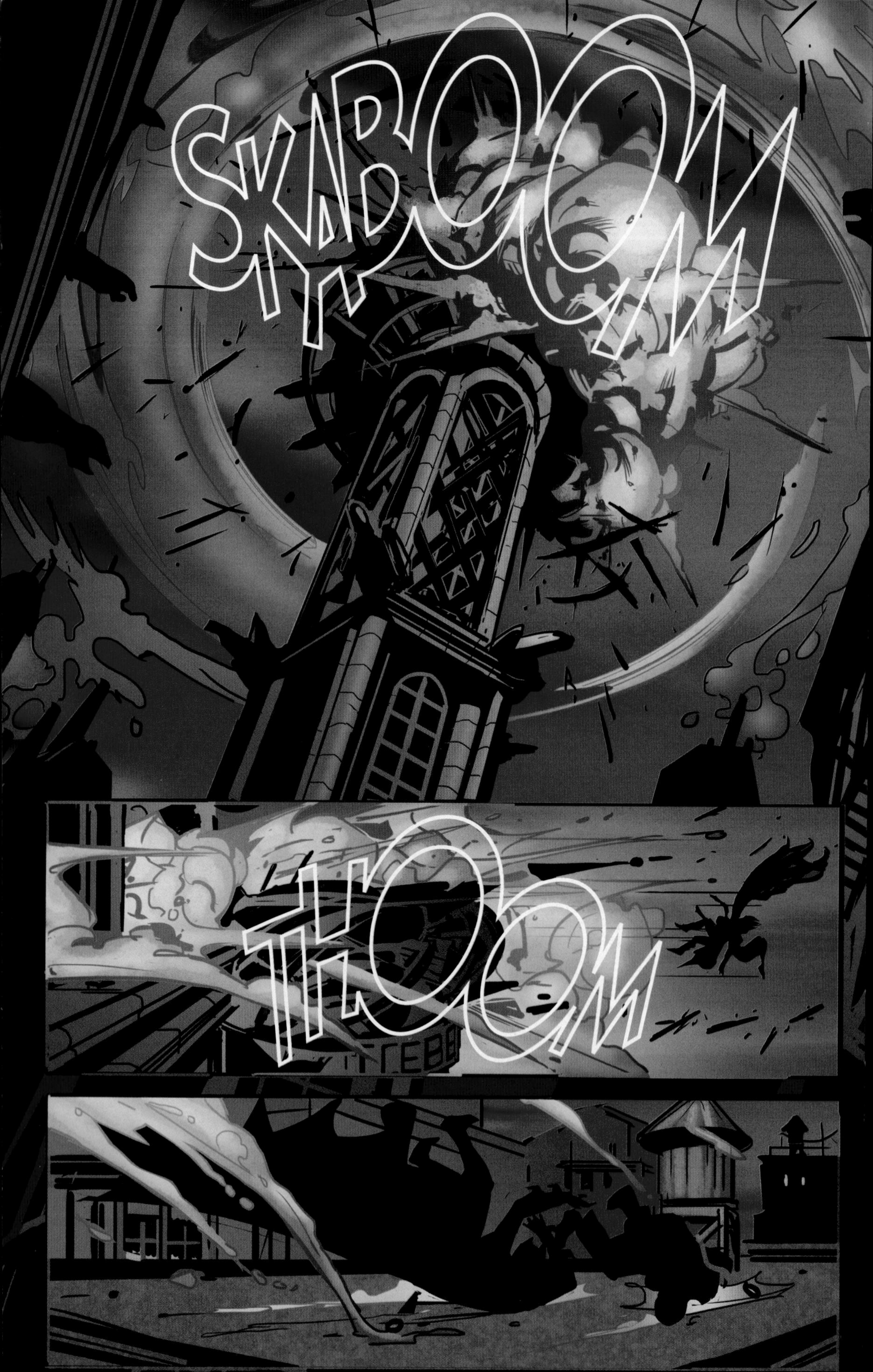
SKABOOM
THOOM

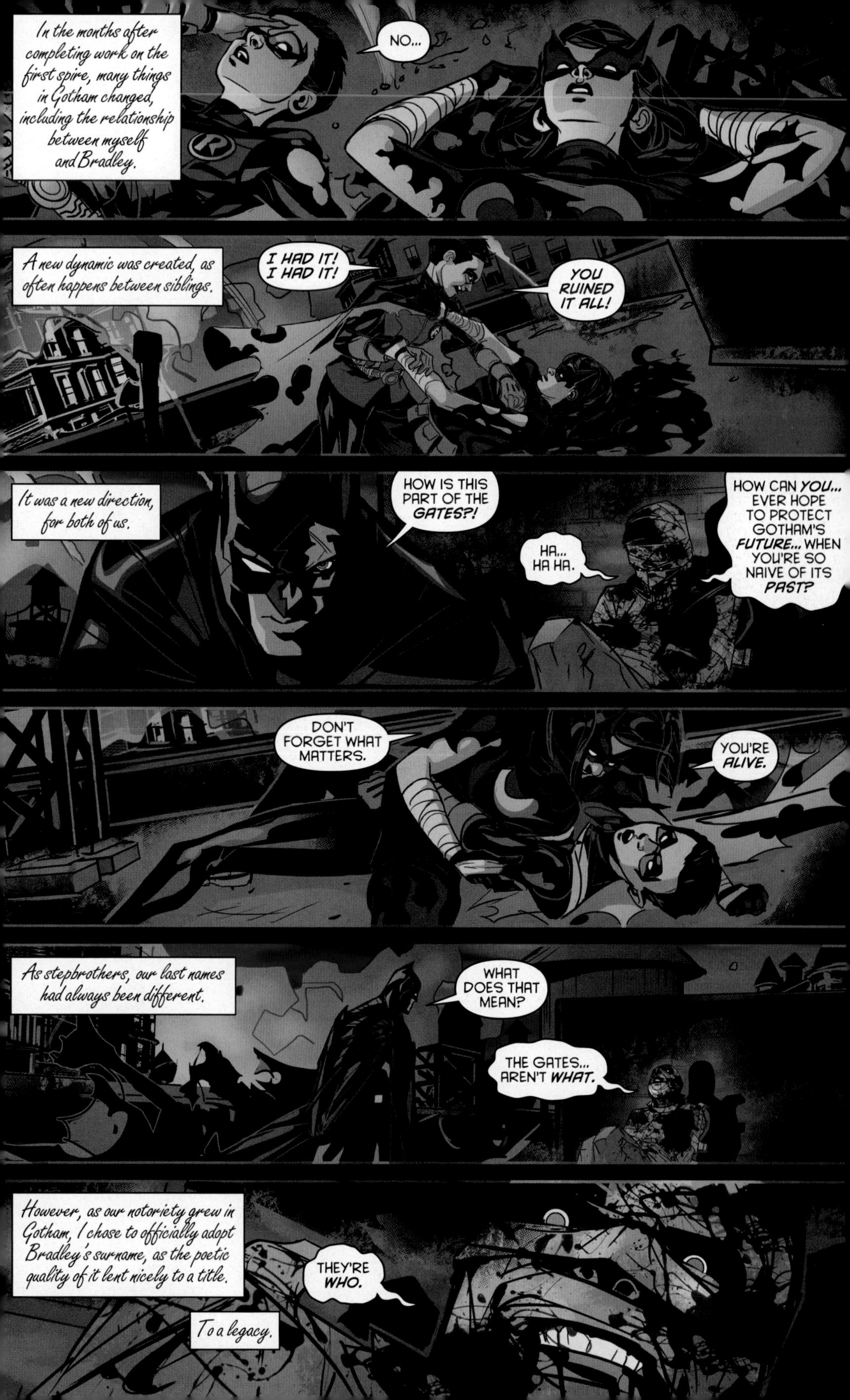
In the months after completing work on the first spire, many things in Gotham changed, including the relationship between myself and Bradley.
NO...
A new dynamic was created, as often happens between siblings.
I HAD IT! I HAD IT!
YOU RUINED IT ALL!
It was a new direction, for both of us.
HOW IS THIS PART OF THE GATES?!
HA... HA HA.
HOW CAN YOU... EVER HOPE TO PROTECT GOTHAM'S FUTURE... WHEN YOU'RE SO NAIVE OF ITS PAST?
DON'T FORGET WHAT MATTERS.
YOU'RE ALIVE.
As stepbrothers, our last names had always been different.
WHAT DOES THAT MEAN?
THE GATES... AREN'T WHAT.
However, as our notoriety grew in Gotham, I chose to officially adopt Bradley's surname, as the poetic quality of it lent nicely to a title.
THEY'RE WHO.
To a legacy.

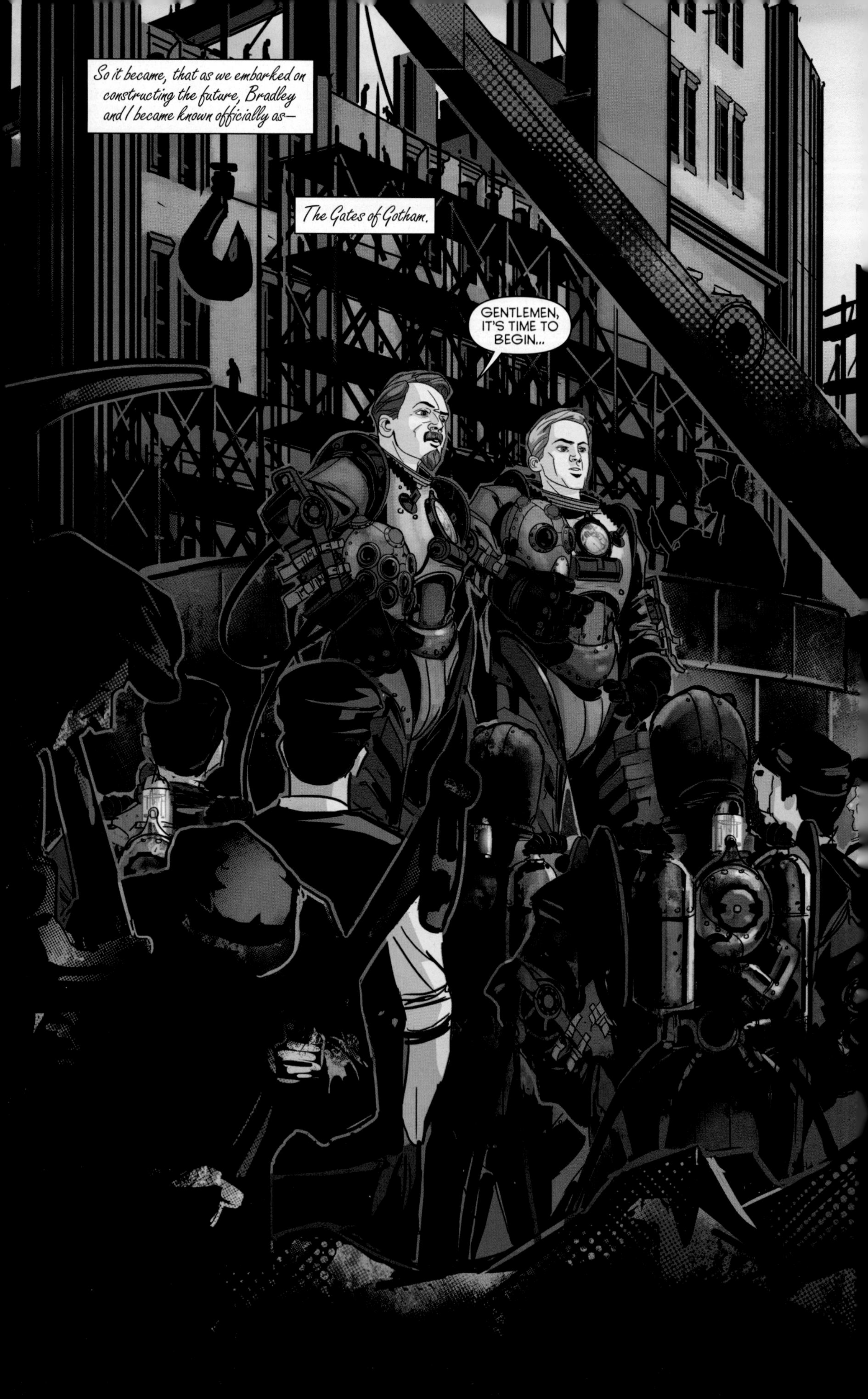
So it became, that as we embarked on constructing the future, Bradley and I became known officially as—
The Gates of Gotham.
GENTLEMEN, IT'S TIME TO BEGIN...

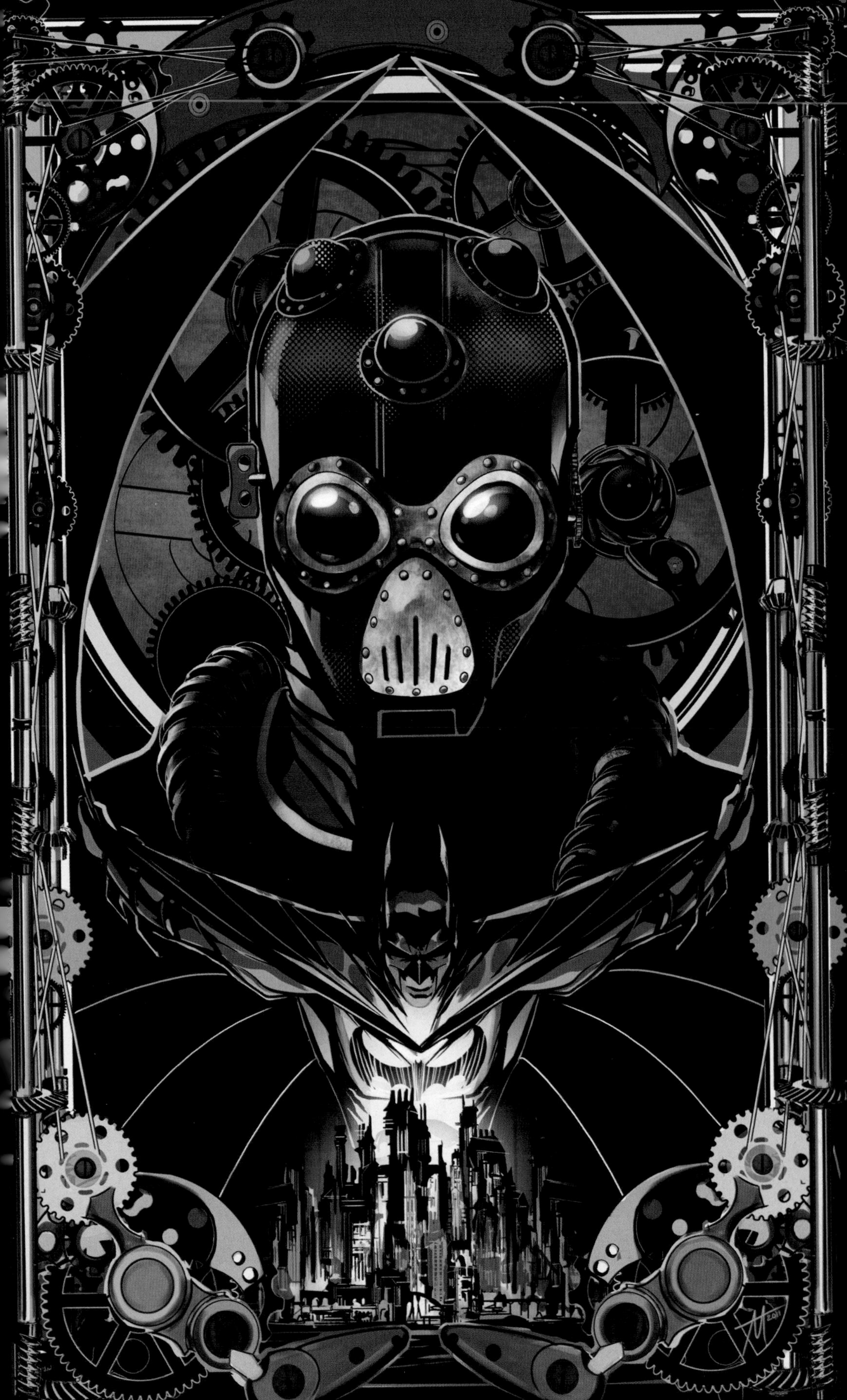

Part Three
THE KEY TO THE CITY

Scott **Snyder** & Kyle **Higgins**
story

Kyle **Higgins** & Ryan **Parrott**
dialogue

Trevor **McCarthy**
art & cover

Graham **Nolan**
layouts

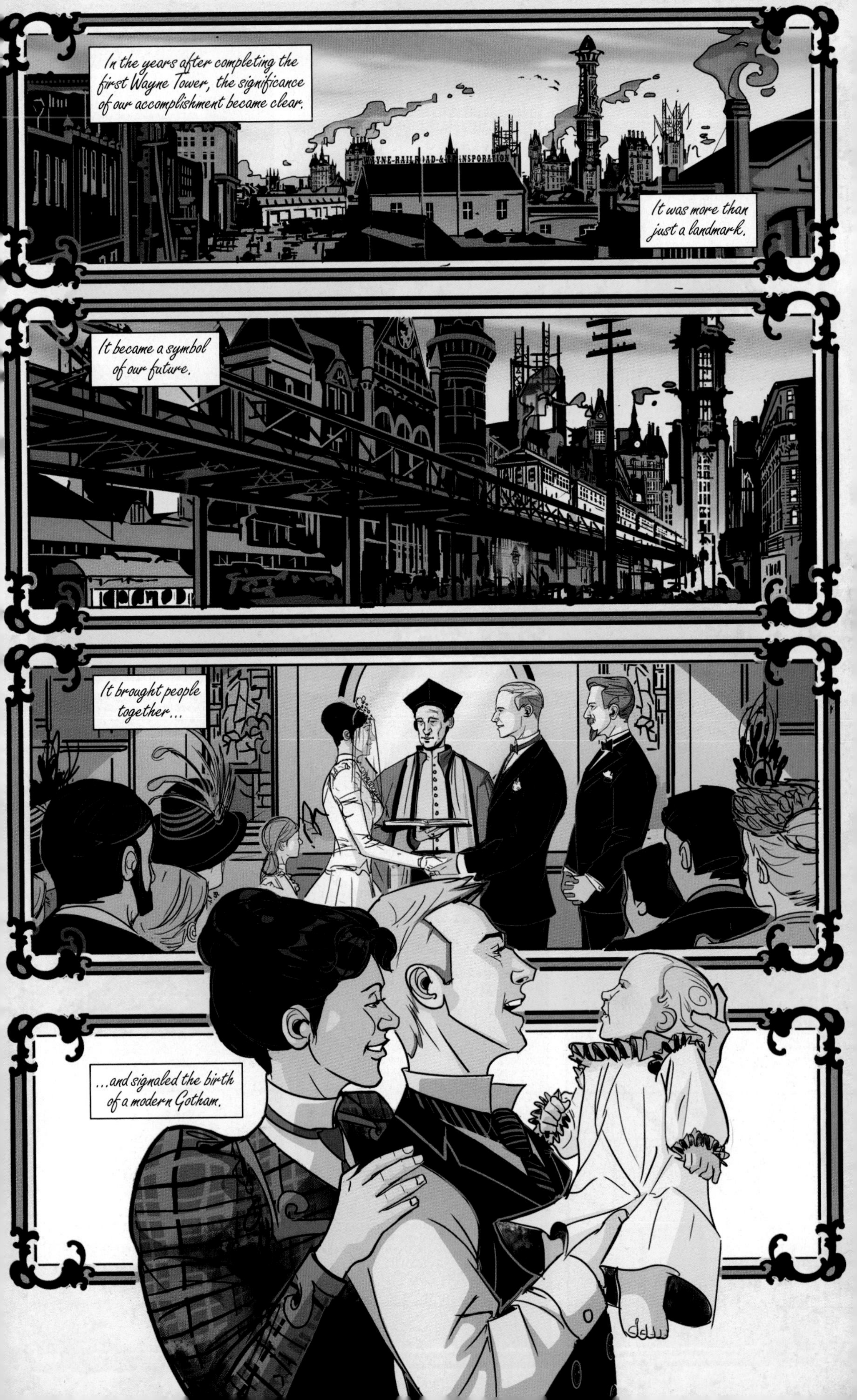
In the years after completing the first Wayne Tower, the significance of our accomplishment became clear.
WAYNE-RAILROAD-&-TRANSPORATION
It was more than just a landmark.
It became a symbol of our future.
It brought people together...
...and signaled the birth of a modern Gotham.

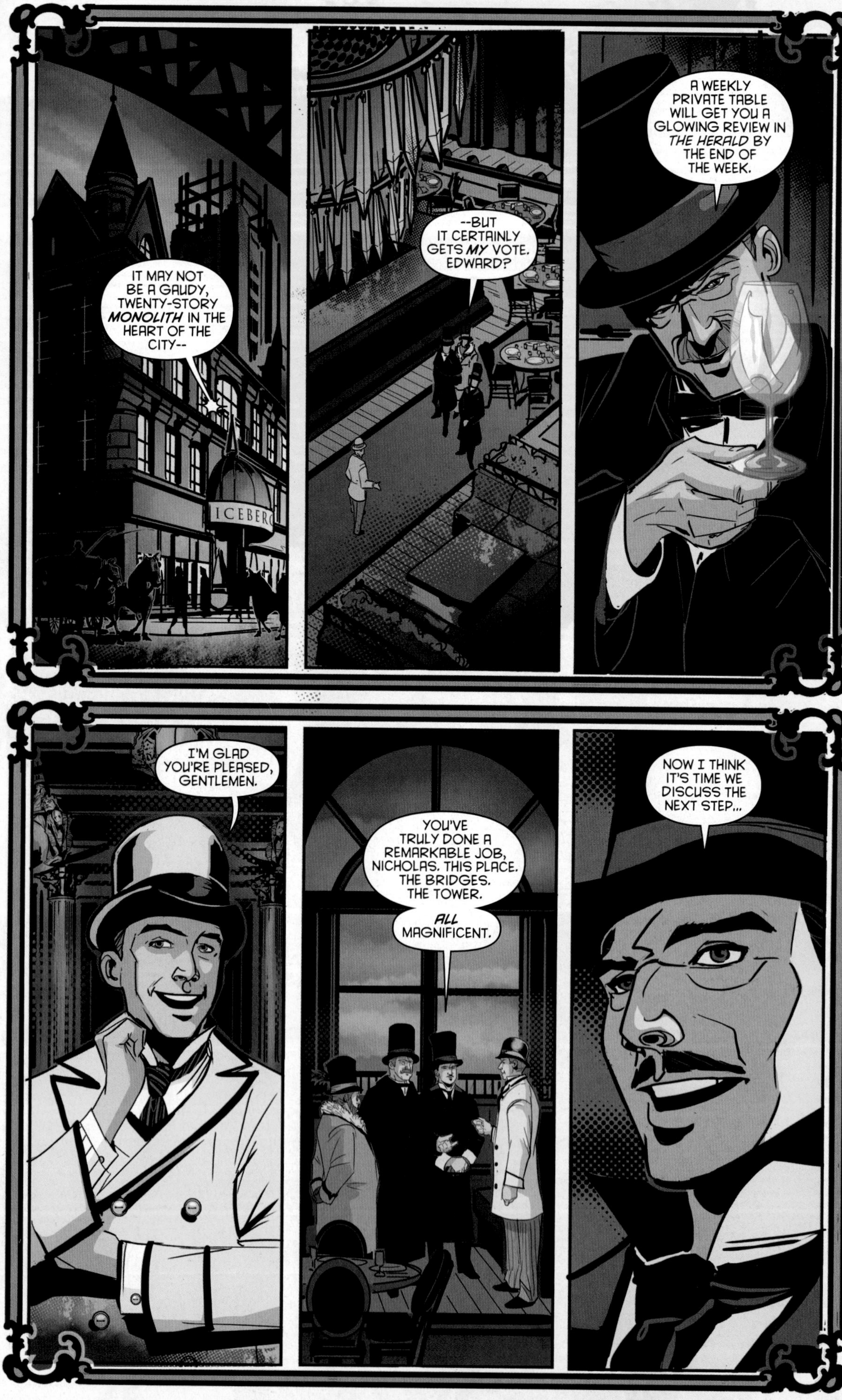
IT MAY NOT BE A GAUDY, TWENTY-STORY *MONOLITH* IN THE HEART OF THE CITY--
ICEBERG
--BUT IT CERTAINLY GETS *MY* VOTE. EDWARD?
A WEEKLY PRIVATE TABLE WILL GET YOU A GLOWING REVIEW IN *THE HERALD* BY THE END OF THE WEEK.
I'M GLAD YOU'RE PLEASED, GENTLEMEN.
YOU'VE TRULY DONE A REMARKABLE JOB, NICHOLAS. THIS PLACE. THE BRIDGES. THE TOWER.
ALL MAGNIFICENT.
NOW I THINK IT'S TIME WE DISCUSS THE NEXT STEP...

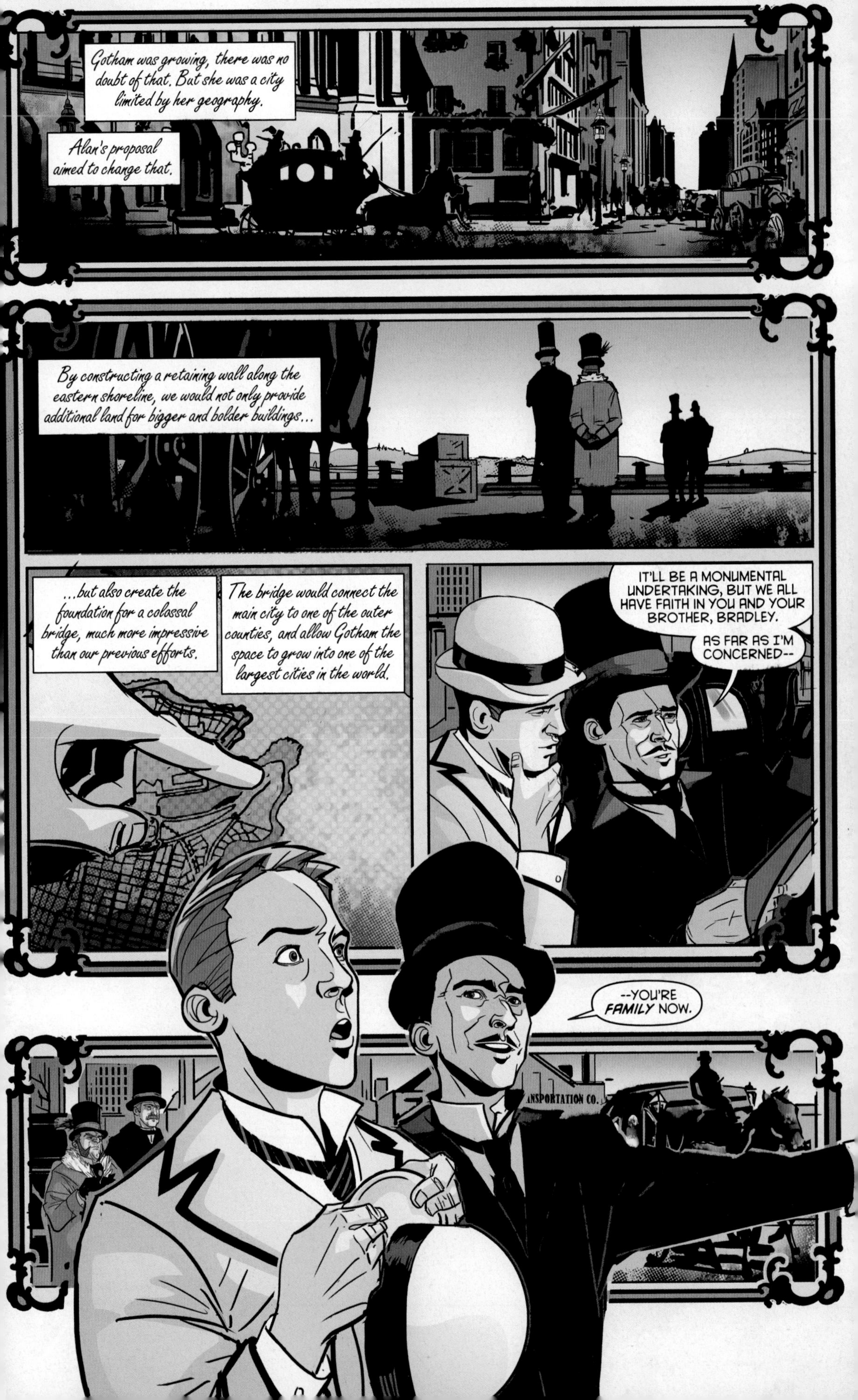
Gotham was growing, there was no doubt of that. But she was a city limited by her geography.
Alan's proposal aimed to change that.
By constructing a retaining wall along the eastern shoreline, we would not only provide additional land for bigger and bolder buildings...
...but also create the foundation for a colossal bridge, much more impressive than our previous efforts.
The bridge would connect the main city to one of the outer counties, and allow Gotham the space to grow into one of the largest cities in the world.
IT'LL BE A MONUMENTAL UNDERTAKING, BUT WE ALL HAVE FAITH IN YOU AND YOUR BROTHER, BRADLEY.
AS FAR AS I'M CONCERNED--
--YOU'RE FAMILY NOW.
ANSPORTATION CO.

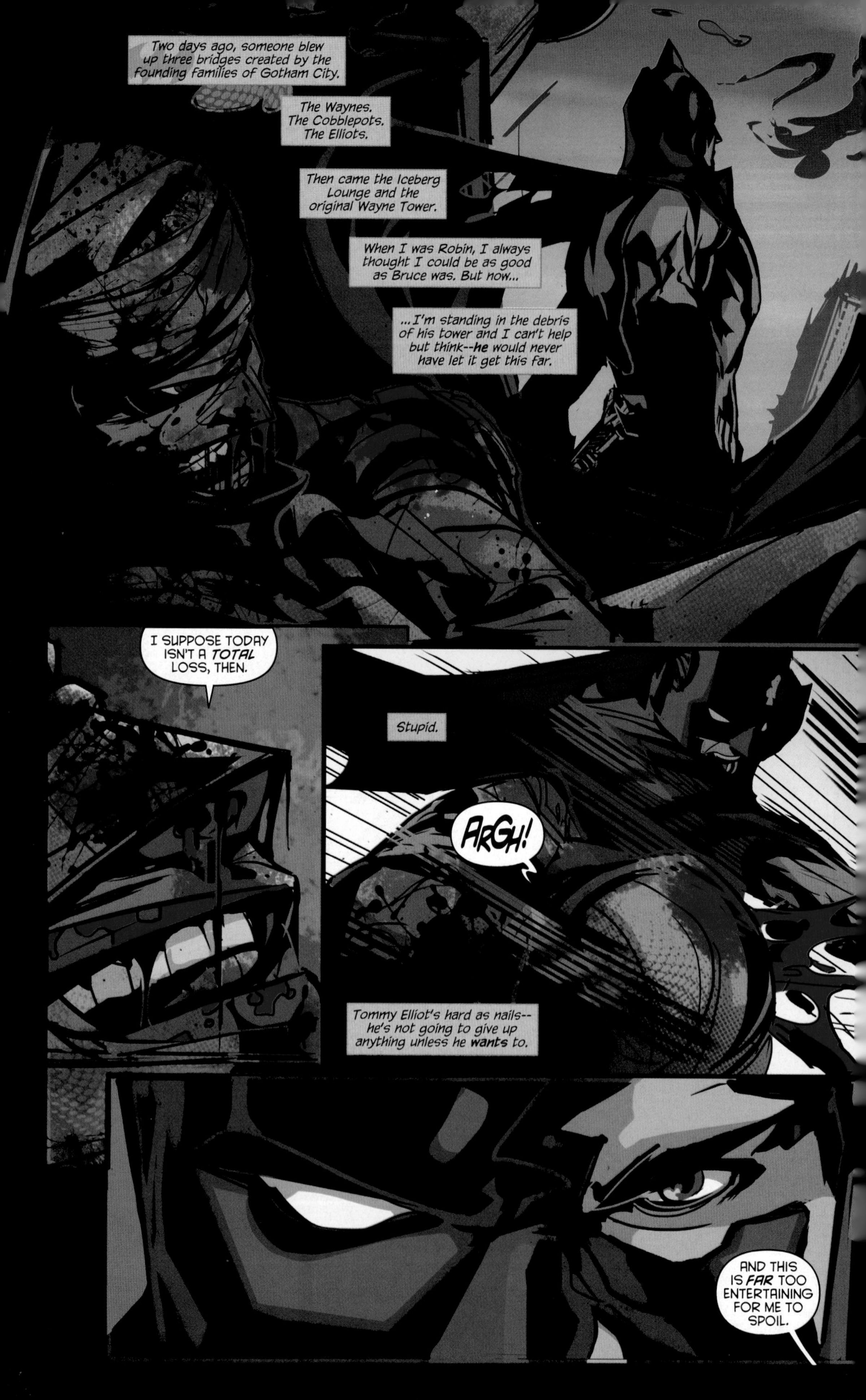

Two days ago, someone blew up three bridges created by the founding families of Gotham City.
The Waynes. The Cobblepots. The Elliots.
Then came the Iceberg Lounge and the original Wayne Tower.
When I was Robin, I always thought I could be as good as Bruce was. But now...
...I'm standing in the debris of his tower and I can't help but think--he would never have let it get this far.
I SUPPOSE TODAY ISN'T A TOTAL LOSS, THEN.
Stupid.
ARGH!
Tommy Elliot's hard as nails--he's not going to give up anything unless he wants to.
AND THIS IS FAR TOO ENTERTAINING FOR ME TO SPOIL.

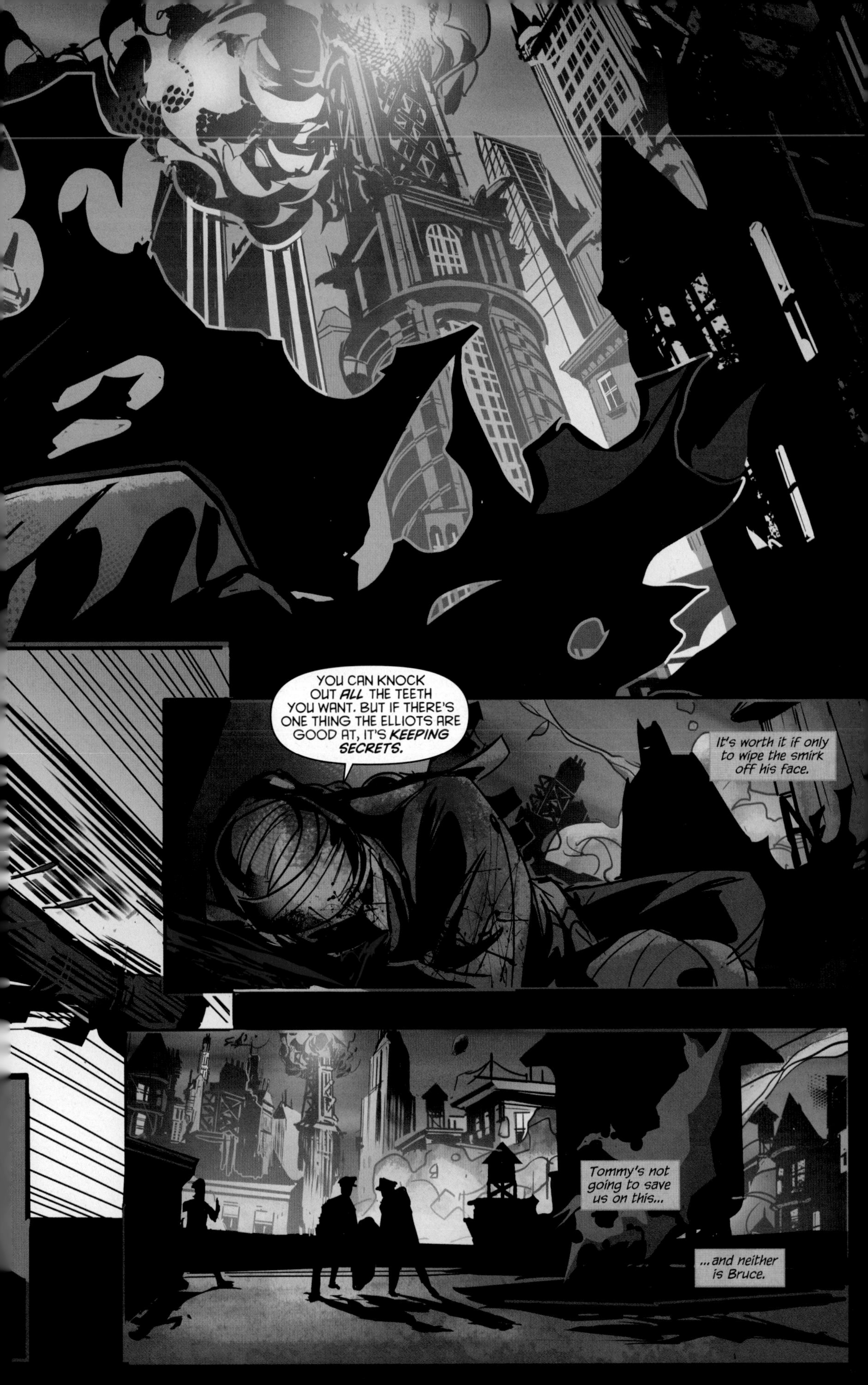
YOU CAN KNOCK OUT ALL THE TEETH YOU WANT. BUT IF THERE'S ONE THING THE ELLIOTS ARE GOOD AT, IT'S KEEPING SECRETS.
It's worth it if only to wipe the smirk off his face.
Tommy's not going to save us on this...
...and neither is Bruce.

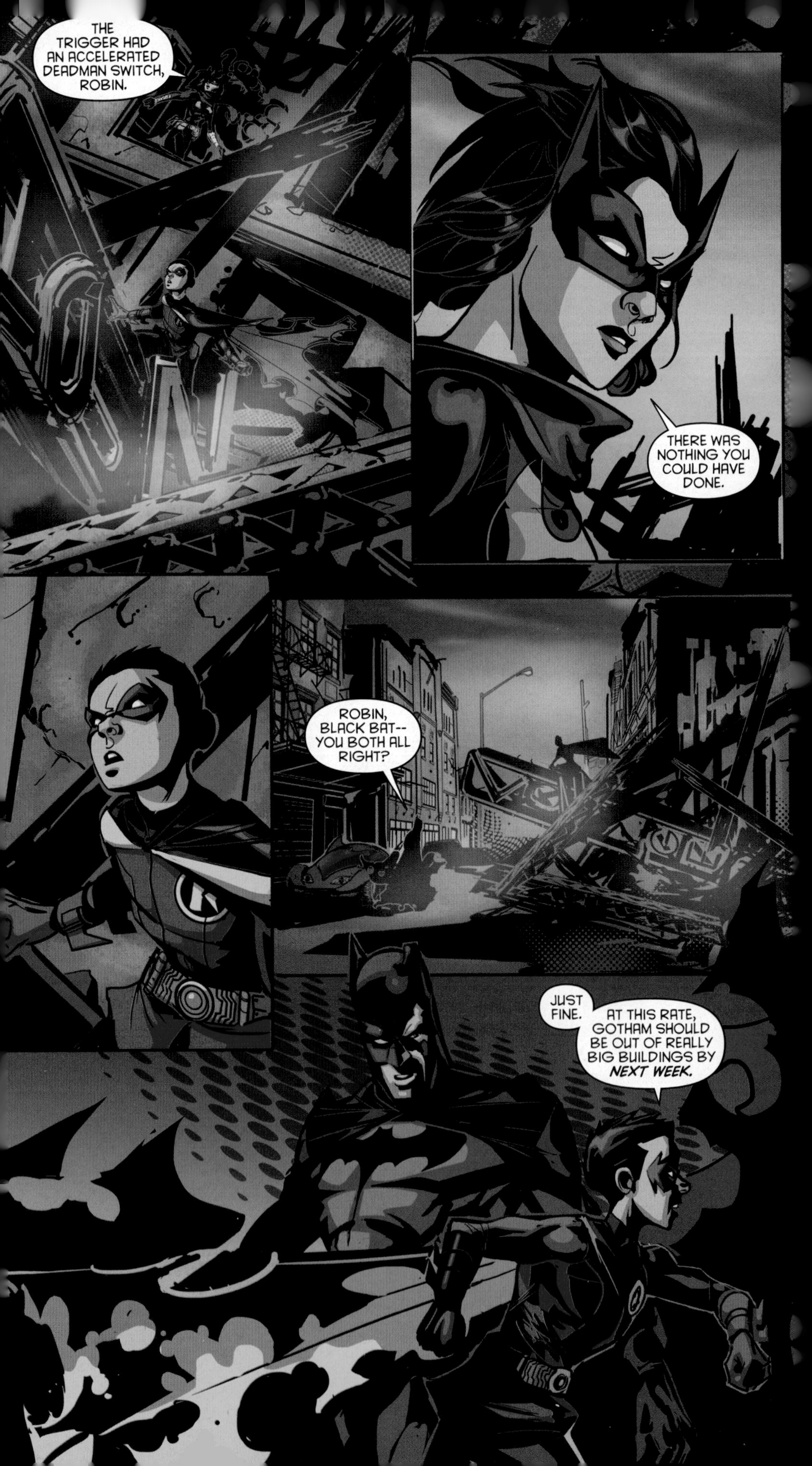
THE TRIGGER HAD AN ACCELERATED DEADMAN SWITCH, ROBIN.
THERE WAS NOTHING YOU COULD HAVE DONE.
ROBIN, BLACK BAT-- YOU BOTH ALL RIGHT?
JUST FINE.
AT THIS RATE, GOTHAM SHOULD BE OUT OF REALLY BIG BUILDINGS BY *NEXT WEEK.*

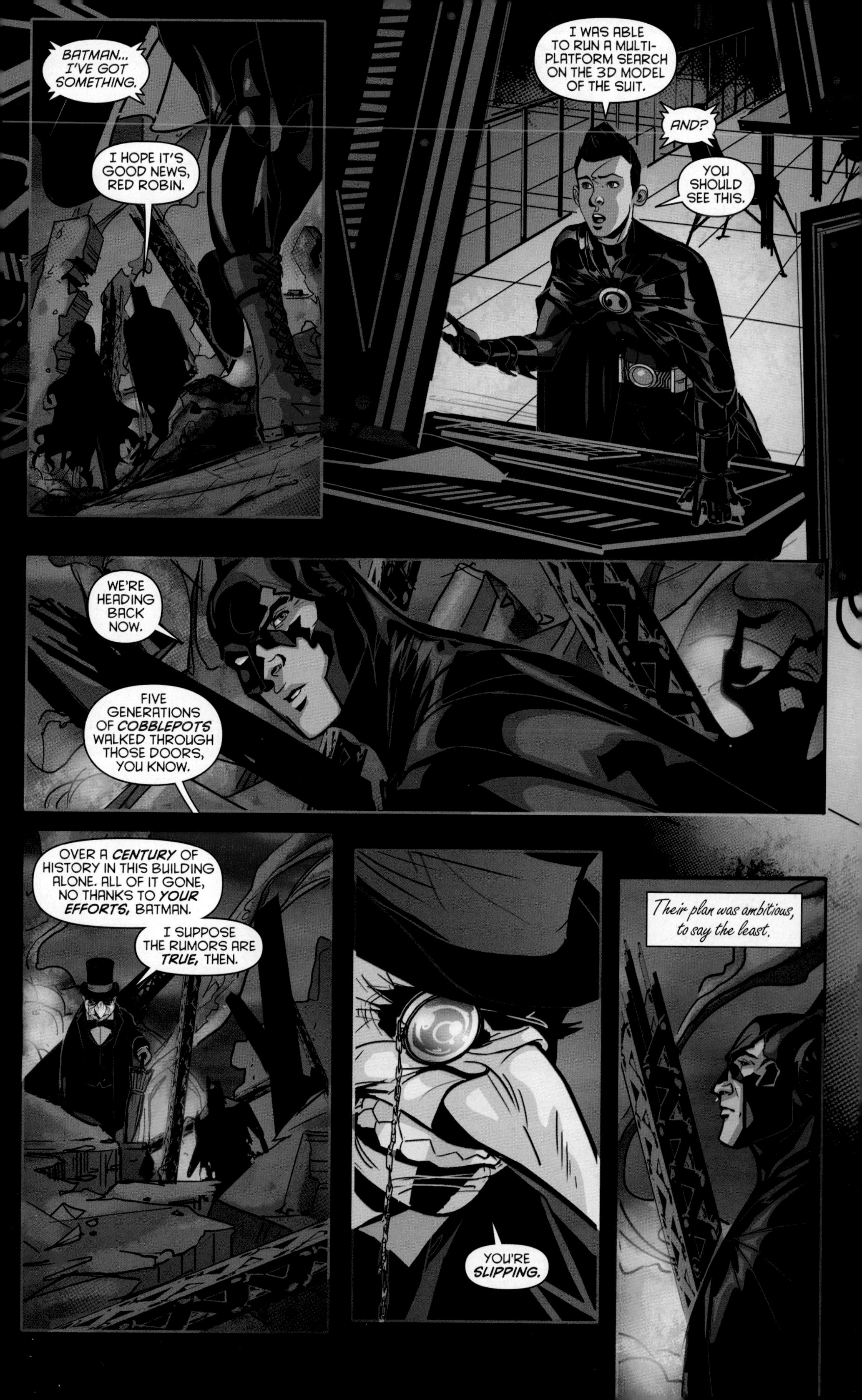
BATMAN... I'VE GOT SOMETHING.
I HOPE IT'S GOOD NEWS, RED ROBIN.
I WAS ABLE TO RUN A MULTI-PLATFORM SEARCH ON THE 3D MODEL OF THE SUIT.
AND?
YOU SHOULD SEE THIS.
WE'RE HEADING BACK NOW.
FIVE GENERATIONS OF COBBLEPOTS WALKED THROUGH THOSE DOORS, YOU KNOW.
OVER A CENTURY OF HISTORY IN THIS BUILDING ALONE. ALL OF IT GONE, NO THANKS TO YOUR EFFORTS, BATMAN.
I SUPPOSE THE RUMORS ARE TRUE, THEN.
YOU'RE SLIPPING.
Their plan was ambitious, to say the least.

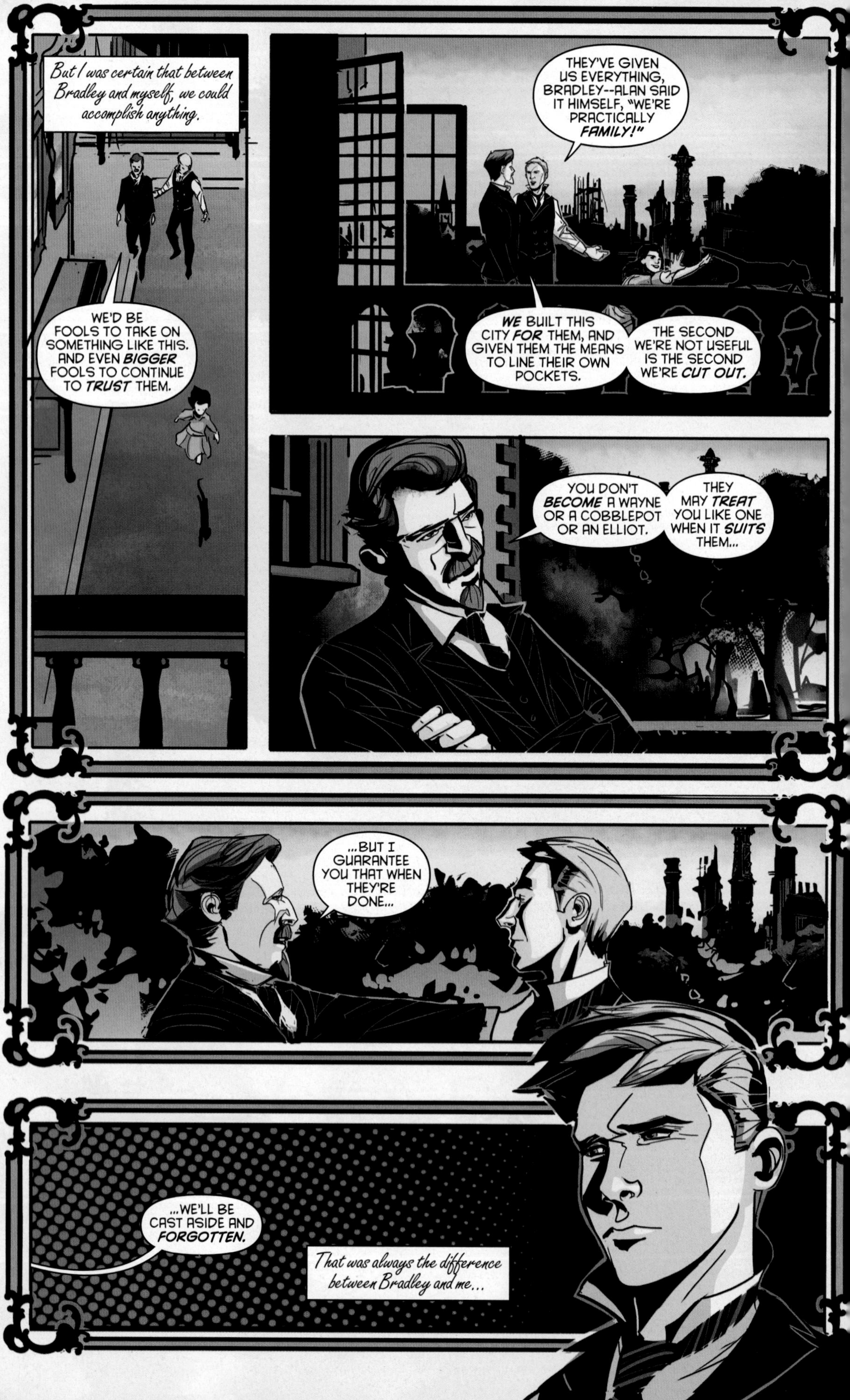
But I was certain that between Bradley and myself, we could accomplish anything.
WE'D BE FOOLS TO TAKE ON SOMETHING LIKE THIS. AND EVEN BIGGER FOOLS TO CONTINUE TO TRUST THEM.
THEY'VE GIVEN US EVERYTHING, BRADLEY--ALAN SAID IT HIMSELF, "WE'RE PRACTICALLY FAMILY!"
WE BUILT THIS CITY FOR THEM, AND GIVEN THEM THE MEANS TO LINE THEIR OWN POCKETS.
THE SECOND WE'RE NOT USEFUL IS THE SECOND WE'RE CUT OUT.
YOU DON'T BECOME A WAYNE OR A COBBLEPOT OR AN ELLIOT.
THEY MAY TREAT YOU LIKE ONE WHEN IT SUITS THEM...
...BUT I GUARANTEE YOU THAT WHEN THEY'RE DONE...
...WE'LL BE CAST ASIDE AND FORGOTTEN.
That was always the difference between Bradley and me...

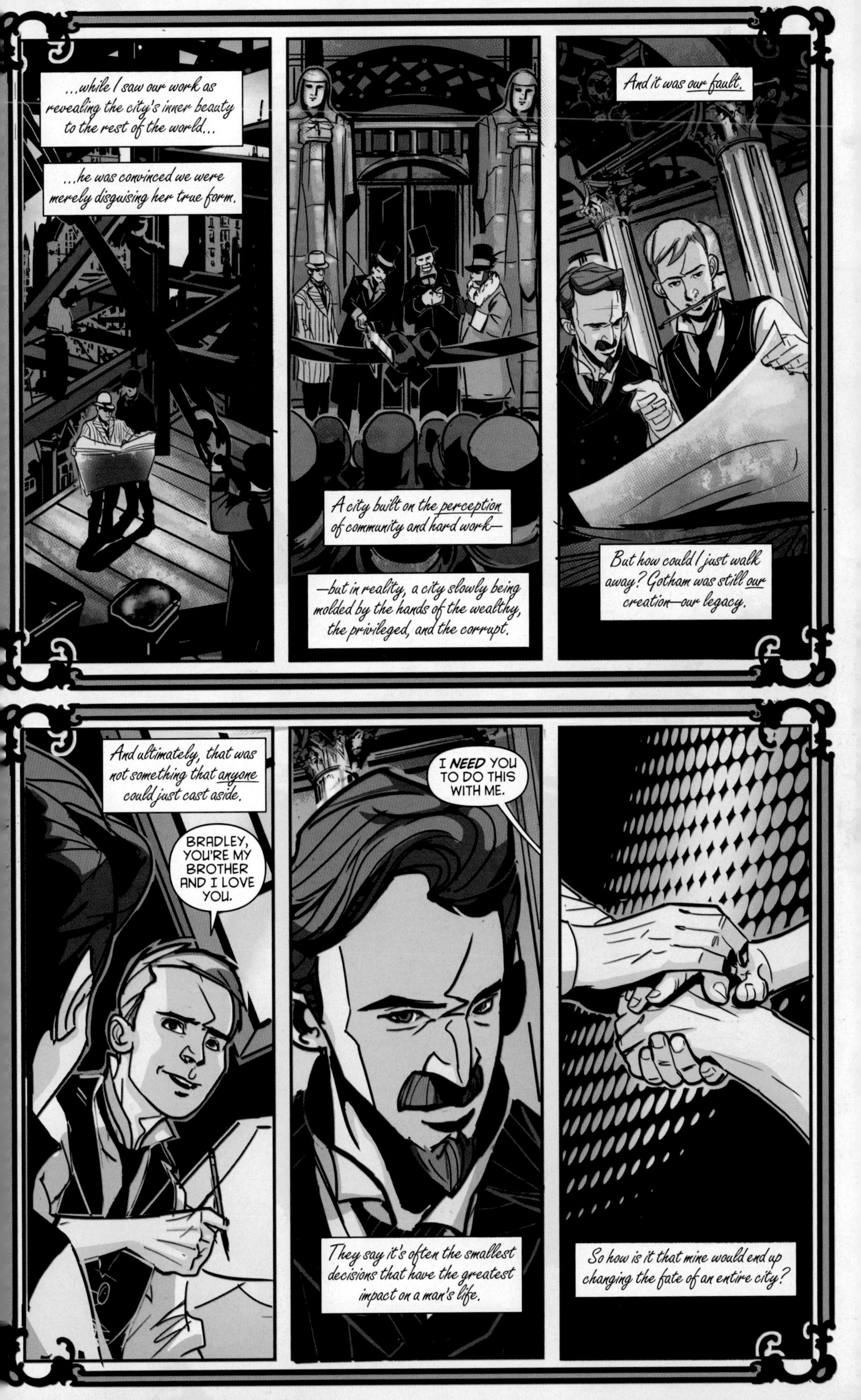
...while I saw our work as revealing the city's inner beauty to the rest of the world...
...he was convinced we were merely disguising her true form.
A city built on the perception of community and hard work—
—but in reality, a city slowly being molded by the hands of the wealthy, the privileged, and the corrupt.
And it was our fault.
But how could I just walk away? Gotham was still our creation—our legacy.
And ultimately, that was not something that anyone could just cast aside.
BRADLEY, YOU'RE MY BROTHER AND I LOVE YOU.
I NEED YOU TO DO THIS WITH ME.
They say it's often the smallest decisions that have the greatest impact on a man's life.
So how is it that mine would end up changing the fate of an entire city?

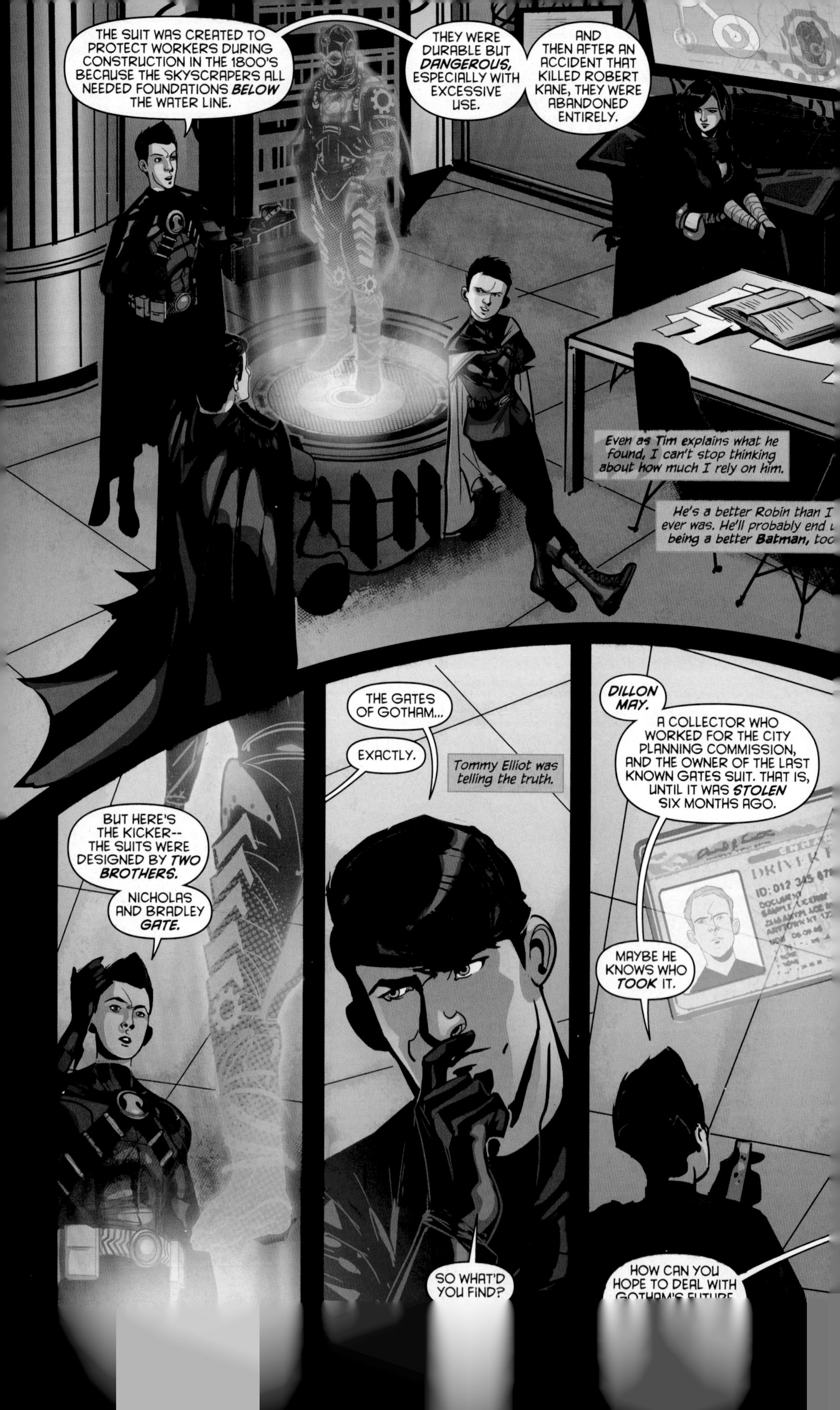
THE SUIT WAS CREATED TO PROTECT WORKERS DURING CONSTRUCTION IN THE 1800'S BECAUSE THE SKYSCRAPERS ALL NEEDED FOUNDATIONS BELOW THE WATER LINE.
THEY WERE DURABLE BUT DANGEROUS, ESPECIALLY WITH EXCESSIVE USE.
AND THEN AFTER AN ACCIDENT THAT KILLED ROBERT KANE, THEY WERE ABANDONED ENTIRELY.
Even as Tim explains what he found, I can't stop thinking about how much I rely on him.
He's a better Robin than I ever was. He'll probably end u being a better Batman, too
BUT HERE'S THE KICKER-- THE SUITS WERE DESIGNED BY TWO BROTHERS.
NICHOLAS AND BRADLEY GATE.
THE GATES OF GOTHAM...
EXACTLY.
Tommy Elliot was telling the truth.
SO WHAT'D YOU FIND?
DILLON MAY.
A COLLECTOR WHO WORKED FOR THE CITY PLANNING COMMISSION, AND THE OWNER OF THE LAST KNOWN GATES SUIT. THAT IS, UNTIL IT WAS STOLEN SIX MONTHS AGO.
MAYBE HE KNOWS WHO TOOK IT.
HOW CAN YOU HOPE TO DEAL WITH

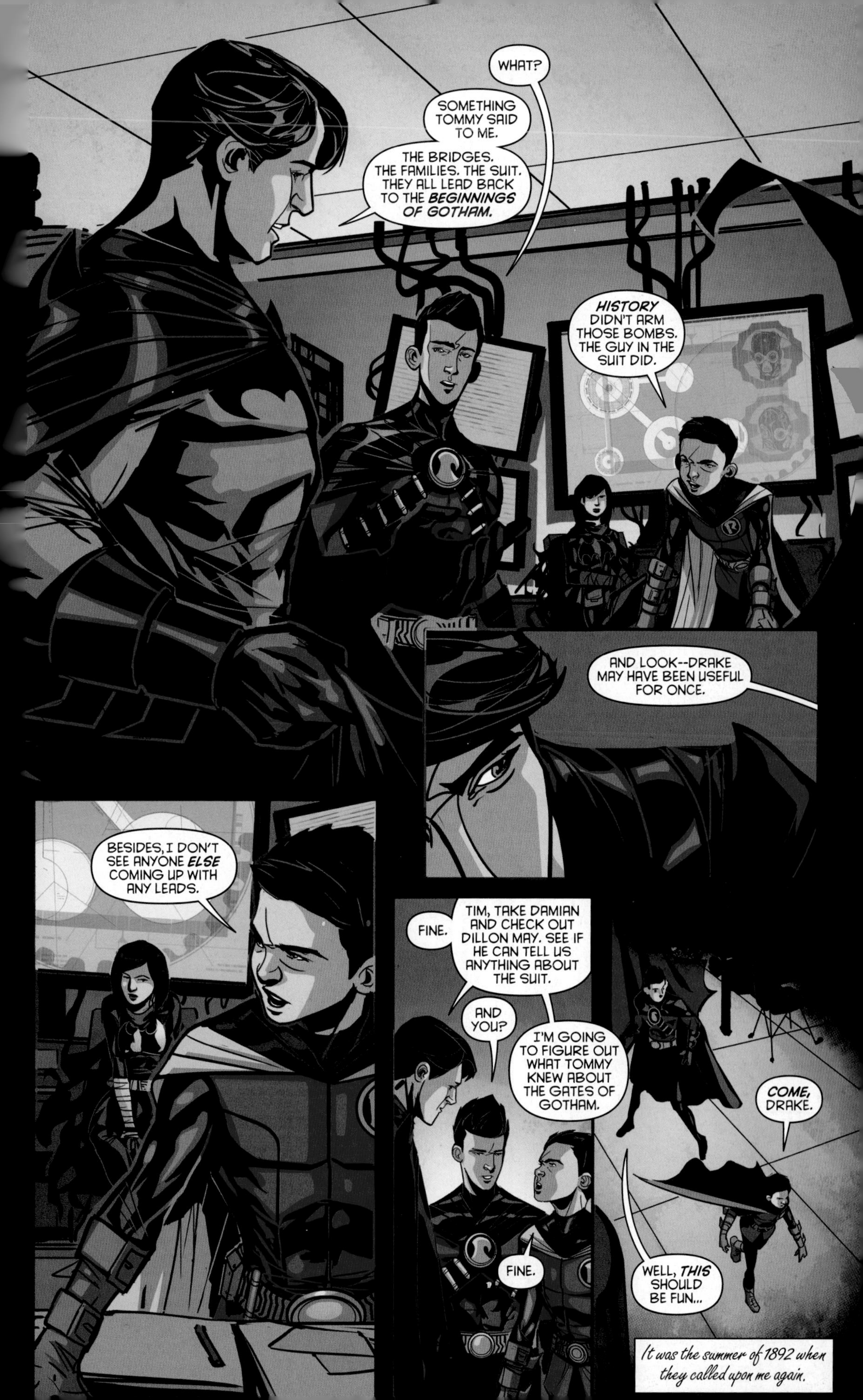
WHAT?
SOMETHING TOMMY SAID TO ME.
THE BRIDGES. THE FAMILIES. THE SUIT. THEY ALL LEAD BACK TO THE *BEGINNINGS OF GOTHAM.*
HISTORY DIDN'T ARM THOSE BOMBS. THE GUY IN THE SUIT DID.
AND LOOK--DRAKE MAY HAVE BEEN USEFUL FOR ONCE.
BESIDES, I DON'T SEE ANYONE *ELSE* COMING UP WITH ANY LEADS.
FINE.
TIM, TAKE DAMIAN AND CHECK OUT DILLON MAY. SEE IF HE CAN TELL US ANYTHING ABOUT THE SUIT.
AND YOU?
I'M GOING TO FIGURE OUT WHAT TOMMY KNEW ABOUT THE GATES OF GOTHAM.
FINE.
COME, DRAKE.
WELL, *THIS* SHOULD BE FUN...
It was the summer of 1892 when they called upon me again.

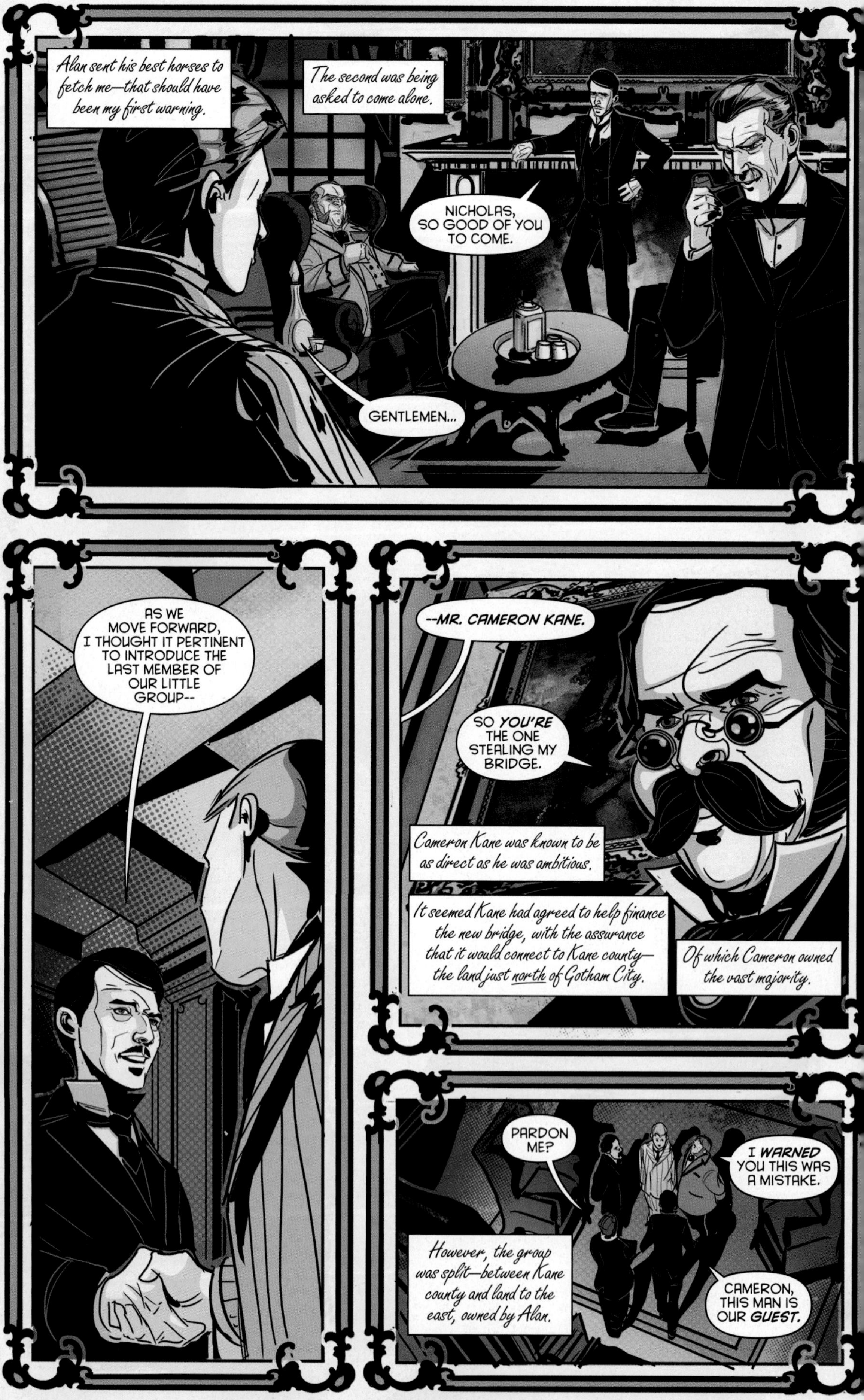
Alan sent his best horses to fetch me—that should have been my first warning.
The second was being asked to come alone.
NICHOLAS, SO GOOD OF YOU TO COME.
GENTLEMEN...
AS WE MOVE FORWARD, I THOUGHT IT PERTINENT TO INTRODUCE THE LAST MEMBER OF OUR LITTLE GROUP--
--MR. CAMERON KANE.
SO YOU'RE THE ONE STEALING MY BRIDGE.
Cameron Kane was known to be as direct as he was ambitious.
It seemed Kane had agreed to help finance the new bridge, with the assurance that it would connect to Kane county—the land just north of Gotham City.
Of which Cameron owned the vast majority.
PARDON ME?
I WARNED YOU THIS WAS A MISTAKE.
However, the group was split—between Kane county and land to the east, owned by Alan.
CAMERON, THIS MAN IS OUR GUEST.

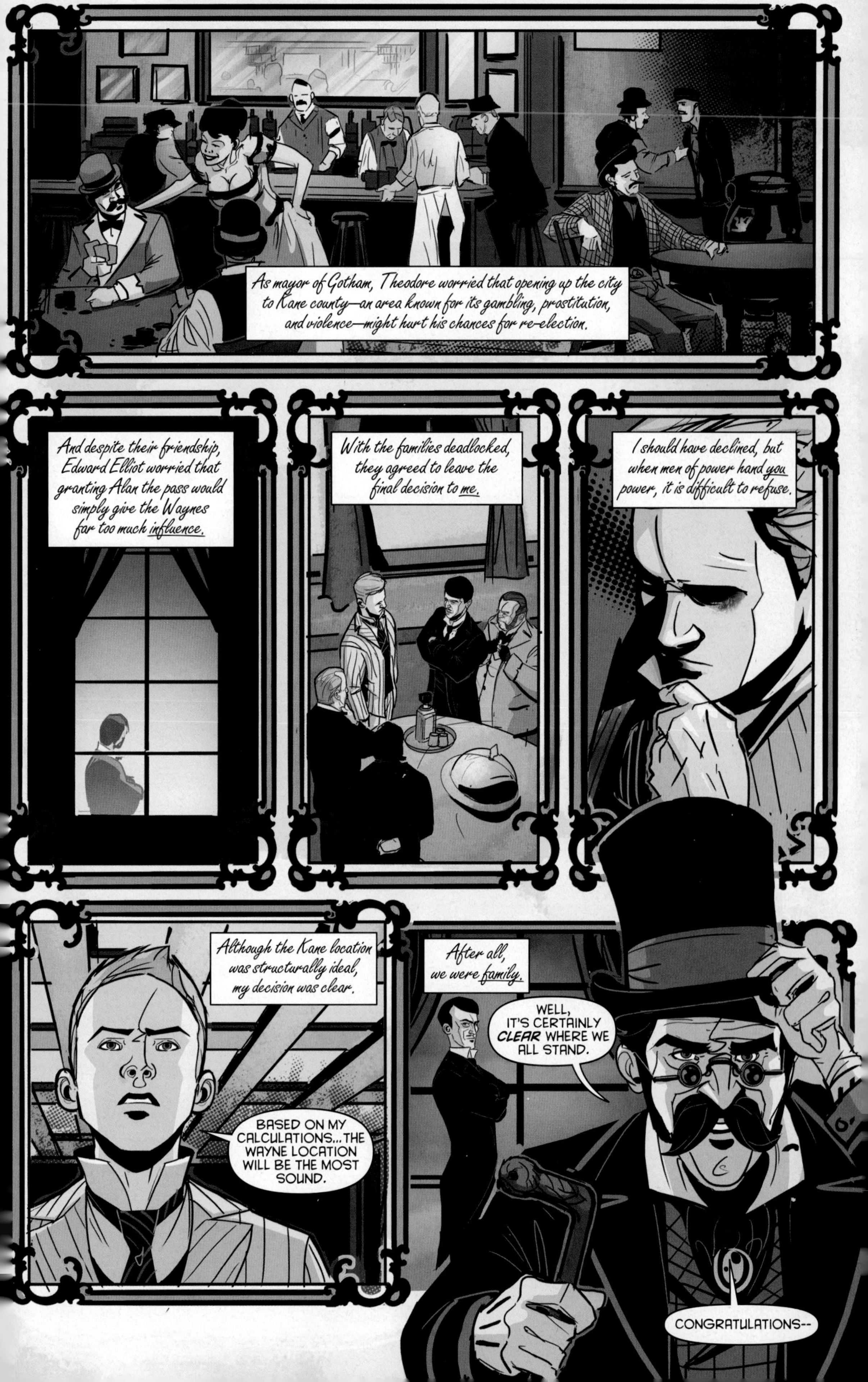
As mayor of Gotham, Theodore worried that opening up the city to Kane county—an area known for its gambling, prostitution, and violence—might hurt his chances for re-election.
And despite their friendship, Edward Elliot worried that granting Alan the pass would simply give the Waynes far too much influence.
With the families deadlocked, they agreed to leave the final decision to me.
I should have declined, but when men of power hand you power, it is difficult to refuse.
Although the Kane location was structurally ideal, my decision was clear.
BASED ON MY CALCULATIONS... THE WAYNE LOCATION WILL BE THE MOST SOUND.
After all, we were family.
WELL, IT'S CERTAINLY CLEAR WHERE WE ALL STAND.
CONGRATULATIONS--

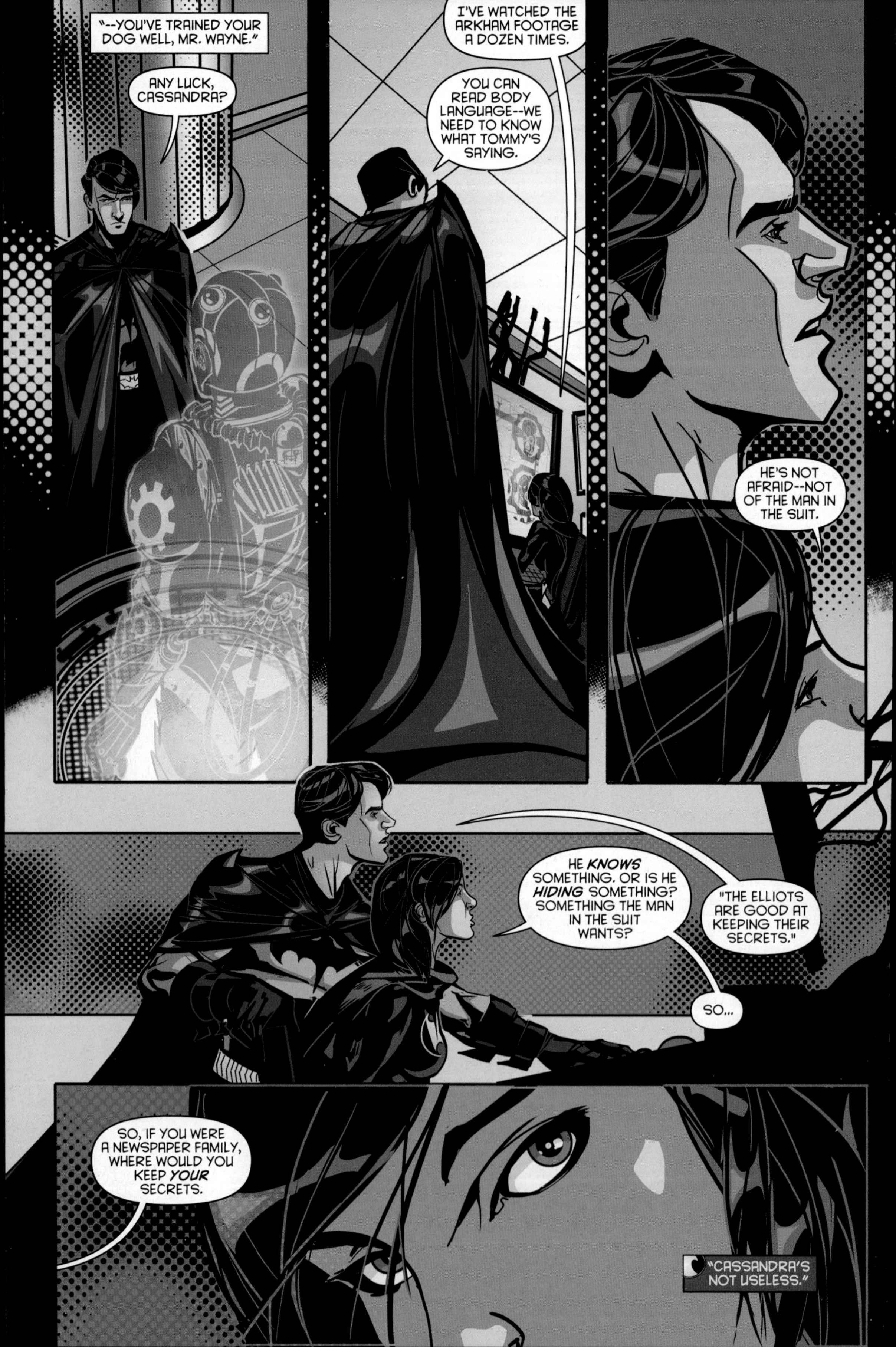
"--YOU'VE TRAINED YOUR DOG WELL, MR. WAYNE."
ANY LUCK, CASSANDRA?
I'VE WATCHED THE ARKHAM FOOTAGE A DOZEN TIMES.
YOU CAN READ BODY LANGUAGE--WE NEED TO KNOW WHAT TOMMY'S SAYING.
HE'S NOT AFRAID--NOT OF THE MAN IN THE SUIT.
HE *KNOWS* SOMETHING. OR IS HE *HIDING* SOMETHING? SOMETHING THE MAN IN THE SUIT WANTS?
"THE ELLIOTS ARE GOOD AT KEEPING THEIR SECRETS."
SO...
SO, IF YOU WERE A NEWSPAPER FAMILY, WHERE WOULD YOU KEEP *YOUR* SECRETS.
"CASSANDRA'S NOT USELESS."

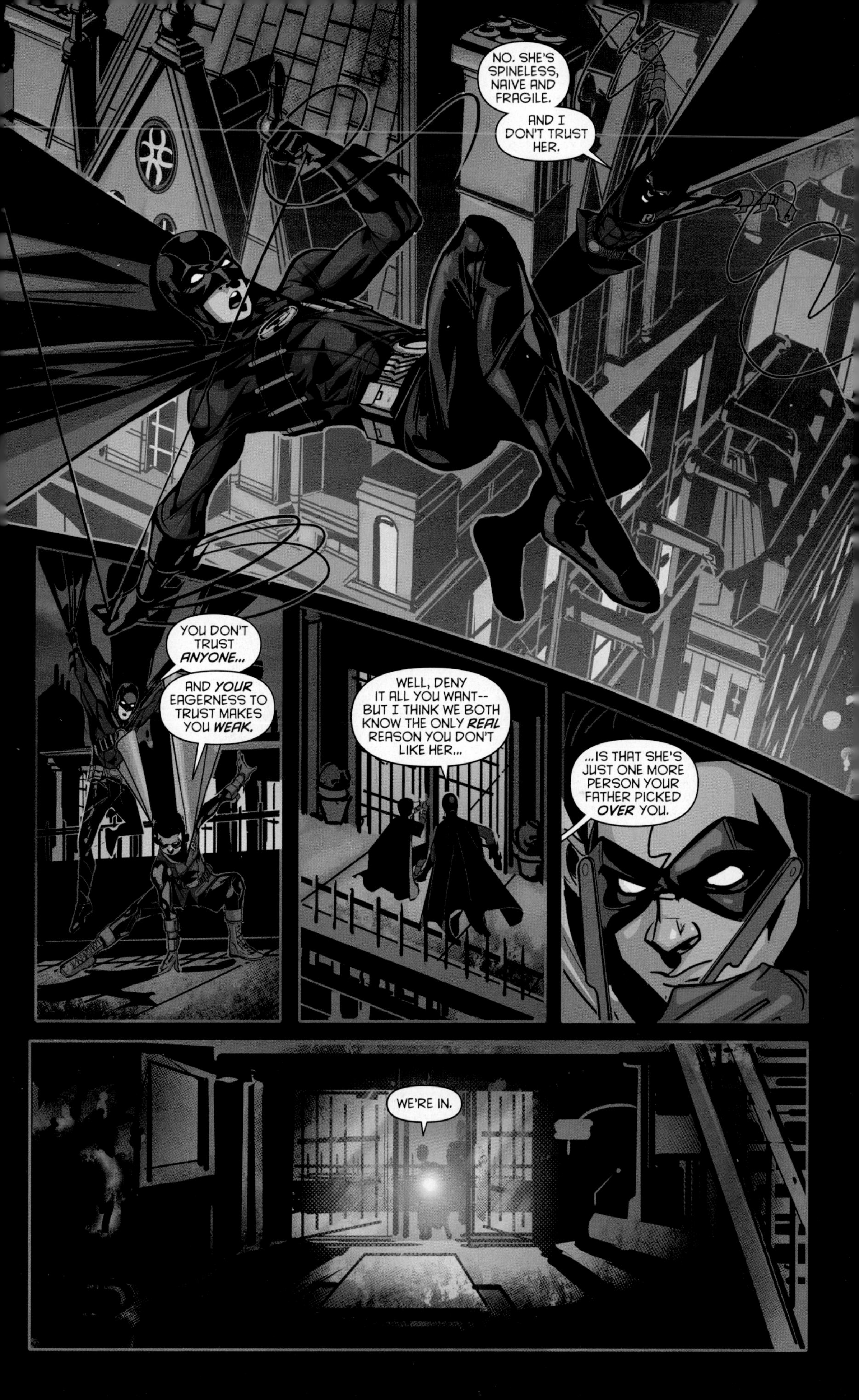
NO. SHE'S SPINELESS, NAIVE AND FRAGILE.
AND I DON'T TRUST HER.
YOU DON'T TRUST *ANYONE...*
AND *YOUR* EAGERNESS TO TRUST MAKES YOU *WEAK.*
WELL, DENY IT ALL YOU WANT-- BUT I THINK WE BOTH KNOW THE ONLY *REAL* REASON YOU DON'T LIKE HER...
...IS THAT SHE'S JUST ONE MORE PERSON YOUR FATHER PICKED *OVER* YOU.
WE'RE IN.

THE ELLIOTS HAVE OWNED THIS BUILDING FOR AS LONG AS THEY'VE LIVED IN GOTHAM.

IF THEY *WERE* HIDING ANYTHING, IT'D BE HERE.

LOOKS LIKE WE'RE TOO LATE.

MAYBE NOT. HOLD STILL.

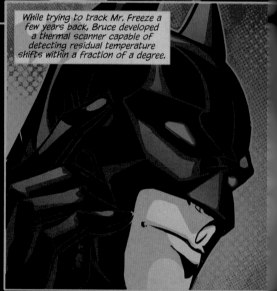

While trying to track Mr. Freeze a few years back, Bruce developed a thermal scanner capable of detecting residual temperature shifts within a fraction of a degree.

And a three-hundred-pound metal suit creates a *lot* of friction.

I guess Bruce is going to help us, after all.

WHAT ARE YOU LOOKING AT?

THE PAST.

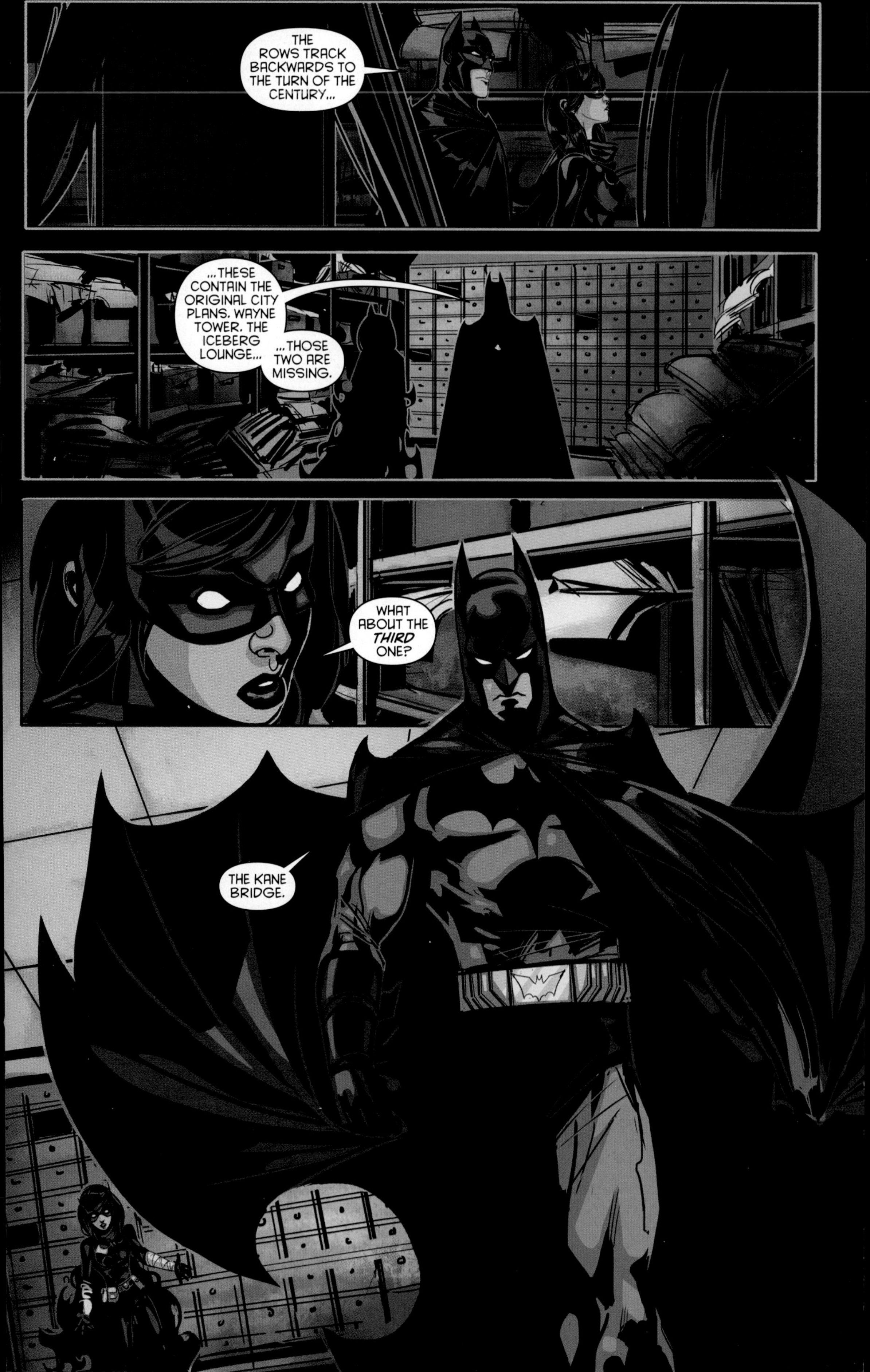

THE ROWS TRACK BACKWARDS TO THE TURN OF THE CENTURY...
...THESE CONTAIN THE ORIGINAL CITY PLANS. WAYNE TOWER. THE ICEBERG LOUNGE...
...THOSE TWO ARE MISSING.
WHAT ABOUT THE *THIRD* ONE?
THE KANE BRIDGE.

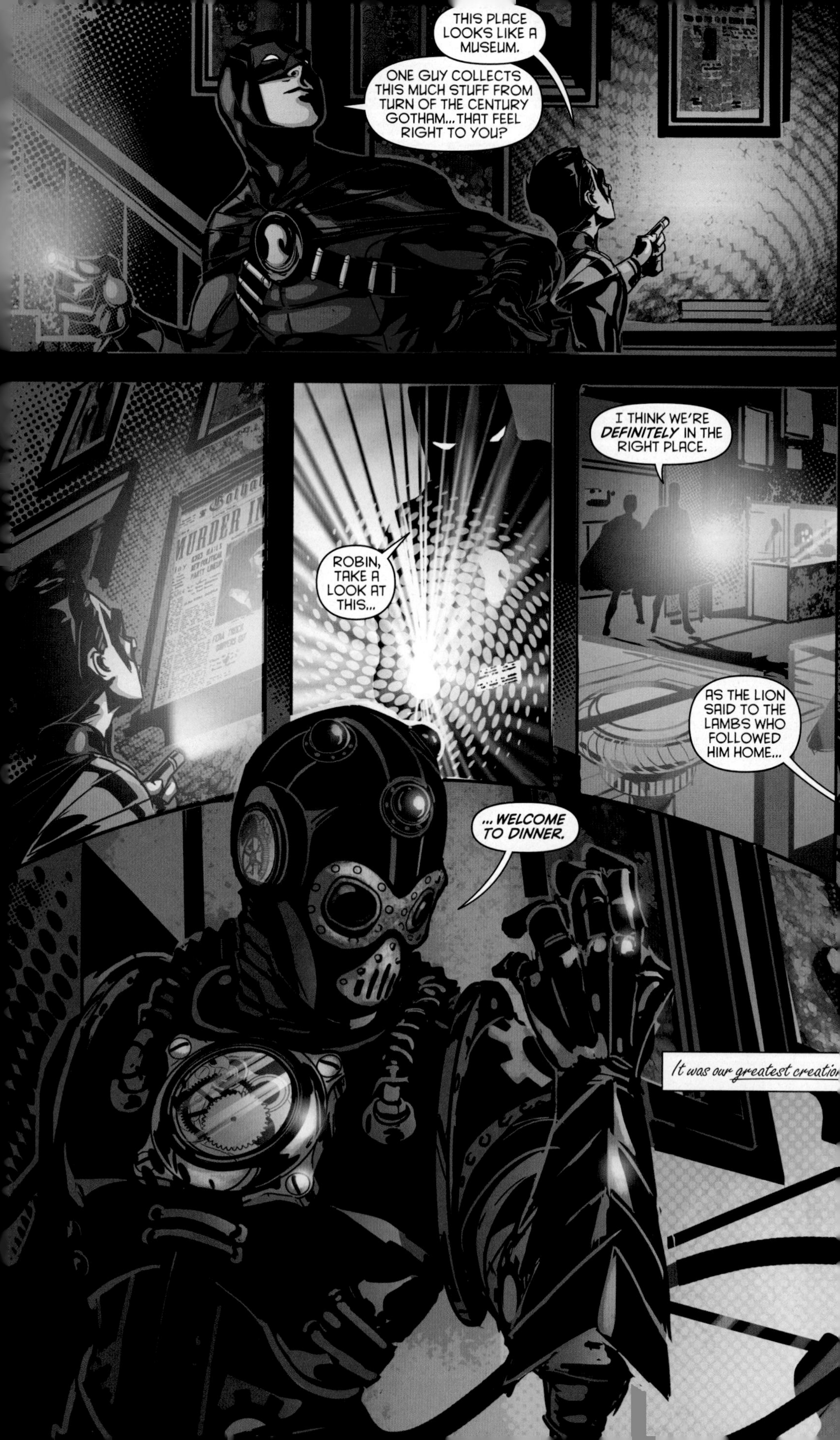
THIS PLACE LOOKS LIKE A MUSEUM.
ONE GUY COLLECTS THIS MUCH STUFF FROM TURN OF THE CENTURY GOTHAM... THAT FEEL RIGHT TO YOU?
MURDER IN
ROBIN, TAKE A LOOK AT THIS...
I THINK WE'RE *DEFINITELY* IN THE RIGHT PLACE.
AS THE LION SAID TO THE LAMBS WHO FOLLOWED HIM HOME...
...WELCOME TO DINNER.
It was our greatest creatio

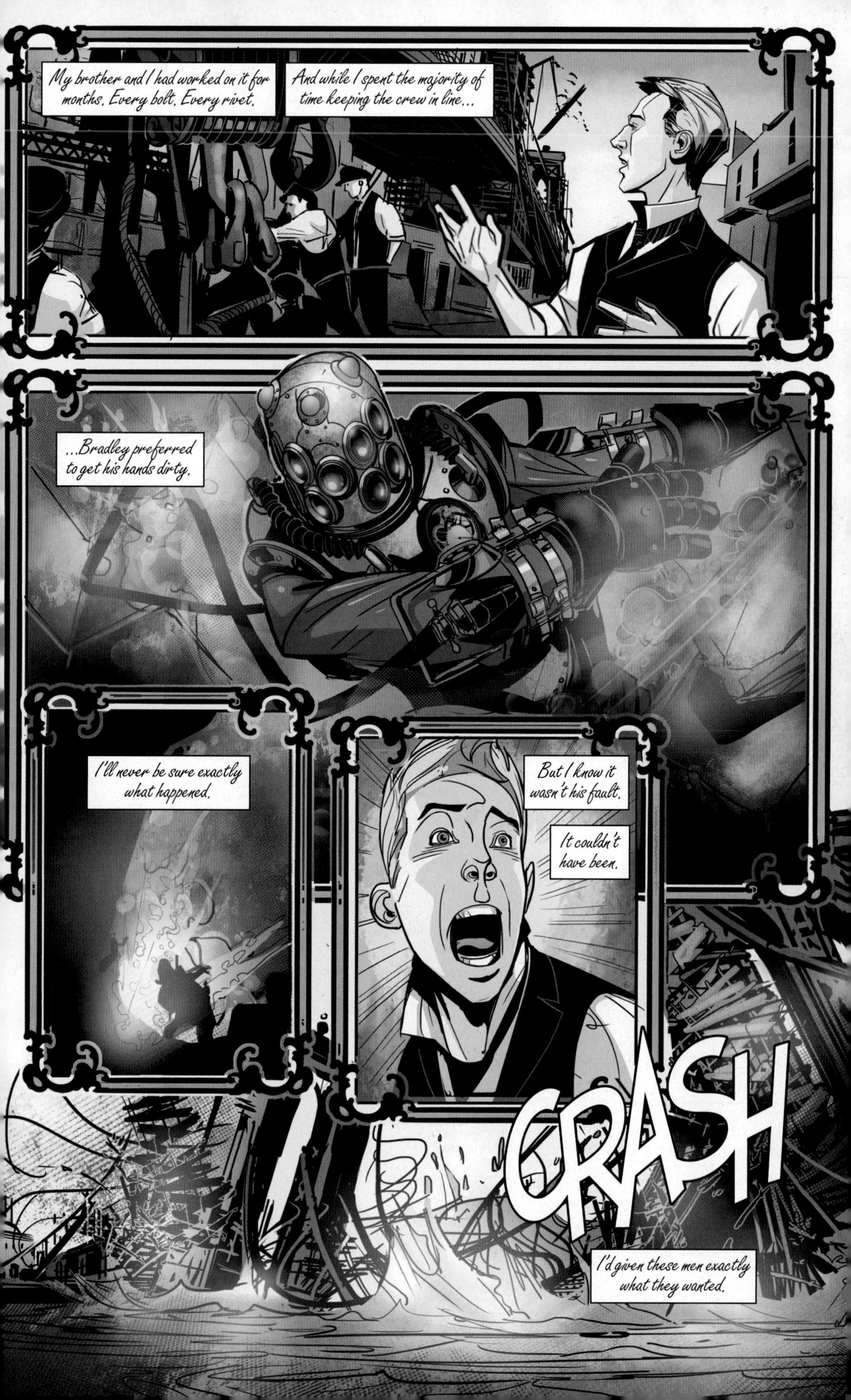
My brother and I had worked on it for months. Every bolt. Every rivet.
And while I spent the majority of time keeping the crew in line...
...Bradley preferred to get his hands dirty.
I'll never be sure exactly what happened.
But I know it wasn't his fault.
It couldn't have been.
CRASH
I'd given these men exactly what they wanted.

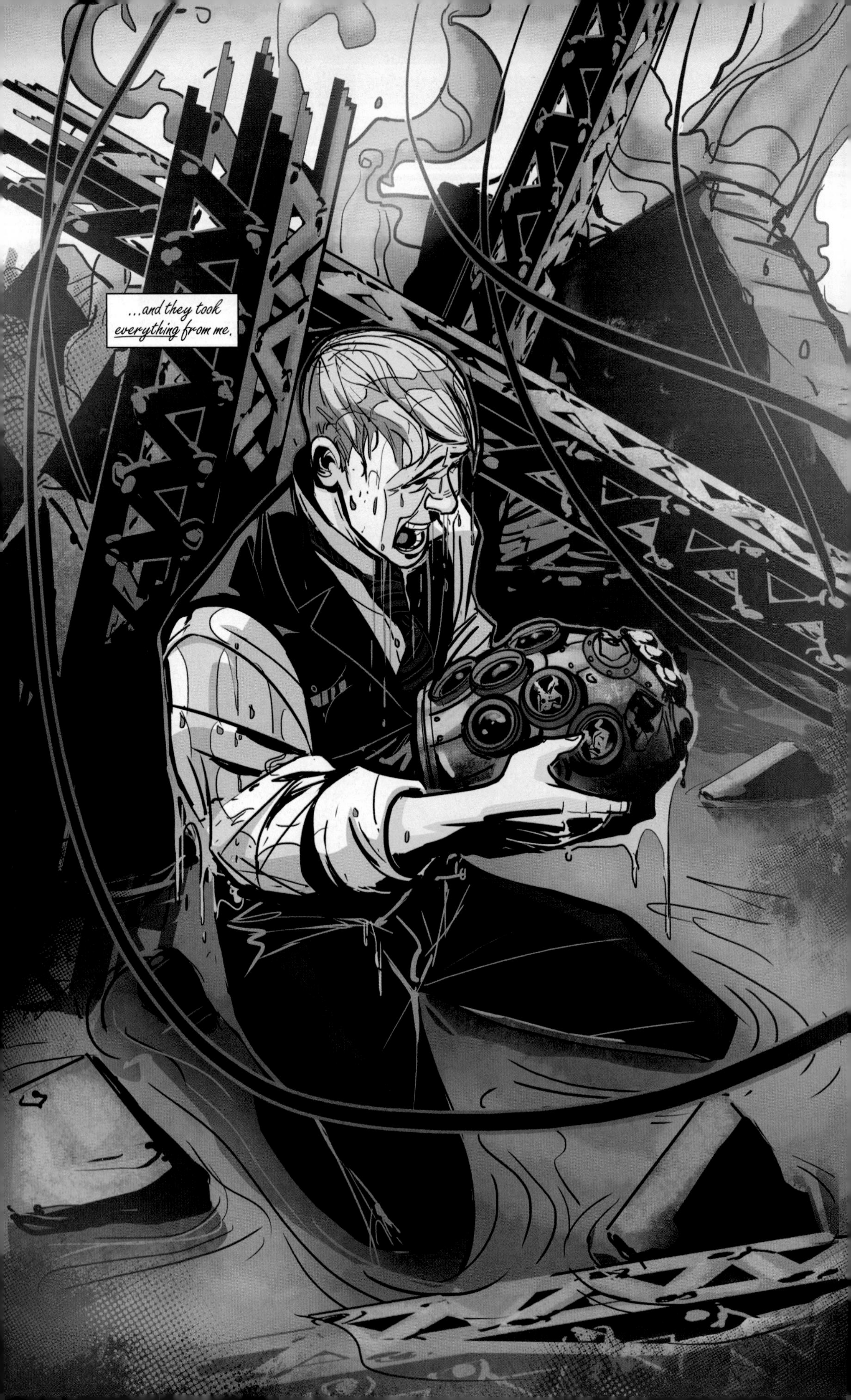
...and they took everything from me.

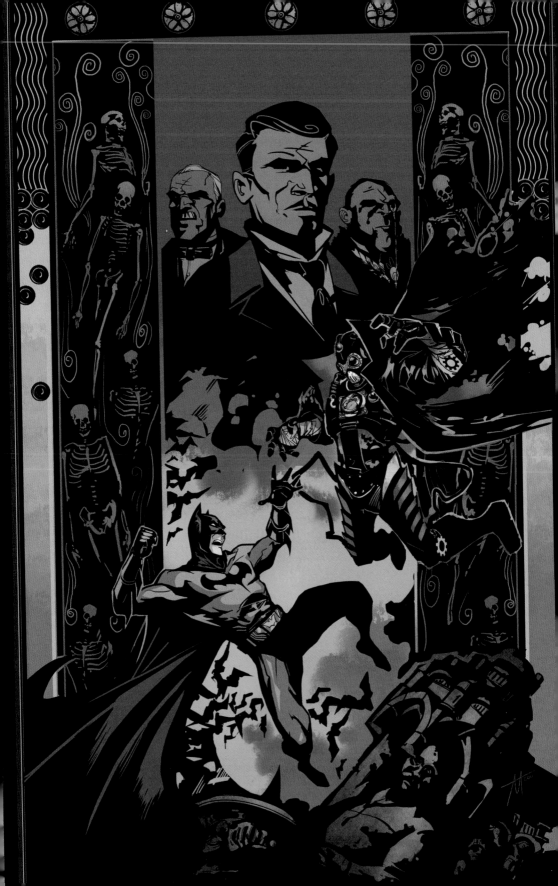

Part Four
THE GOTHAM CITY MASSACRE

Scott **Snyder** & Kyle **Higgins**
story

Kyle **Higgins** & Ryan **Parrott**
dialogue

Dustin **Nguyen** & Derec **Donovan**
art

Graham **Nolan**
layouts

Trevor **McCarthy**
cover

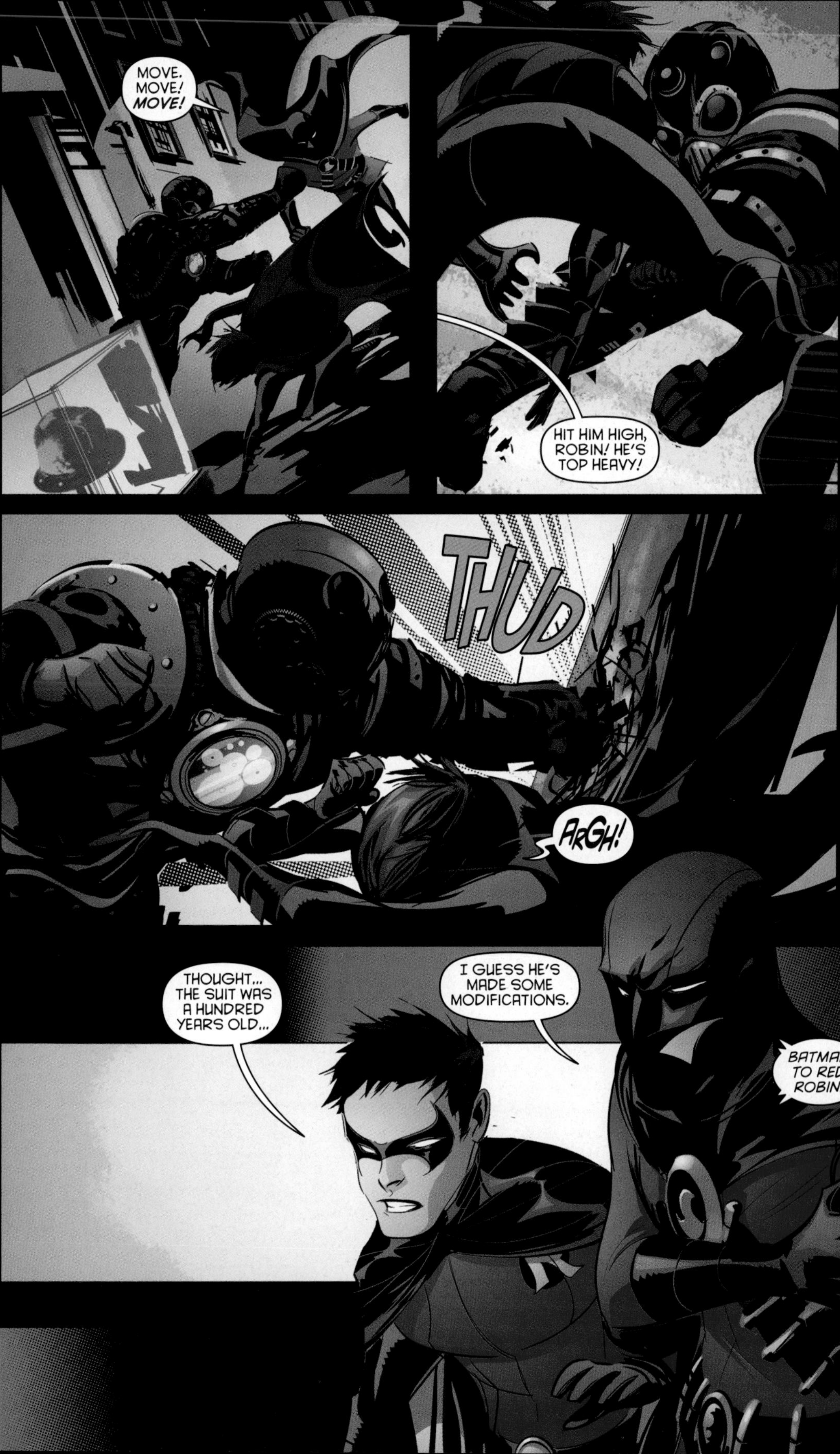
MOVE. MOVE! MOVE!
HIT HIM HIGH, ROBIN! HE'S TOP HEAVY!
THUD
ARGH!
THOUGHT... THE SUIT WAS A HUNDRED YEARS OLD...
I GUESS HE'S MADE SOME MODIFICATIONS.
BATMAN TO RED ROBIN.

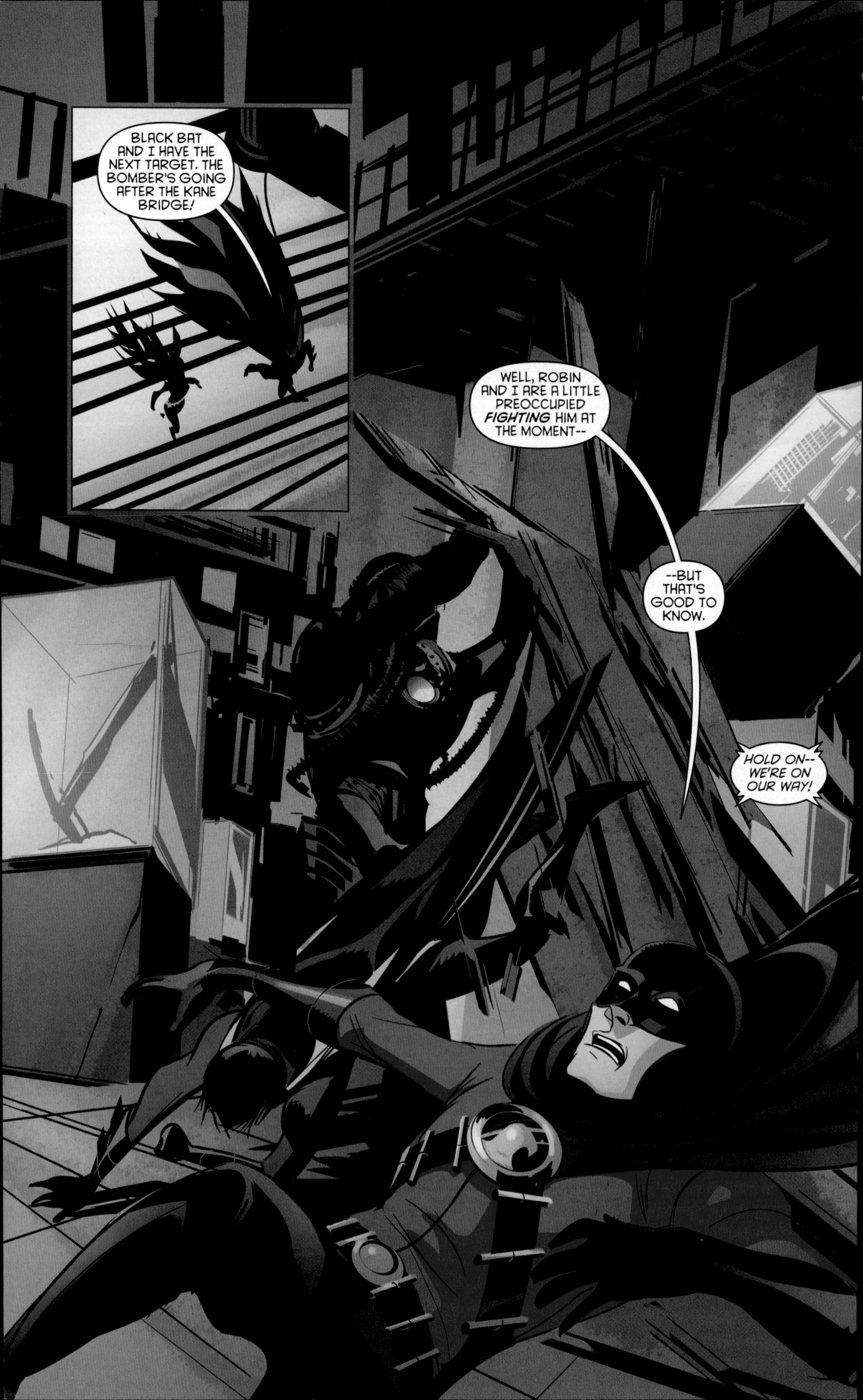
BLACK BAT AND I HAVE THE NEXT TARGET. THE BOMBER'S GOING AFTER THE KANE BRIDGE!
WELL, ROBIN AND I ARE A LITTLE PREOCCUPIED *FIGHTING* HIM AT THE MOMENT--
--BUT THAT'S GOOD TO KNOW.
HOLD ON-- WE'RE ON OUR WAY!

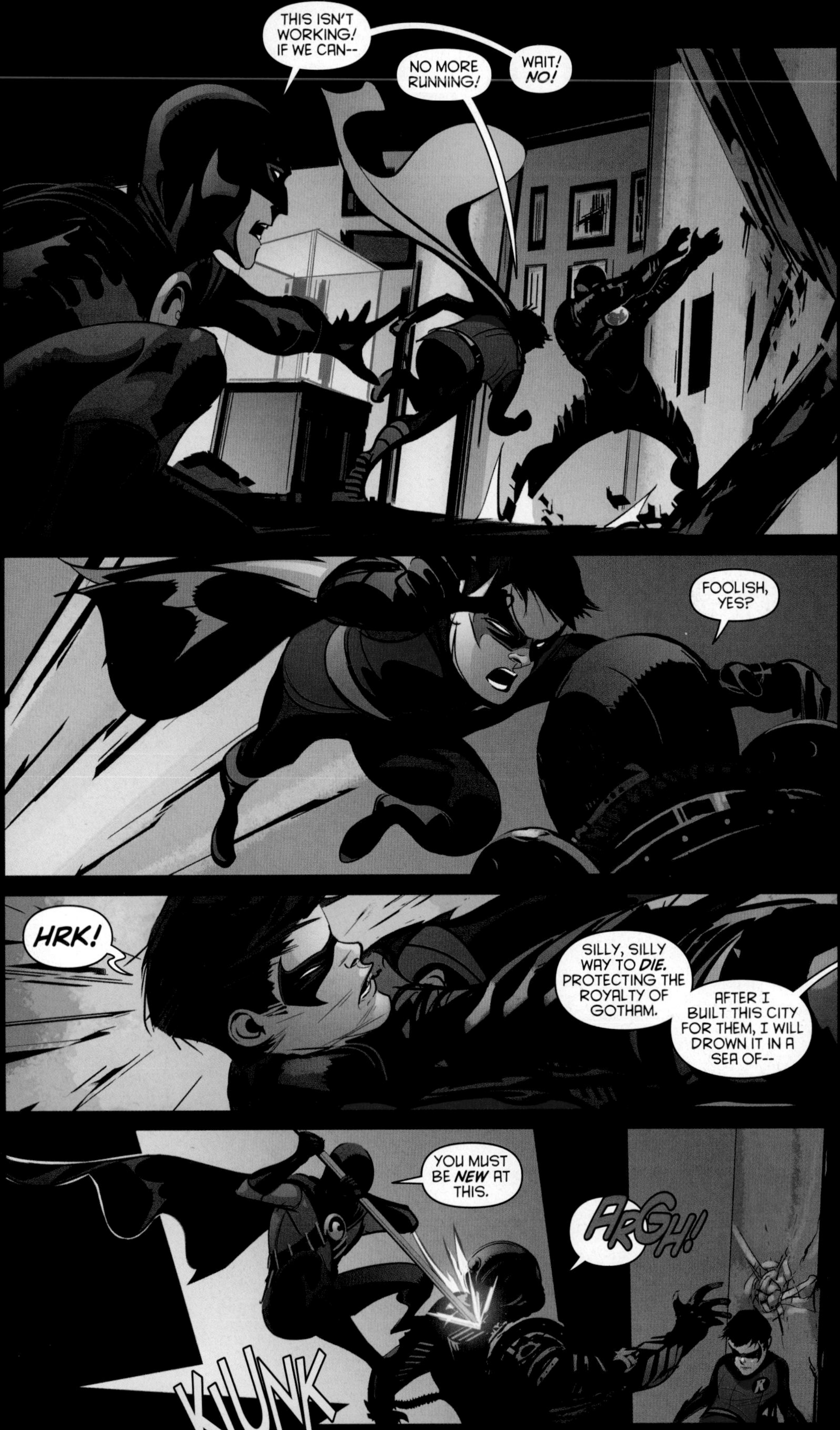

THIS ISN'T WORKING! IF WE CAN--
NO MORE RUNNING!
WAIT! NO!
FOOLISH, YES?
HRK!
SILLY, SILLY WAY TO DIE. PROTECTING THE ROYALTY OF GOTHAM.
AFTER I BUILT THIS CITY FOR THEM, I WILL DROWN IT IN A SEA OF--
YOU MUST BE NEW AT THIS.
ARGH!
KLUNK

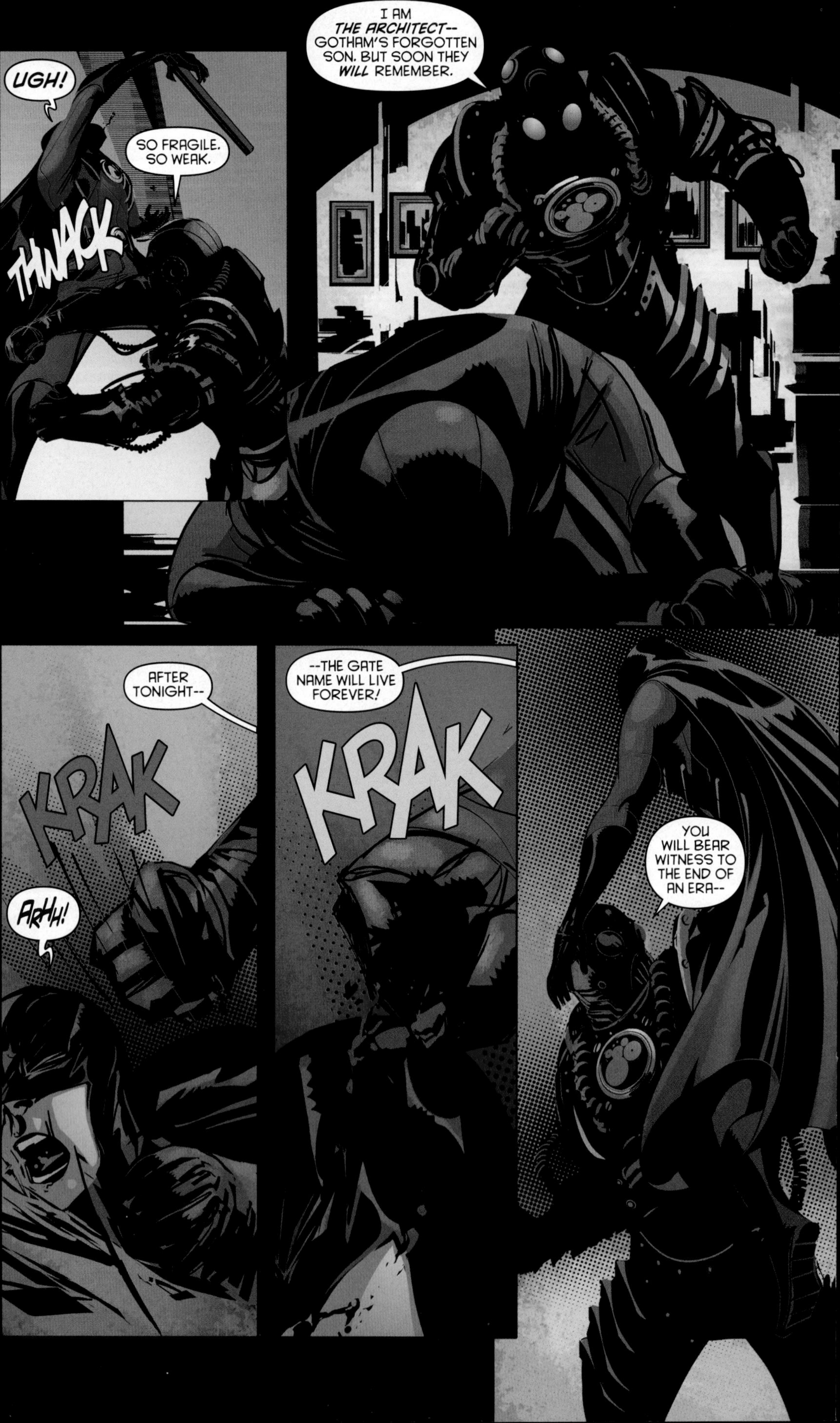

UGH!
SO FRAGILE. SO WEAK.
THWACK
I AM THE ARCHITECT-- GOTHAM'S FORGOTTEN SON. BUT SOON THEY WILL REMEMBER.
AFTER TONIGHT--
KRAK
ARHH!
--THE GATE NAME WILL LIVE FOREVER!
KRAK
YOU WILL BEAR WITNESS TO THE END OF AN ERA--

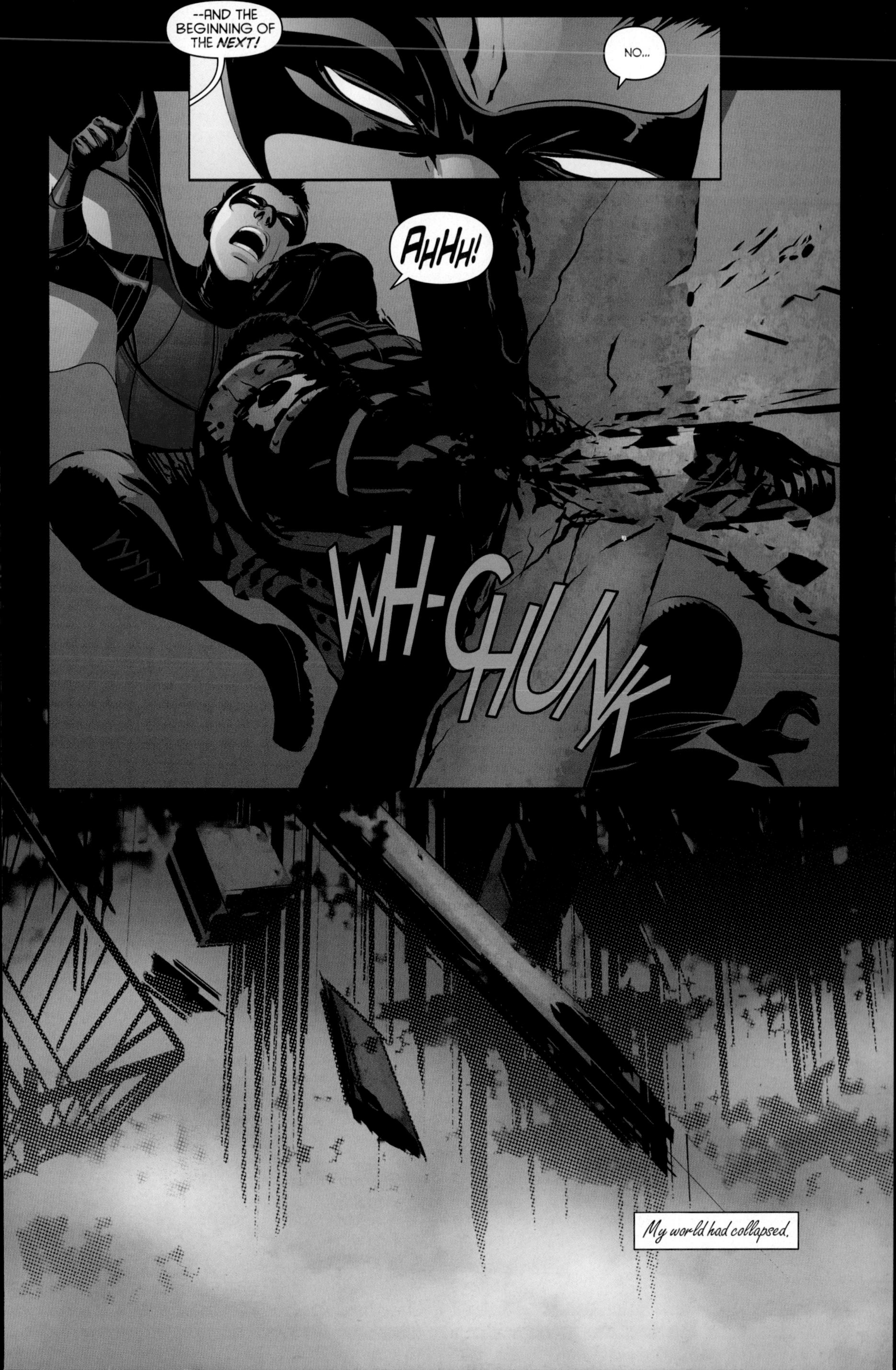
--AND THE BEGINNING OF THE *NEXT!*
NO...
AHHH!
WH-CHUNK
My world had collapsed.

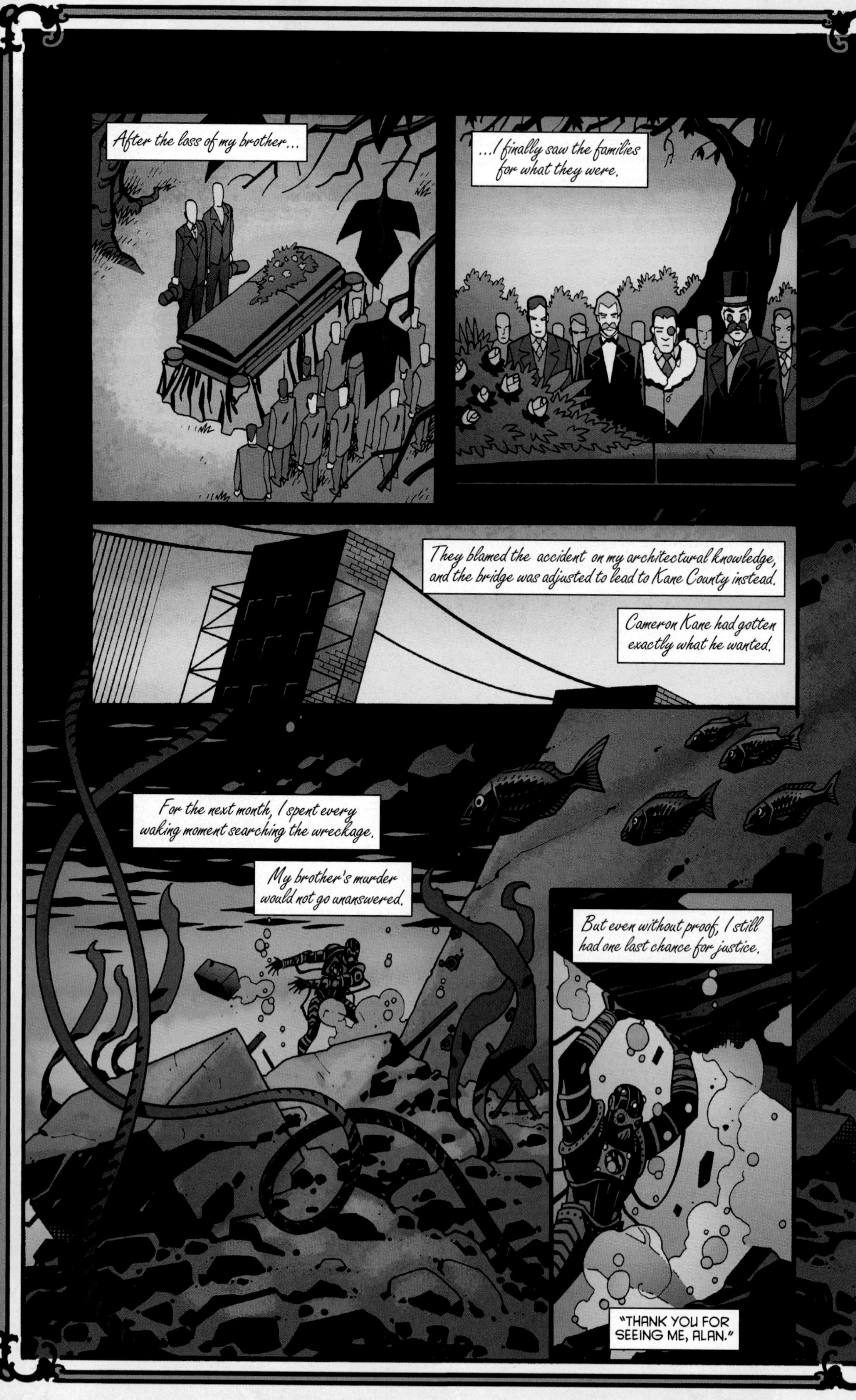
After the loss of my brother...
...I finally saw the families for what they were.
They blamed the accident on my architectural knowledge, and the bridge was adjusted to lead to Kane County instead.
Cameron Kane had gotten exactly what he wanted.
For the next month, I spent every waking moment searching the wreckage.
My brother's murder would not go unanswered.
But even without proof, I still had one last chance for justice.
"THANK YOU FOR SEEING ME, ALAN."

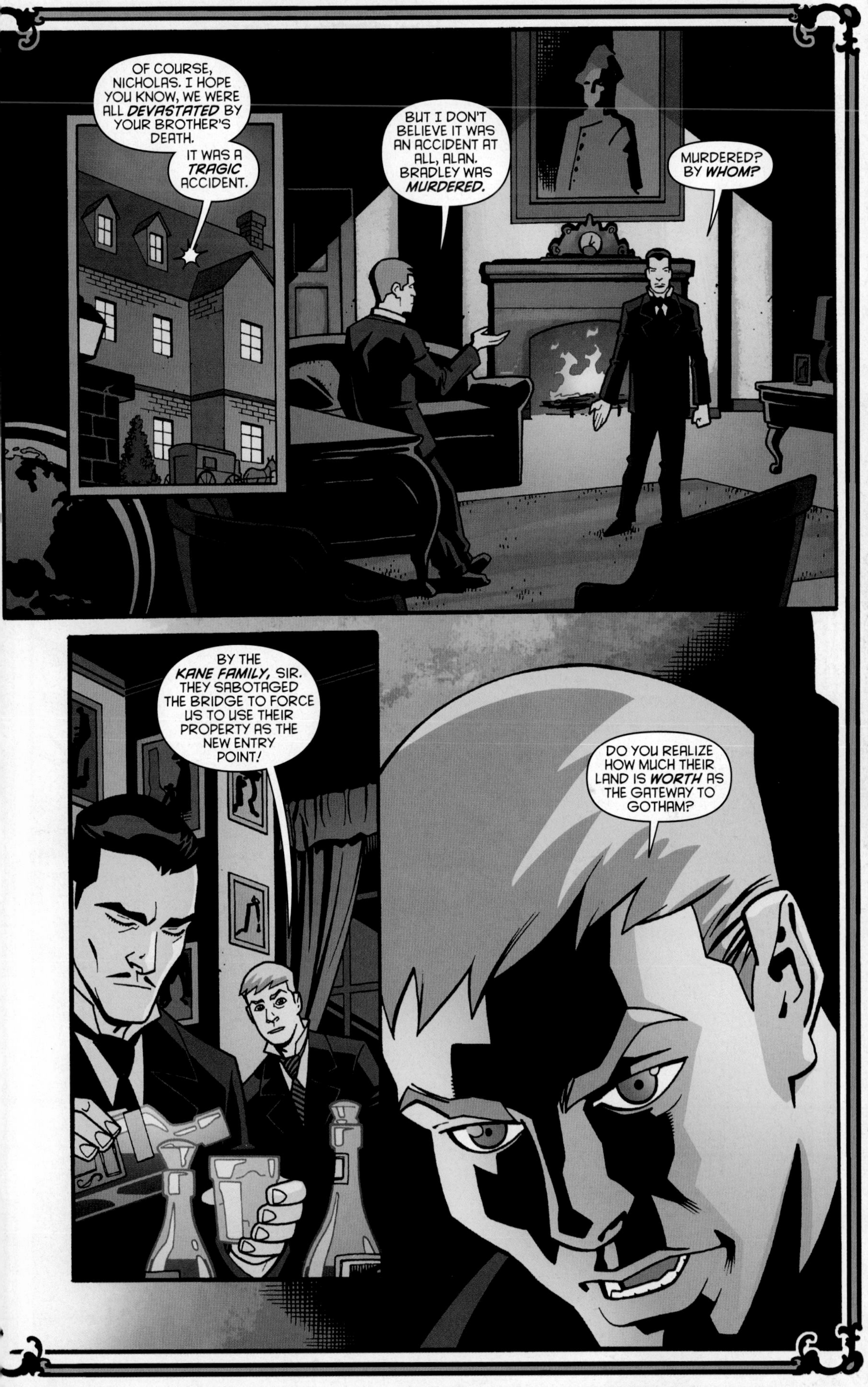

OF COURSE, NICHOLAS. I HOPE YOU KNOW, WE WERE ALL DEVASTATED BY YOUR BROTHER'S DEATH.
IT WAS A TRAGIC ACCIDENT.
BUT I DON'T BELIEVE IT WAS AN ACCIDENT AT ALL, ALAN. BRADLEY WAS MURDERED.
MURDERED? BY WHOM?
BY THE KANE FAMILY, SIR. THEY SABOTAGED THE BRIDGE TO FORCE US TO USE THEIR PROPERTY AS THE NEW ENTRY POINT!
DO YOU REALIZE HOW MUCH THEIR LAND IS WORTH AS THE GATEWAY TO GOTHAM?

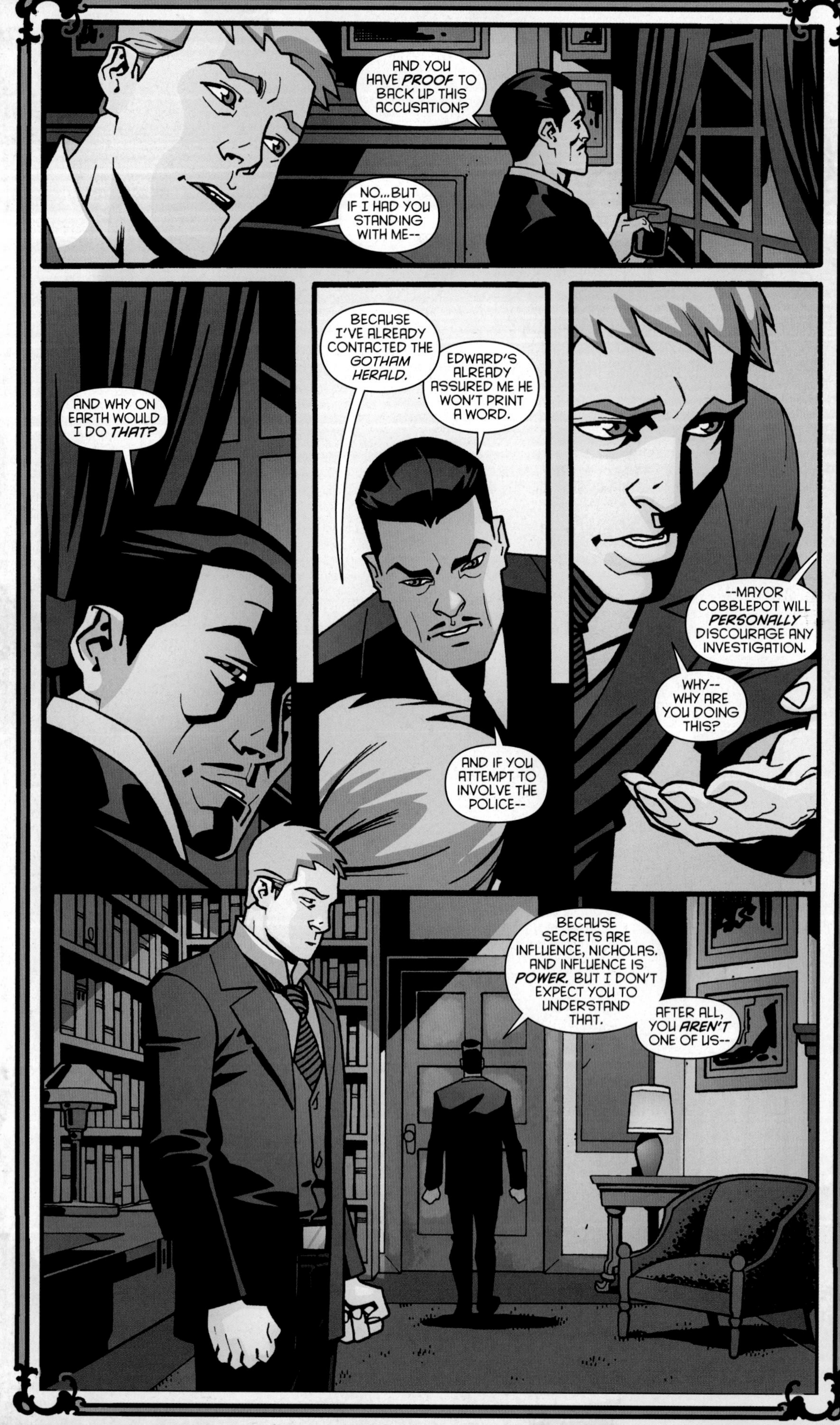

AND YOU HAVE *PROOF* TO BACK UP THIS ACCUSATION?
NO...BUT IF I HAD YOU STANDING WITH ME--
AND WHY ON EARTH WOULD I DO *THAT?*
BECAUSE I'VE ALREADY CONTACTED THE *GOTHAM HERALD.*
EDWARD'S ALREADY ASSURED ME HE WON'T PRINT A WORD.
AND IF YOU ATTEMPT TO INVOLVE THE POLICE--
--MAYOR COBBLEPOT WILL *PERSONALLY* DISCOURAGE ANY INVESTIGATION.
WHY--WHY ARE YOU DOING THIS?
BECAUSE SECRETS ARE INFLUENCE, NICHOLAS. AND INFLUENCE IS *POWER.* BUT I DON'T EXPECT YOU TO UNDERSTAND THAT.
AFTER ALL, YOU *AREN'T* ONE OF US--

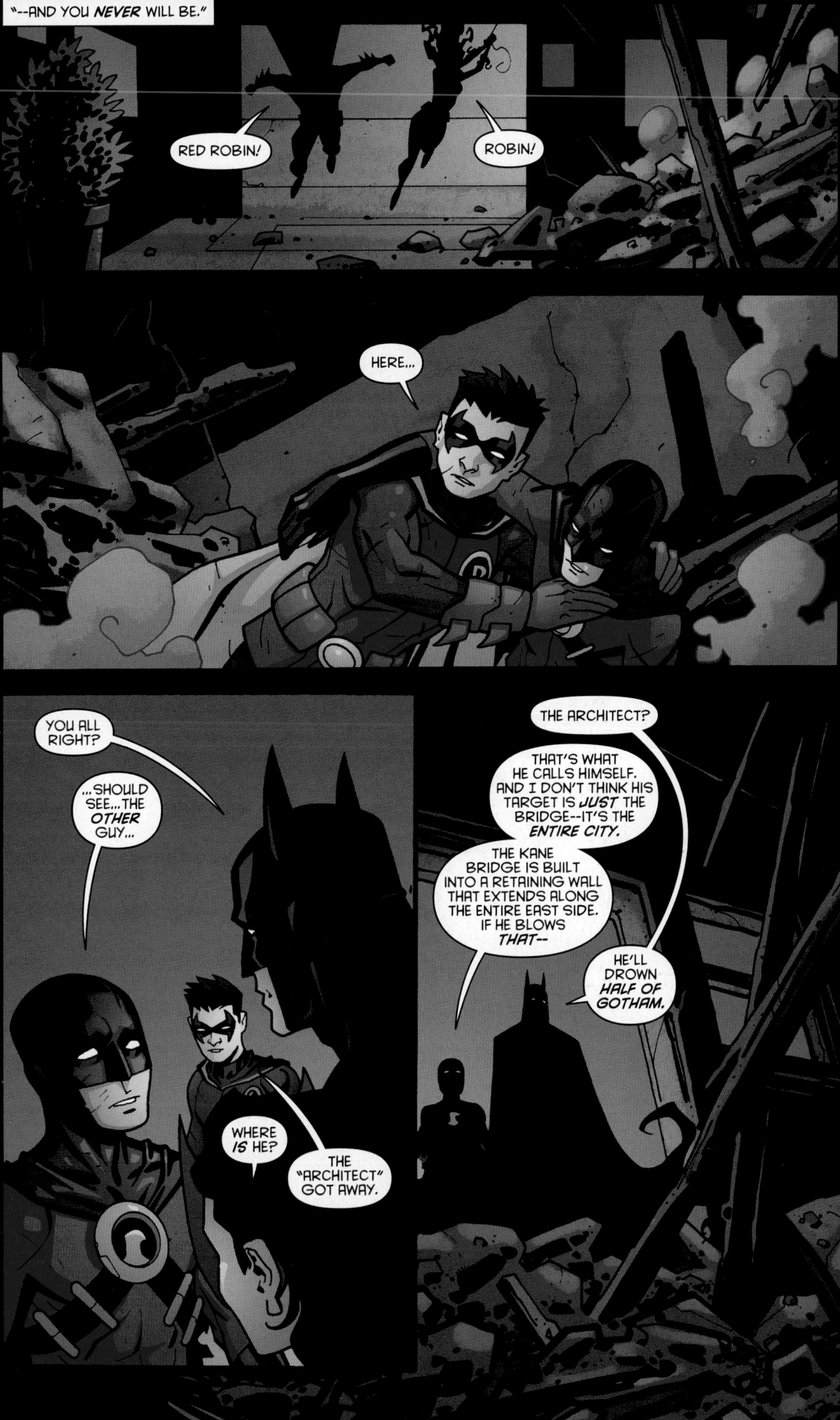
"--AND YOU NEVER WILL BE."
RED ROBIN!
ROBIN!
HERE...
YOU ALL RIGHT?
...SHOULD SEE...THE OTHER GUY...
WHERE IS HE?
THE "ARCHITECT" GOT AWAY.
THE ARCHITECT?
THAT'S WHAT HE CALLS HIMSELF. AND I DON'T THINK HIS TARGET IS JUST THE BRIDGE--IT'S THE ENTIRE CITY.
THE KANE BRIDGE IS BUILT INTO A RETAINING WALL THAT EXTENDS ALONG THE ENTIRE EAST SIDE. IF HE BLOWS THAT--
HE'LL DROWN HALF OF GOTHAM.

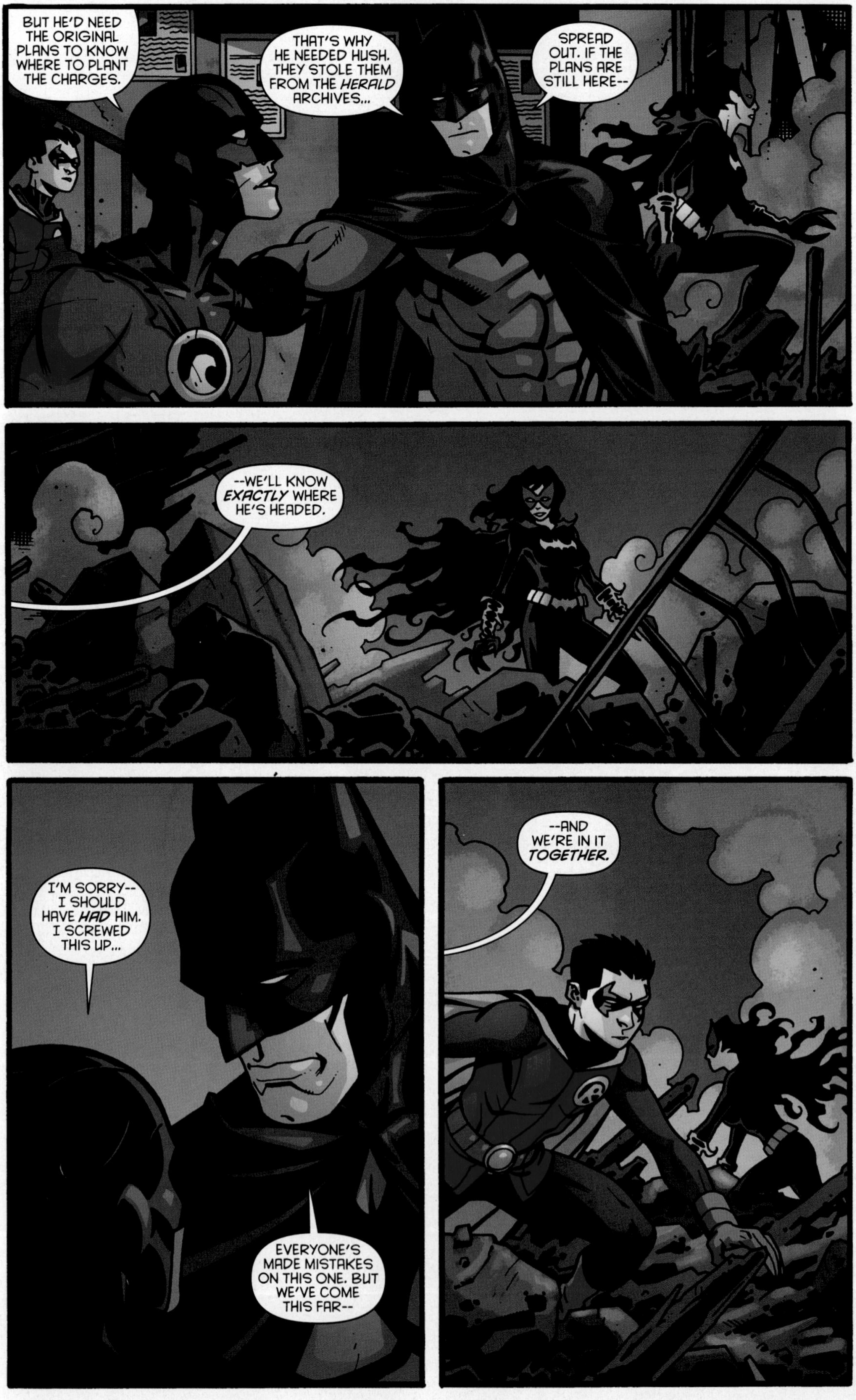
BUT HE'D NEED THE ORIGINAL PLANS TO KNOW WHERE TO PLANT THE CHARGES.
THAT'S WHY HE NEEDED HUSH. THEY STOLE THEM FROM THE *HERALD* ARCHIVES...
SPREAD OUT. IF THE PLANS ARE STILL HERE--
--WE'LL KNOW *EXACTLY* WHERE HE'S HEADED.
I'M SORRY-- I SHOULD HAVE *HAD* HIM. I SCREWED THIS UP...
EVERYONE'S MADE MISTAKES ON THIS ONE. BUT WE'VE COME THIS FAR--
--AND WE'RE IN IT *TOGETHER.*

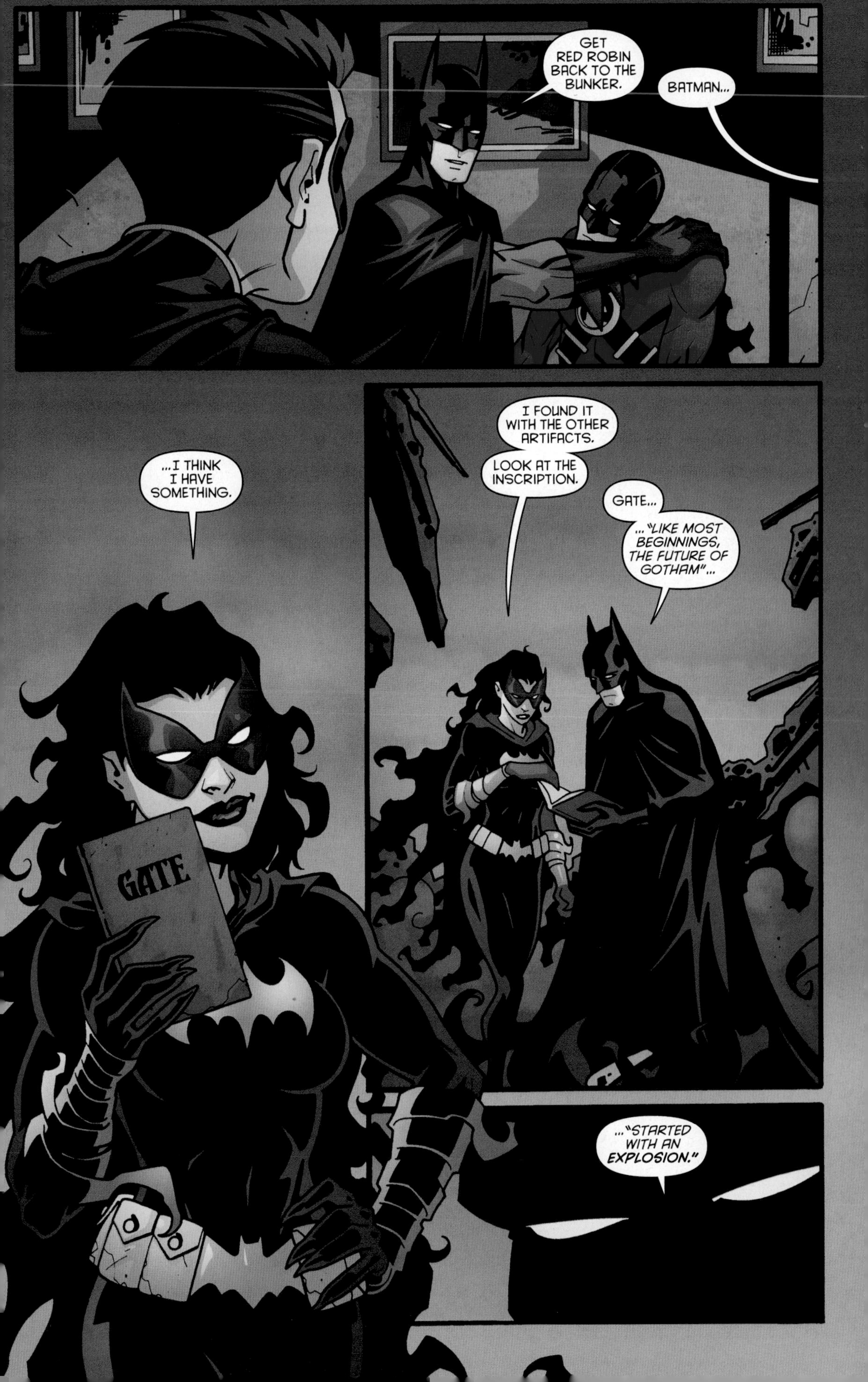
GET RED ROBIN BACK TO THE BUNKER.
BATMAN...
...I THINK I HAVE SOMETHING.
I FOUND IT WITH THE OTHER ARTIFACTS.
LOOK AT THE INSCRIPTION.
GATE...
..."LIKE MOST BEGINNINGS, THE FUTURE OF GOTHAM"...
GATE
..."STARTED WITH AN EXPLOSION."

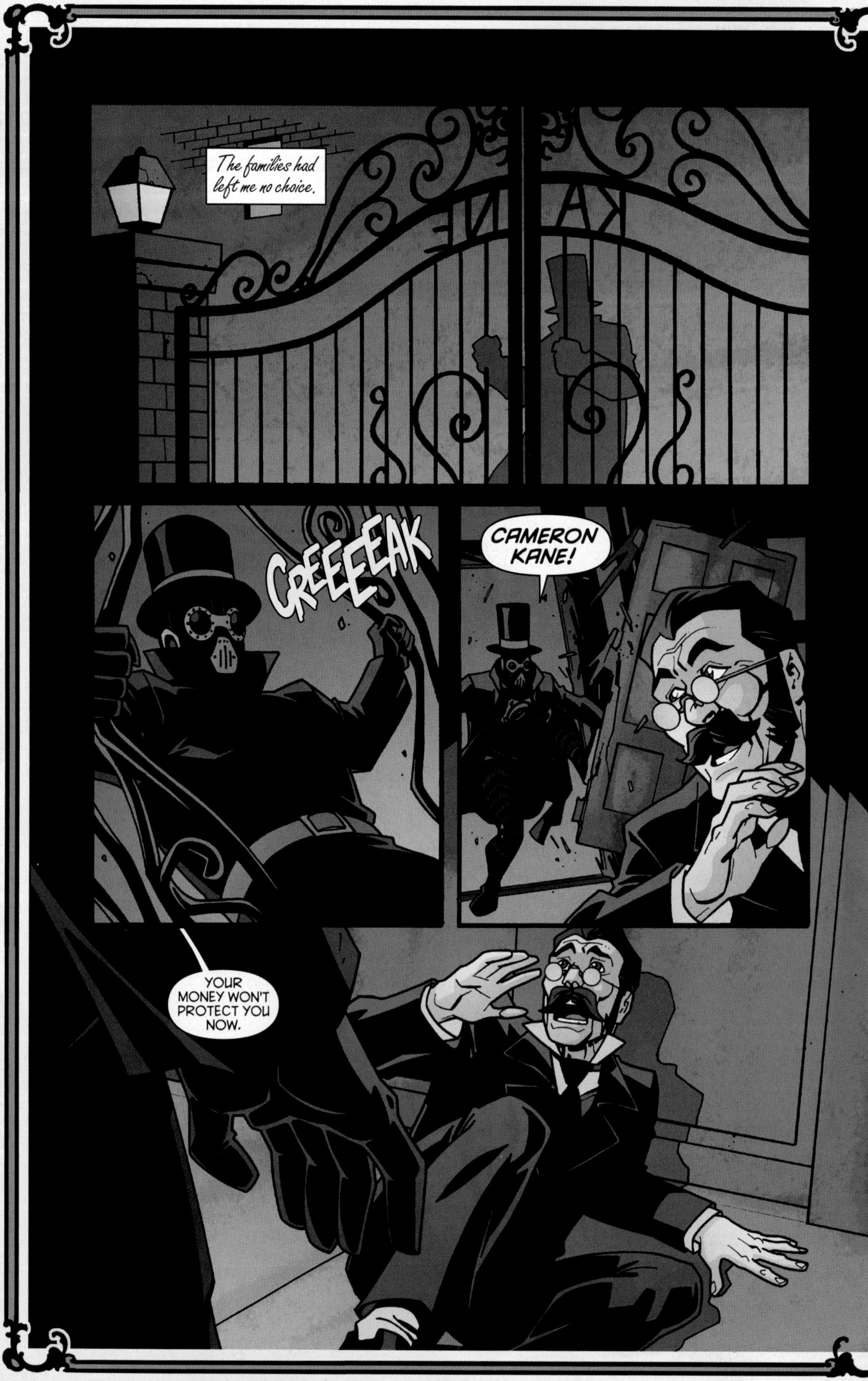
The families had left me no choice.
KANE
CREEEEAK
CAMERON KANE!
YOUR MONEY WON'T PROTECT YOU NOW.

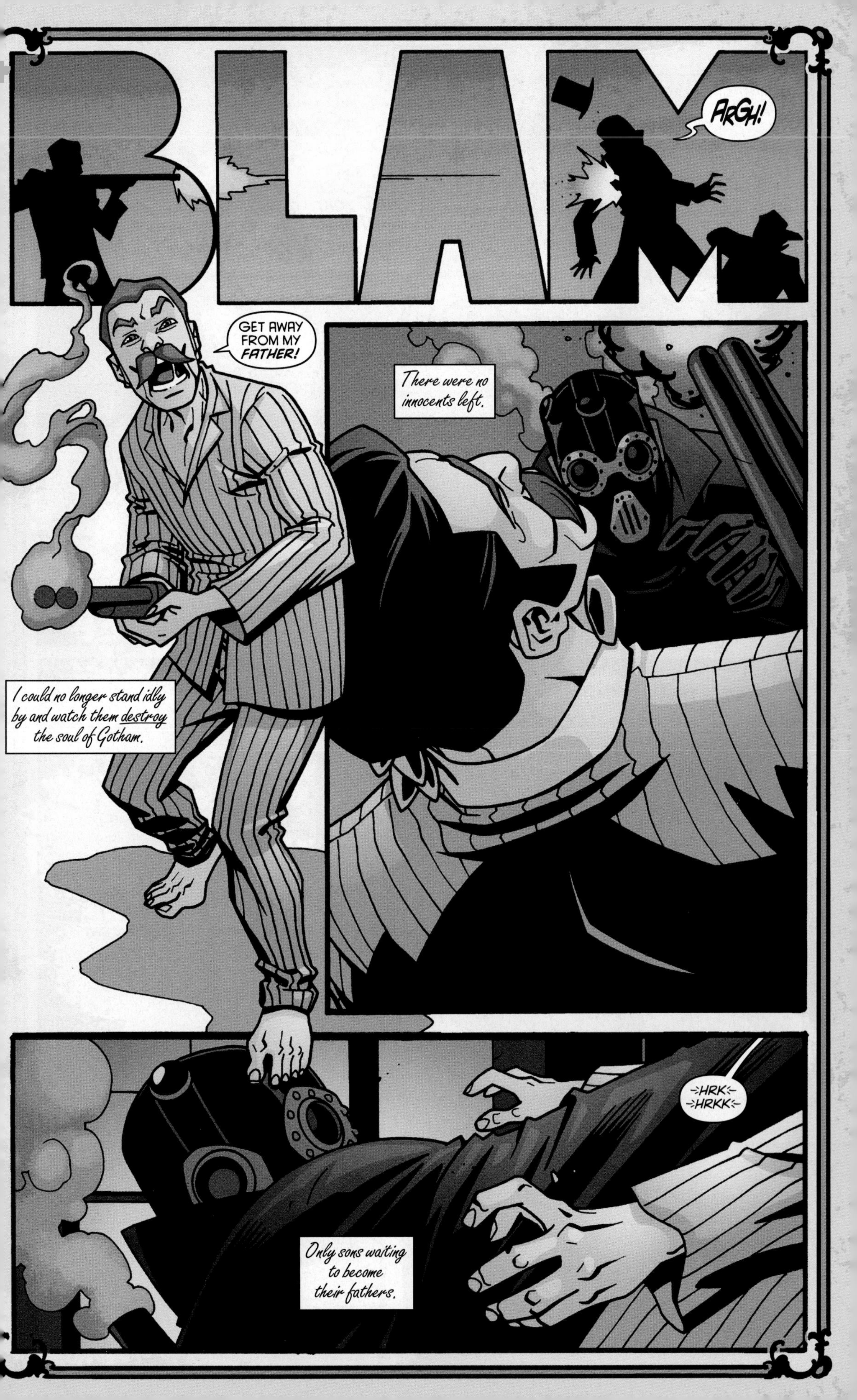

BLAM
ARGH!
GET AWAY FROM MY FATHER!
There were no innocents left.
I could no longer stand idly by and watch them destroy the soul of Gotham.
HRK HRKK
Only sons waiting to become their fathers.

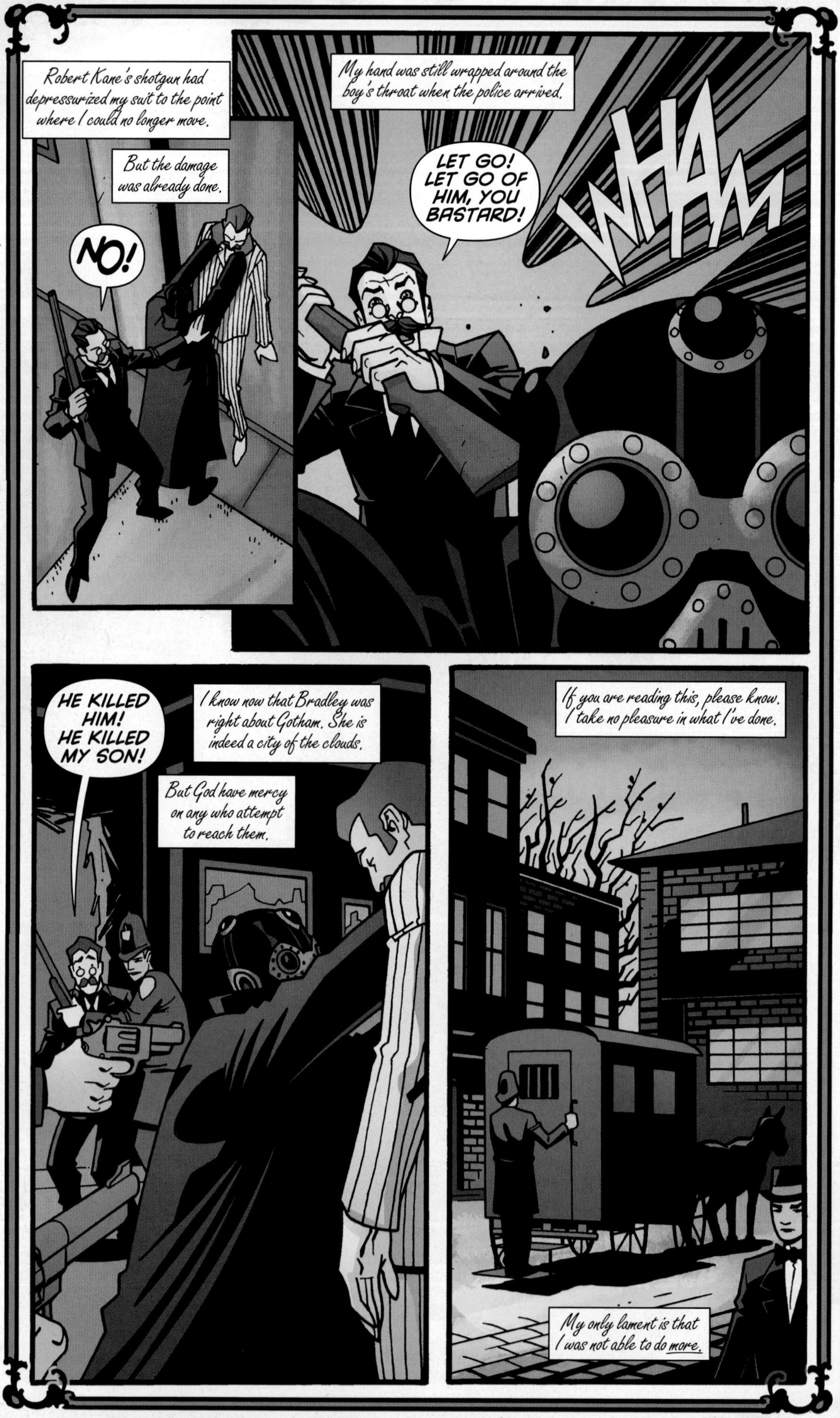
Robert Kane's shotgun had depressurized my suit to the point where I could no longer move.
But the damage was already done.
NO!
My hand was still wrapped around the boy's throat when the police arrived.
LET GO! LET GO OF HIM, YOU BASTARD!
WHAM
HE KILLED HIM! HE KILLED MY SON!
I know now that Bradley was right about Gotham. She is indeed a city of the clouds.
But God have mercy on any who attempt to reach them.
If you are reading this, please know. I take no pleasure in what I've done.
My only lament is that I was not able to do more.

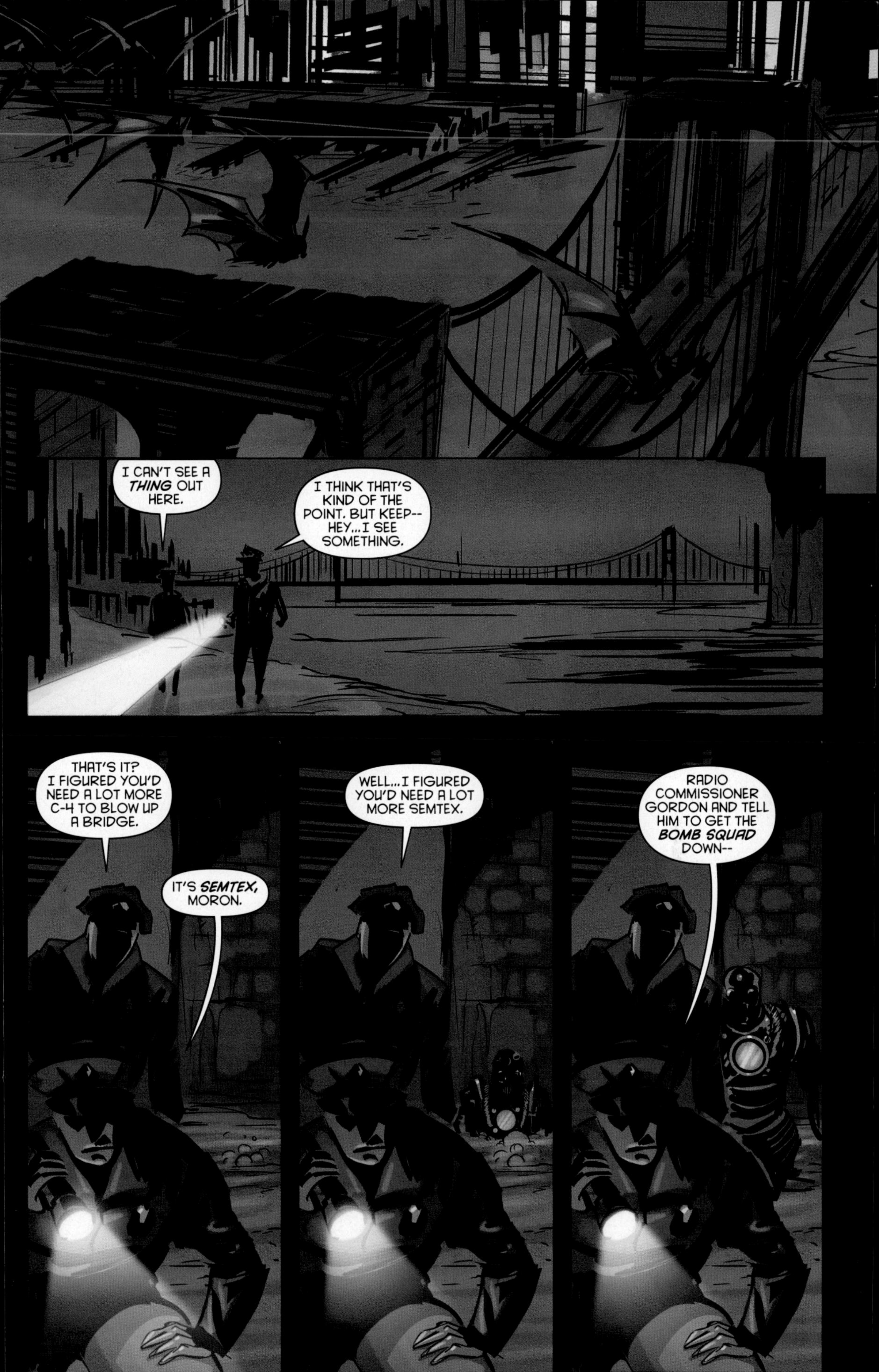
I CAN'T SEE A *THING* OUT HERE.
I THINK THAT'S KIND OF THE POINT. BUT KEEP-- HEY...I SEE SOMETHING.
THAT'S IT? I FIGURED YOU'D NEED A LOT MORE C-4 TO BLOW UP A BRIDGE.
IT'S *SEMTEX,* MORON.
WELL...I FIGURED YOU'D NEED A LOT MORE SEMTEX.
RADIO COMMISSIONER GORDON AND TELL HIM TO GET THE *BOMB SQUAD* DOWN--

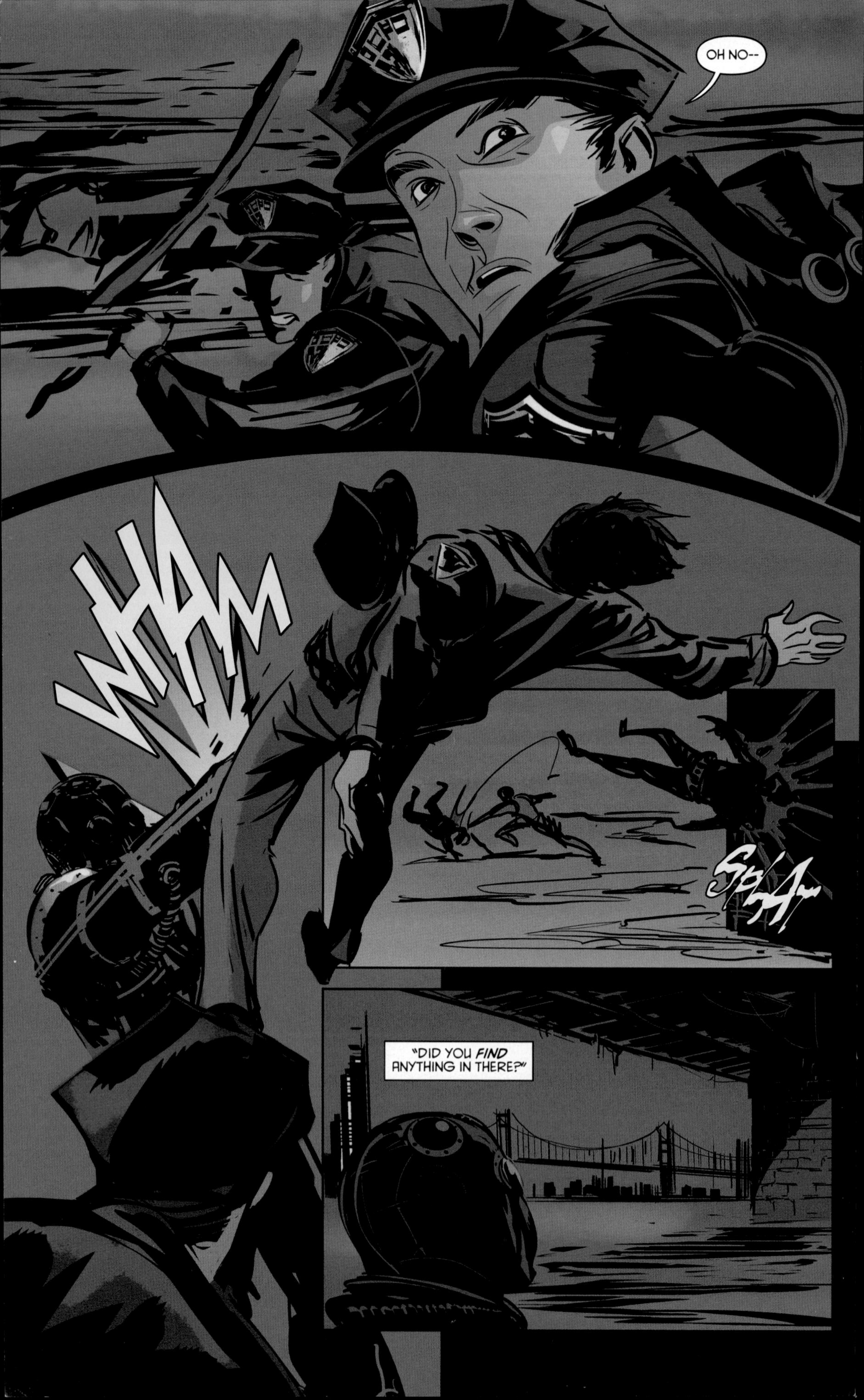
OH NO--
WHAM
"DID YOU FIND ANYTHING IN THERE?"

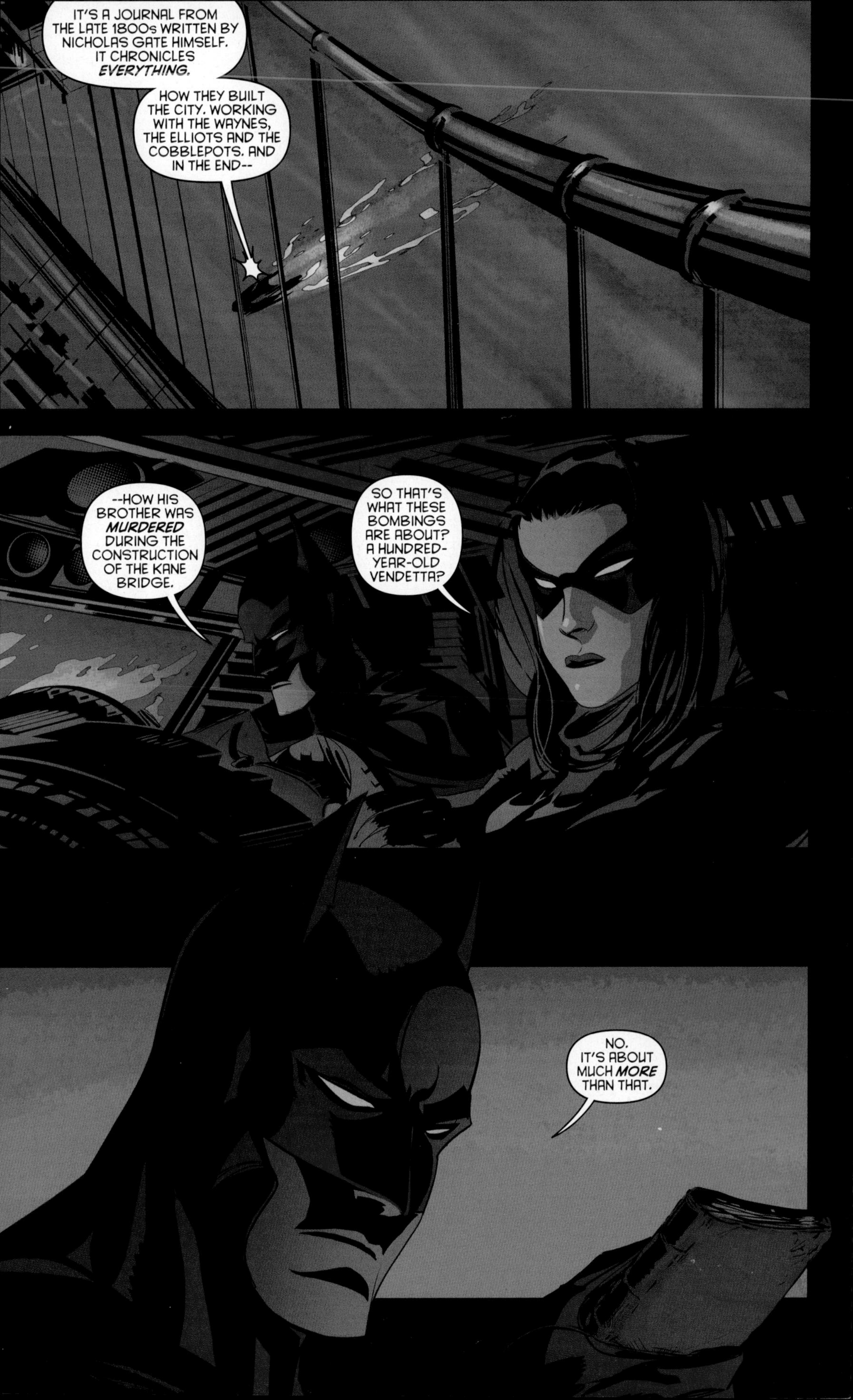
IT'S A JOURNAL FROM THE LATE 1800s WRITTEN BY NICHOLAS GATE HIMSELF. IT CHRONICLES *EVERYTHING.*
HOW THEY BUILT THE CITY. WORKING WITH THE WAYNES, THE ELLIOTS AND THE COBBLEPOTS. AND IN THE END--
--HOW HIS BROTHER WAS *MURDERED* DURING THE CONSTRUCTION OF THE KANE BRIDGE.
SO THAT'S WHAT THESE BOMBINGS ARE ABOUT? A HUNDRED-YEAR-OLD VENDETTA?
NO. IT'S ABOUT MUCH *MORE* THAN THAT.

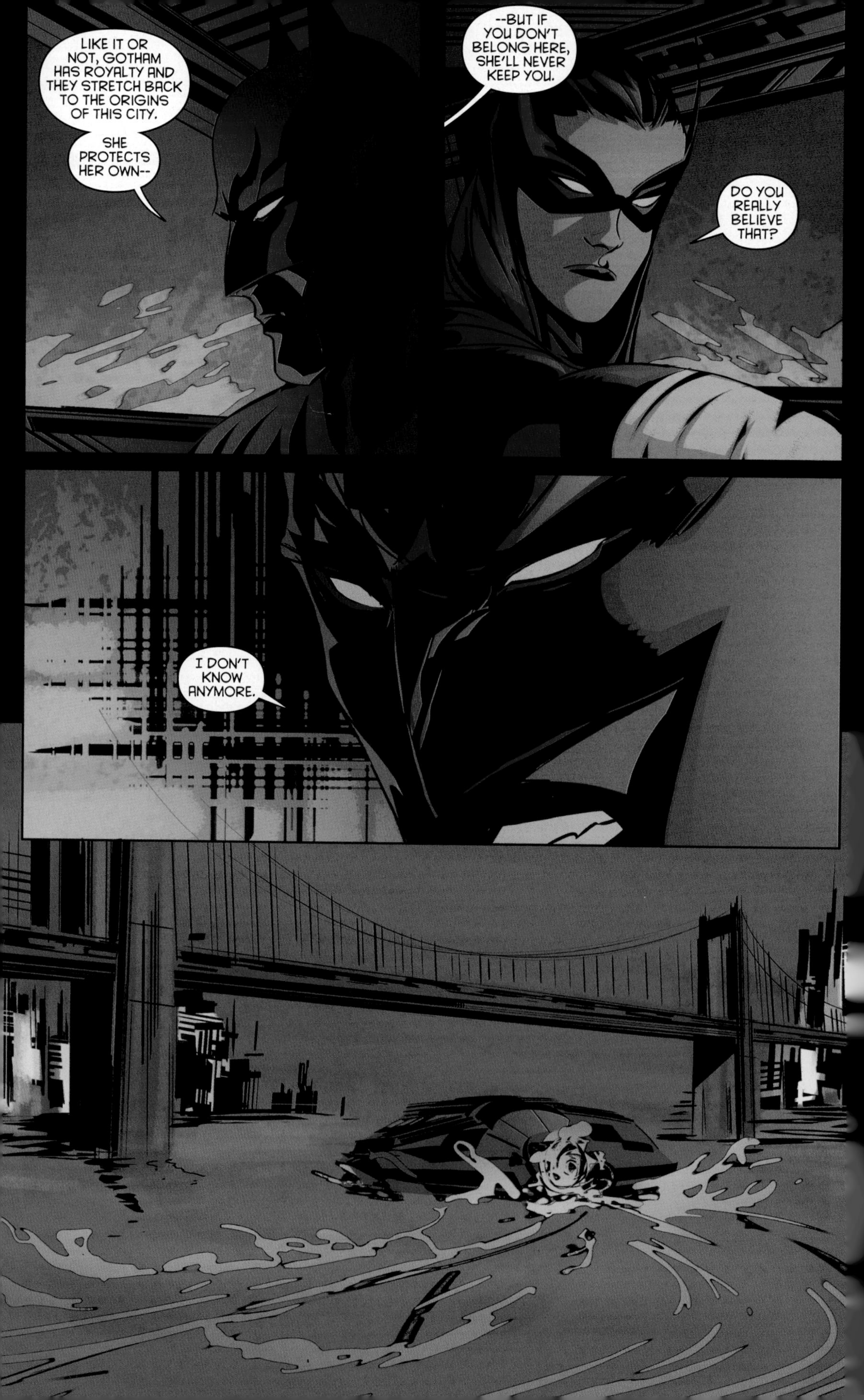
LIKE IT OR NOT, GOTHAM HAS ROYALTY AND THEY STRETCH BACK TO THE ORIGINS OF THIS CITY.
SHE PROTECTS HER OWN--
--BUT IF YOU DON'T BELONG HERE, SHE'LL NEVER KEEP YOU.
DO YOU REALLY BELIEVE THAT?
I DON'T KNOW ANYMORE.

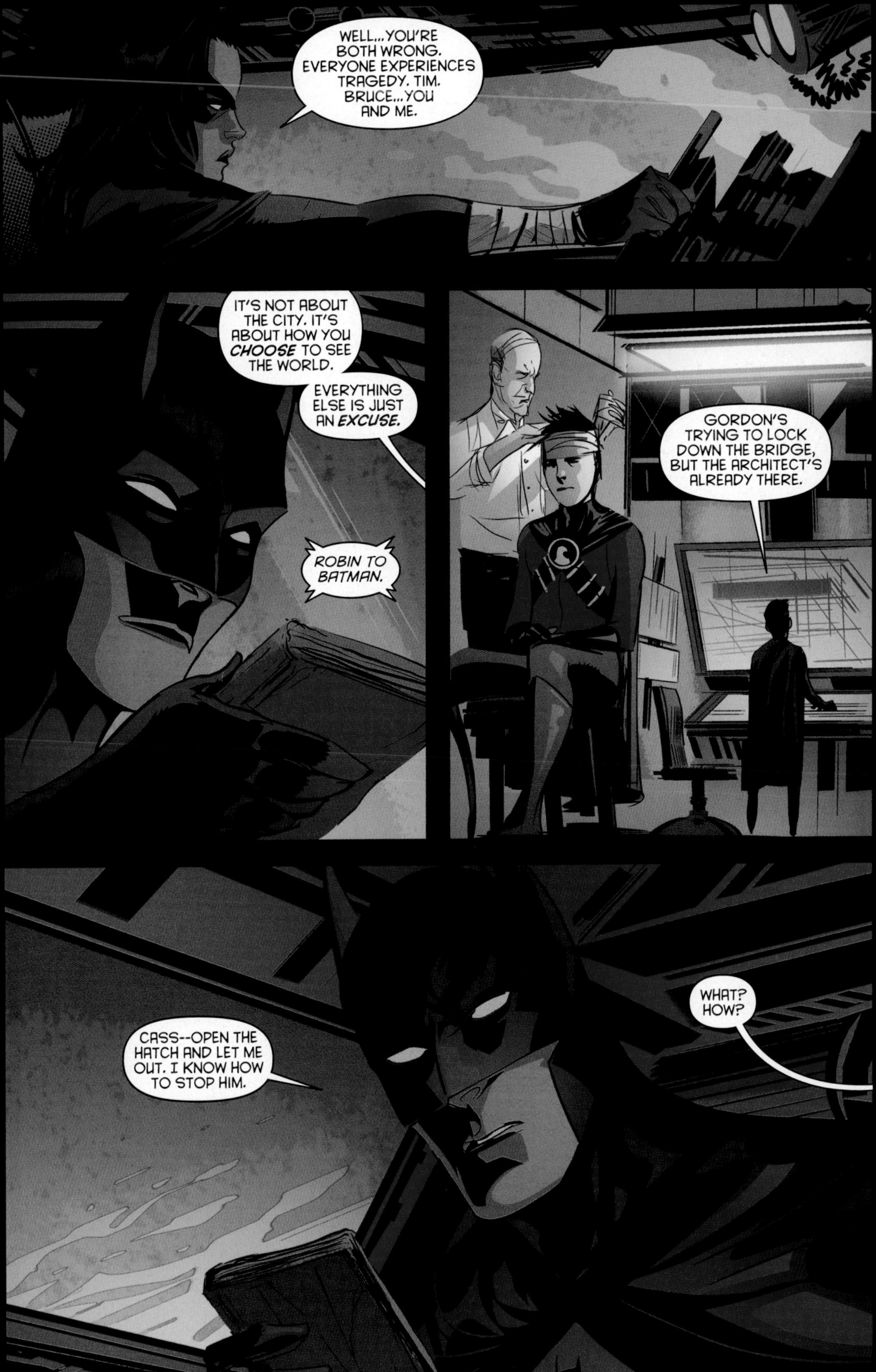
WELL...YOU'RE BOTH WRONG. EVERYONE EXPERIENCES TRAGEDY. TIM. BRUCE...YOU AND ME.
IT'S NOT ABOUT THE CITY. IT'S ABOUT HOW YOU *CHOOSE* TO SEE THE WORLD.
EVERYTHING ELSE IS JUST AN *EXCUSE.*
ROBIN TO BATMAN.
GORDON'S TRYING TO LOCK DOWN THE BRIDGE, BUT THE ARCHITECT'S ALREADY THERE.
WHAT? HOW?
CASS--OPEN THE HATCH AND LET ME OUT. I KNOW HOW TO STOP HIM.

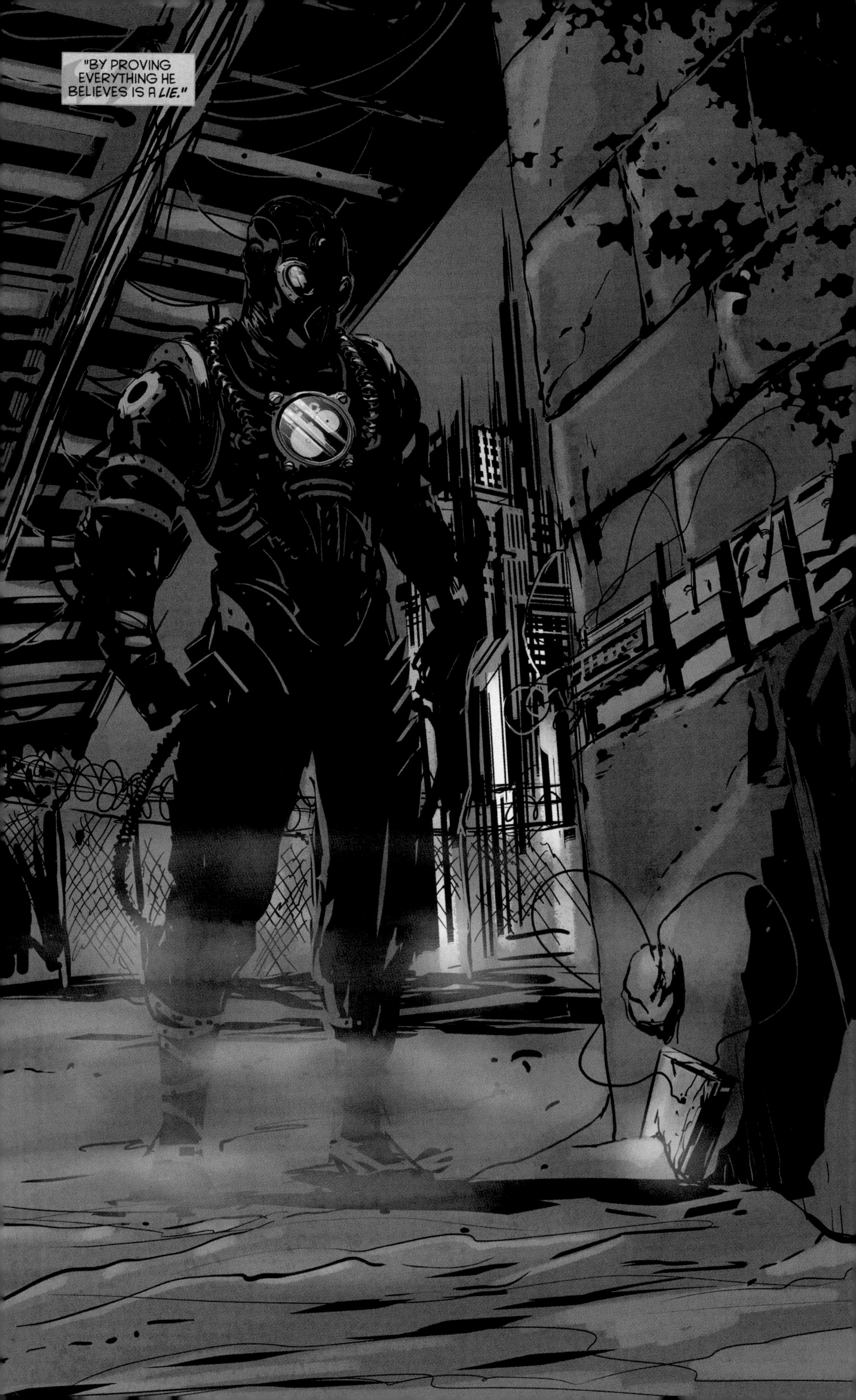
"BY PROVING EVERYTHING HE BELIEVES IS A *LIE.*"

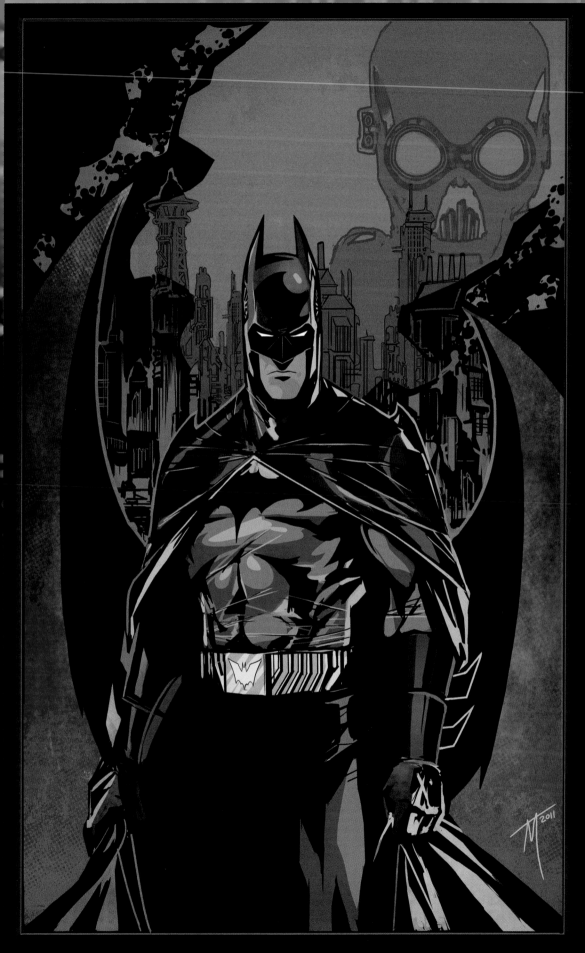

Part Five
WELCOME TO THE FUTURE

Scott **Snyder** & Kyle **Higgins**
story

Kyle **Higgins** & Ryan **Parrott**
dialogue

Trevor **McCarthy**
art & cover

Graham **Nolan**
layouts

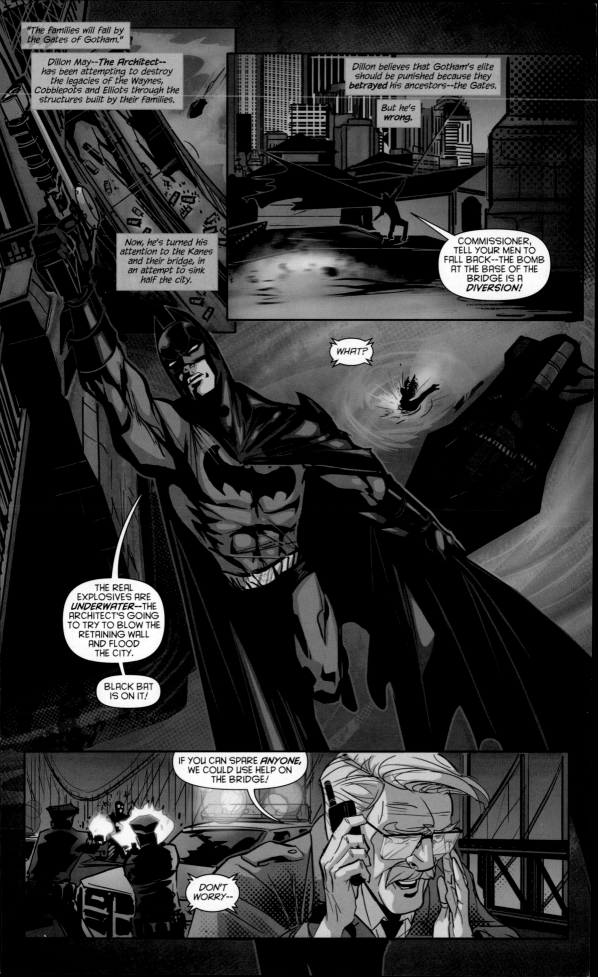

"The families will fall by the Gates of Gotham."

Dillon May--*The Architect*-- has been attempting to destroy the legacies of the Waynes, Cobblepots and Elliots through the structures built by their families.

Now, he's turned his attention to the Kanes and their bridge, in an attempt to sink half the city.

Dillon believes that Gotham's elite should be punished because they *betrayed* his ancestors--the Gates.

But he's *wrong.*

COMMISSIONER, TELL YOUR MEN TO FALL BACK--THE BOMB AT THE BASE OF THE BRIDGE IS A *DIVERSION!*

WHAT?

THE REAL EXPLOSIVES ARE *UNDERWATER*--THE ARCHITECT'S GOING TO TRY TO BLOW THE RETAINING WALL AND FLOOD THE CITY.

BLACK BAT IS ON IT!

IF YOU CAN SPARE *ANYONE,* WE COULD USE HELP ON THE BRIDGE!

DON'T WORRY--

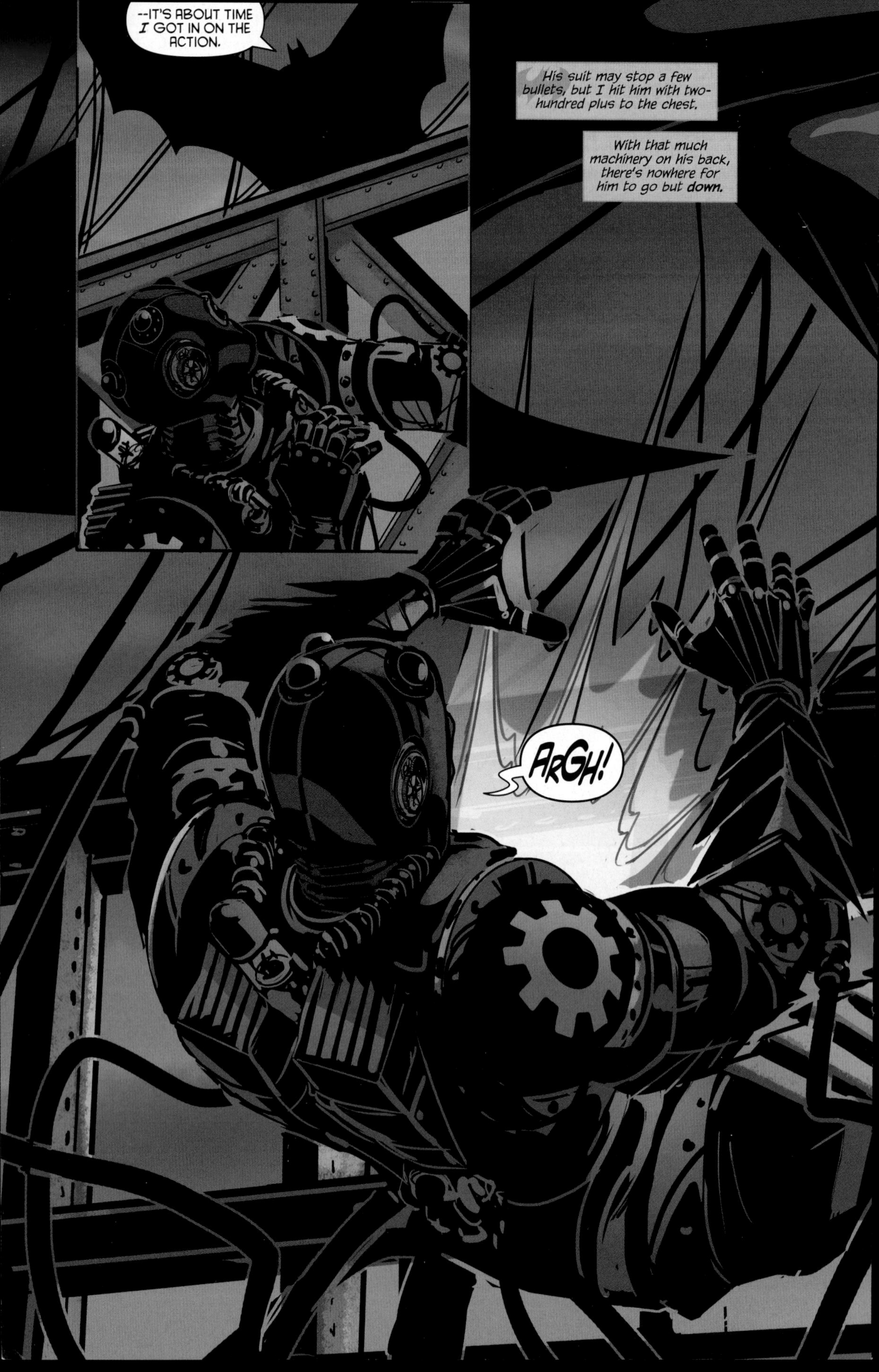
--IT'S ABOUT TIME *I* GOT IN ON THE ACTION.
His suit may stop a few bullets, but I hit him with two-hundred plus to the chest.
With that much machinery on his back, there's nowhere for him to go but **down.**
ARGH!

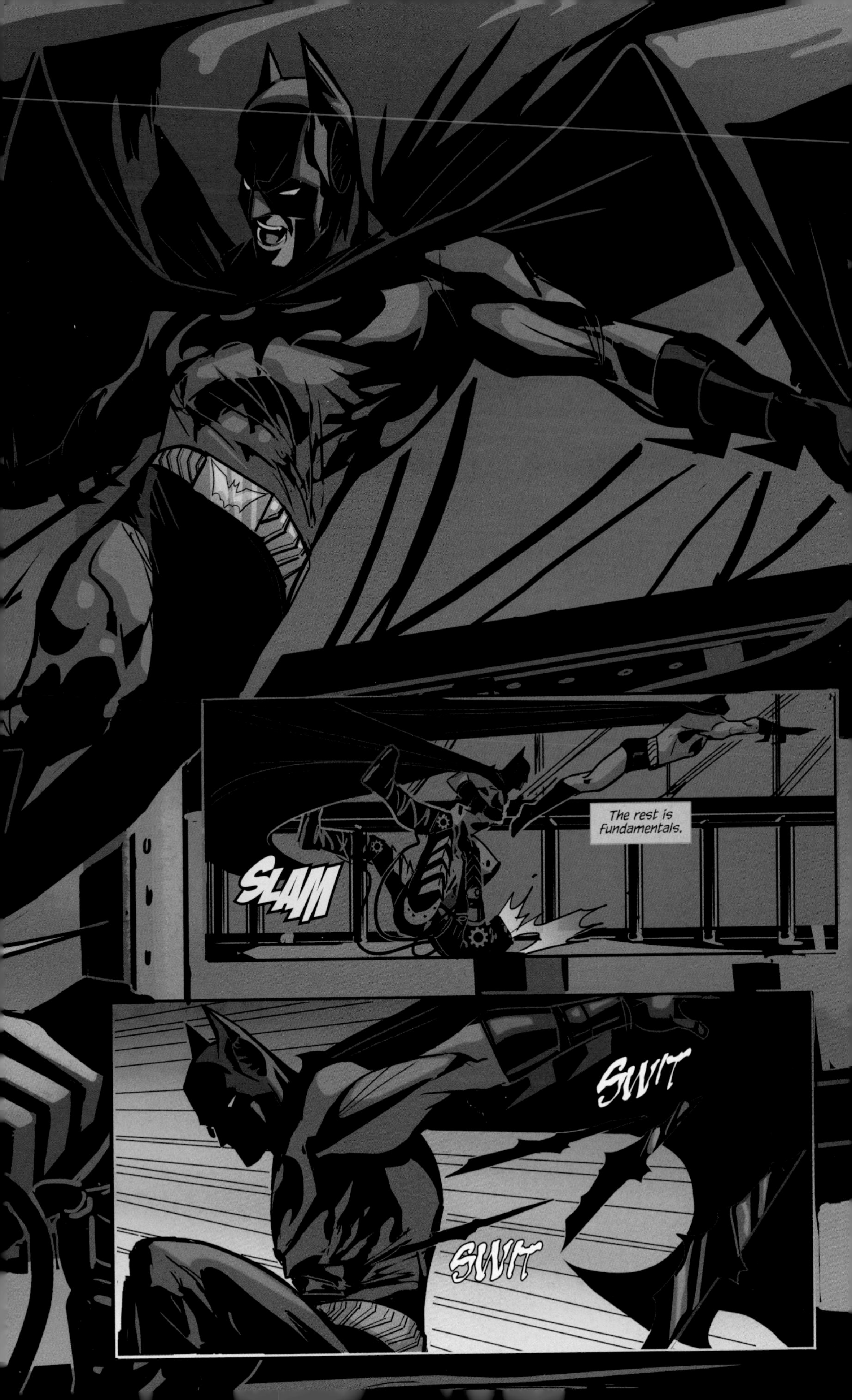
SLAM
The rest is fundamentals.
SWIT
SWIT

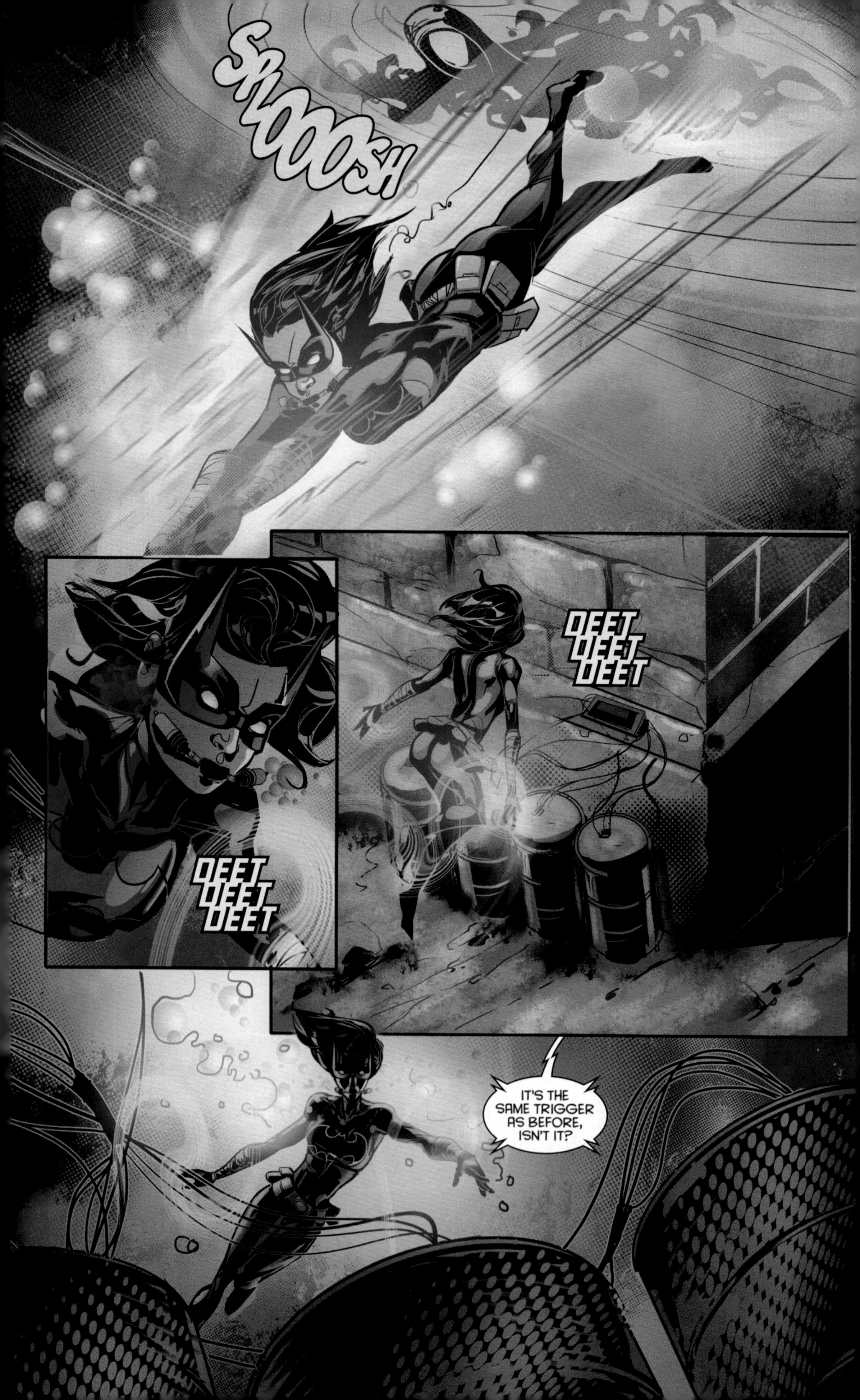
SPLOOOSH
DEET DEET DEET
DEET DEET DEET
IT'S THE SAME TRIGGER AS BEFORE, ISN'T IT?

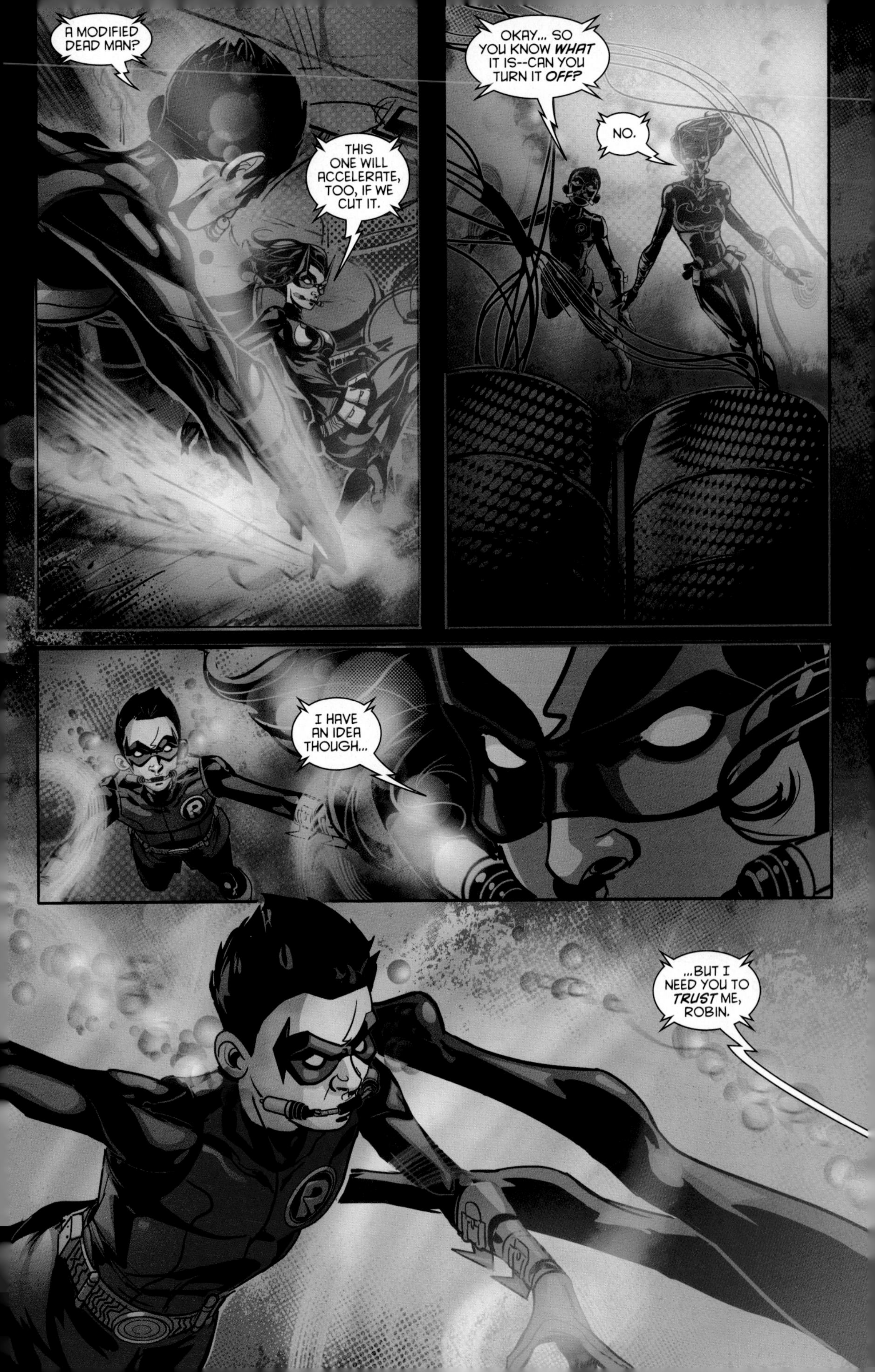
A MODIFIED DEAD MAN?
THIS ONE WILL ACCELERATE, TOO, IF WE CUT IT.
OKAY... SO YOU KNOW WHAT IT IS--CAN YOU TURN IT OFF?
NO.
I HAVE AN IDEA THOUGH...
...BUT I NEED YOU TO TRUST ME, ROBIN.

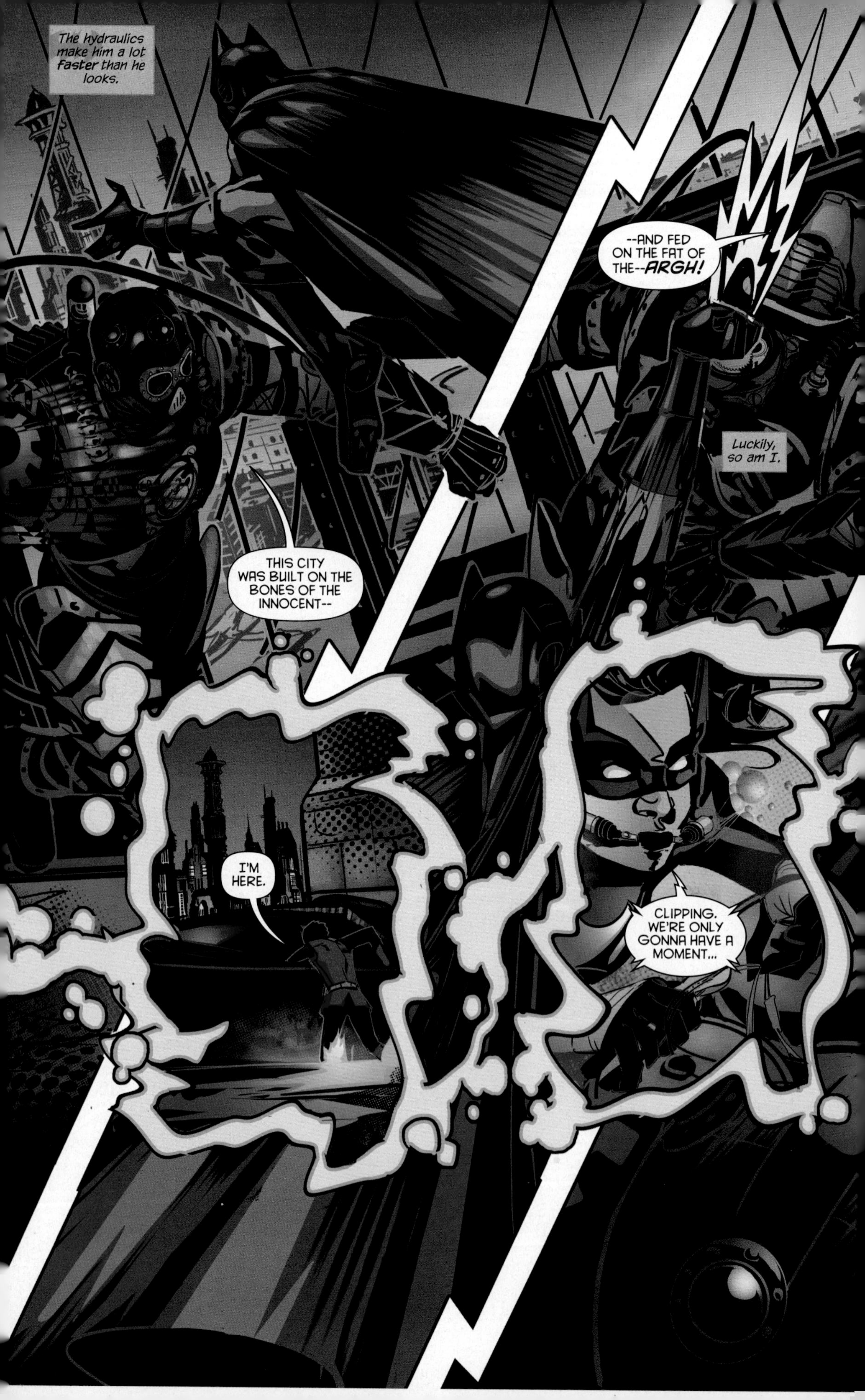
The hydraulics make him a lot faster than he looks.
THIS CITY WAS BUILT ON THE BONES OF THE INNOCENT--
--AND FED ON THE FAT OF THE--ARGH!
Luckily, so am I.
I'M HERE.
CLIPPING. WE'RE ONLY GONNA HAVE A MOMENT...

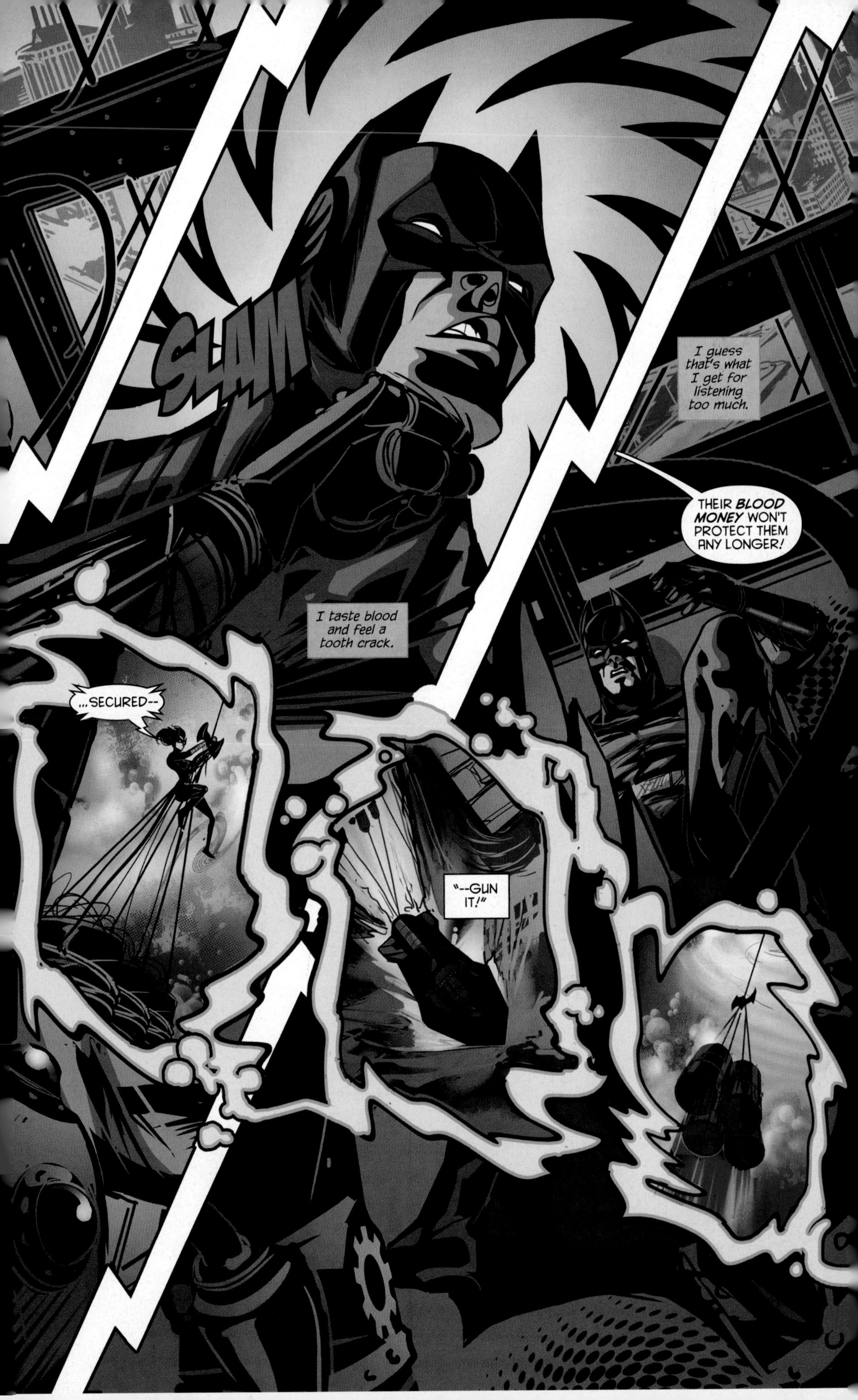
SLAM
I taste blood and feel a tooth crack.
I guess that's what I get for listening too much.
THEIR BLOOD MONEY WON'T PROTECT THEM ANY LONGER!
...SECURED--
"--GUN IT!"

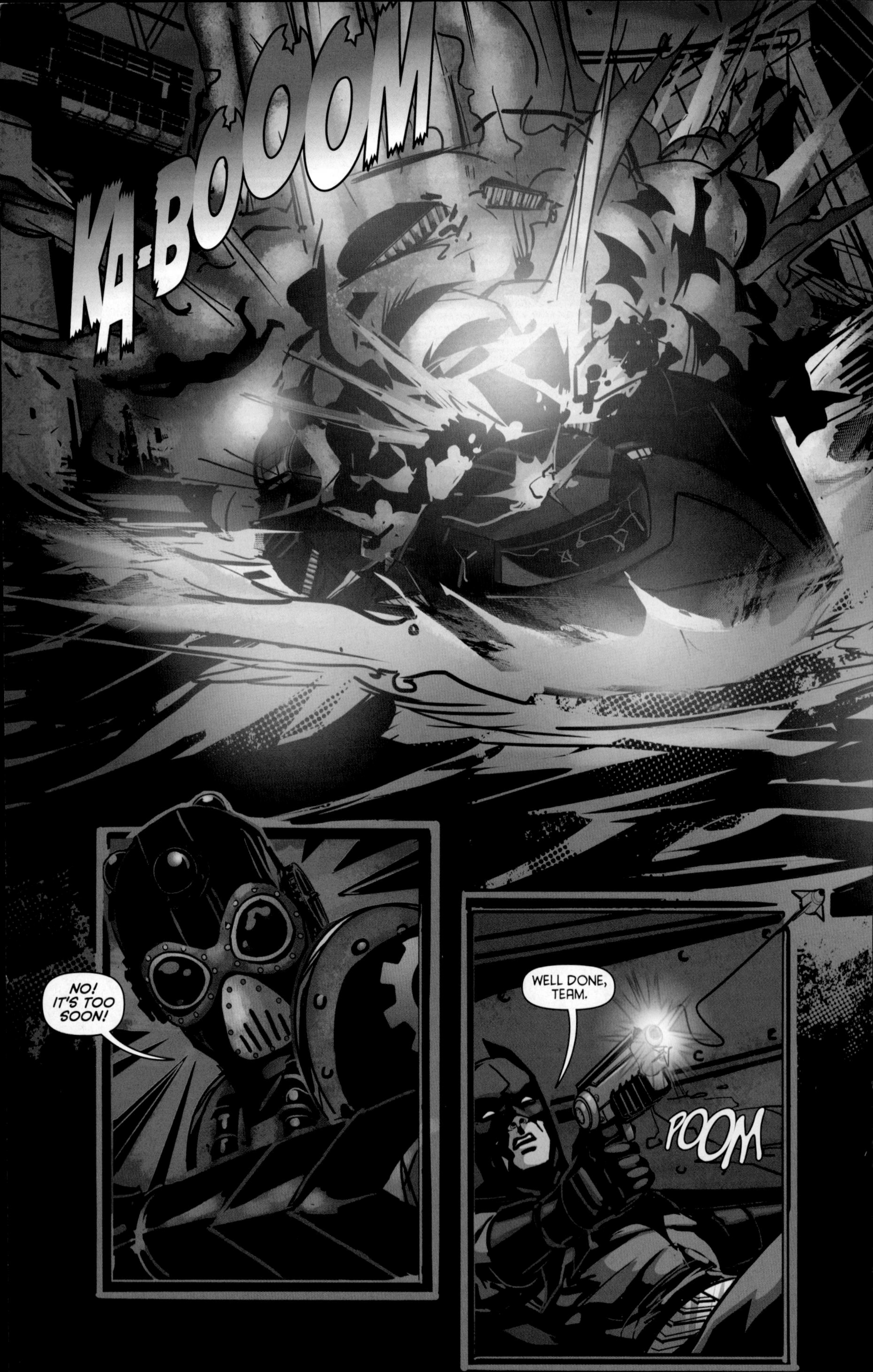
KA-BOOOM
NO! IT'S TOO SOON!
WELL DONE, TEAM.
POOM

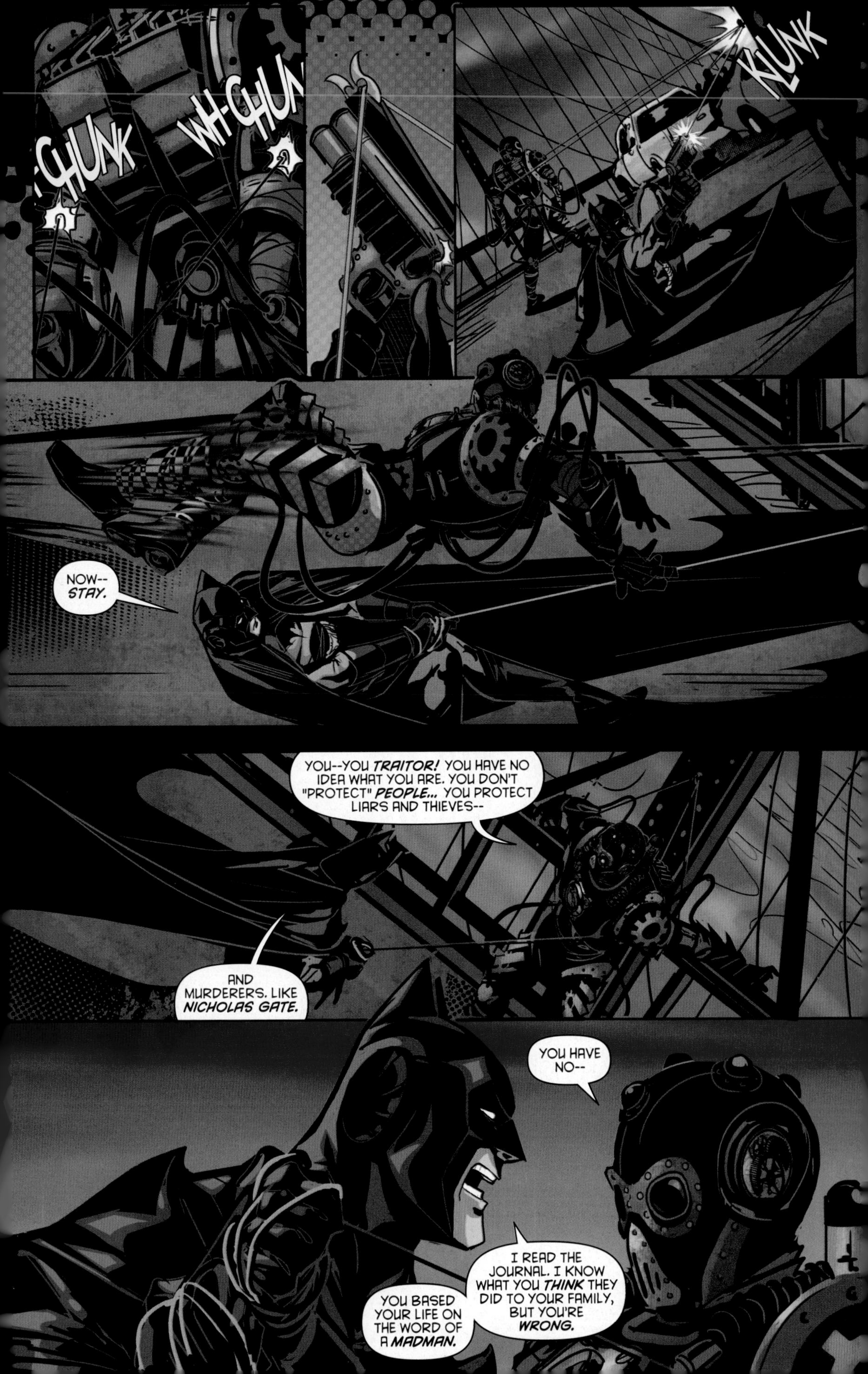
CHUNK
WH-CHUNK
KLUNK
NOW-- STAY.
YOU--YOU TRAITOR! YOU HAVE NO IDEA WHAT YOU ARE. YOU DON'T "PROTECT" PEOPLE... YOU PROTECT LIARS AND THIEVES--
AND MURDERERS. LIKE NICHOLAS GATE.
YOU HAVE NO--
I READ THE JOURNAL. I KNOW WHAT YOU THINK THEY DID TO YOUR FAMILY, BUT YOU'RE WRONG.
YOU BASED YOUR LIFE ON THE WORD OF A MADMAN.

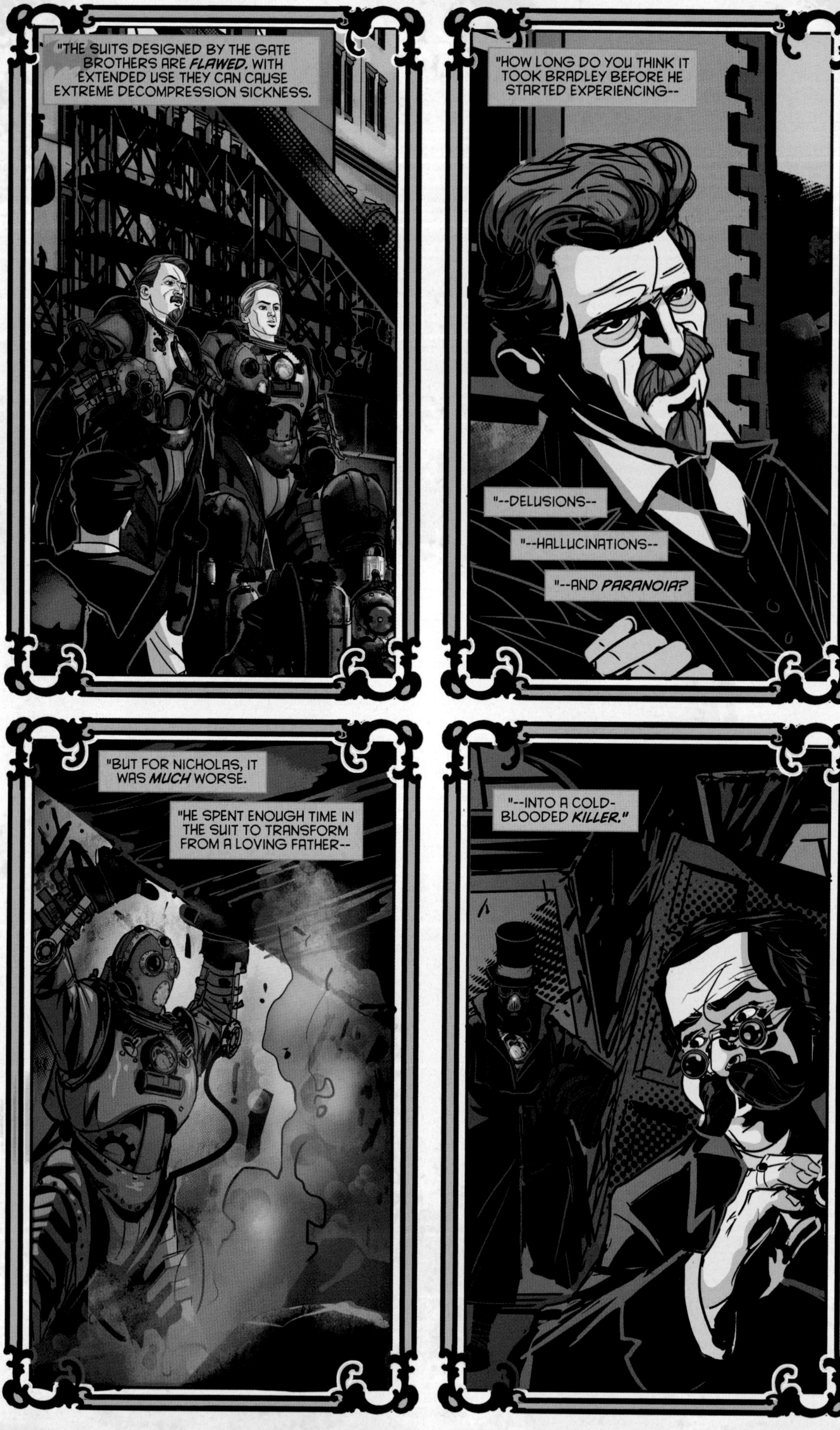
"THE SUITS DESIGNED BY THE GATE BROTHERS ARE *FLAWED.* WITH EXTENDED USE THEY CAN CAUSE EXTREME DECOMPRESSION SICKNESS.
"HOW LONG DO YOU THINK IT TOOK BRADLEY BEFORE HE STARTED EXPERIENCING--
"--DELUSIONS--
"--HALLUCINATIONS--
"--AND *PARANOIA?*
"BUT FOR NICHOLAS, IT WAS *MUCH* WORSE.
"HE SPENT ENOUGH TIME IN THE SUIT TO TRANSFORM FROM A LOVING FATHER--
"--INTO A COLD-BLOODED *KILLER.*"

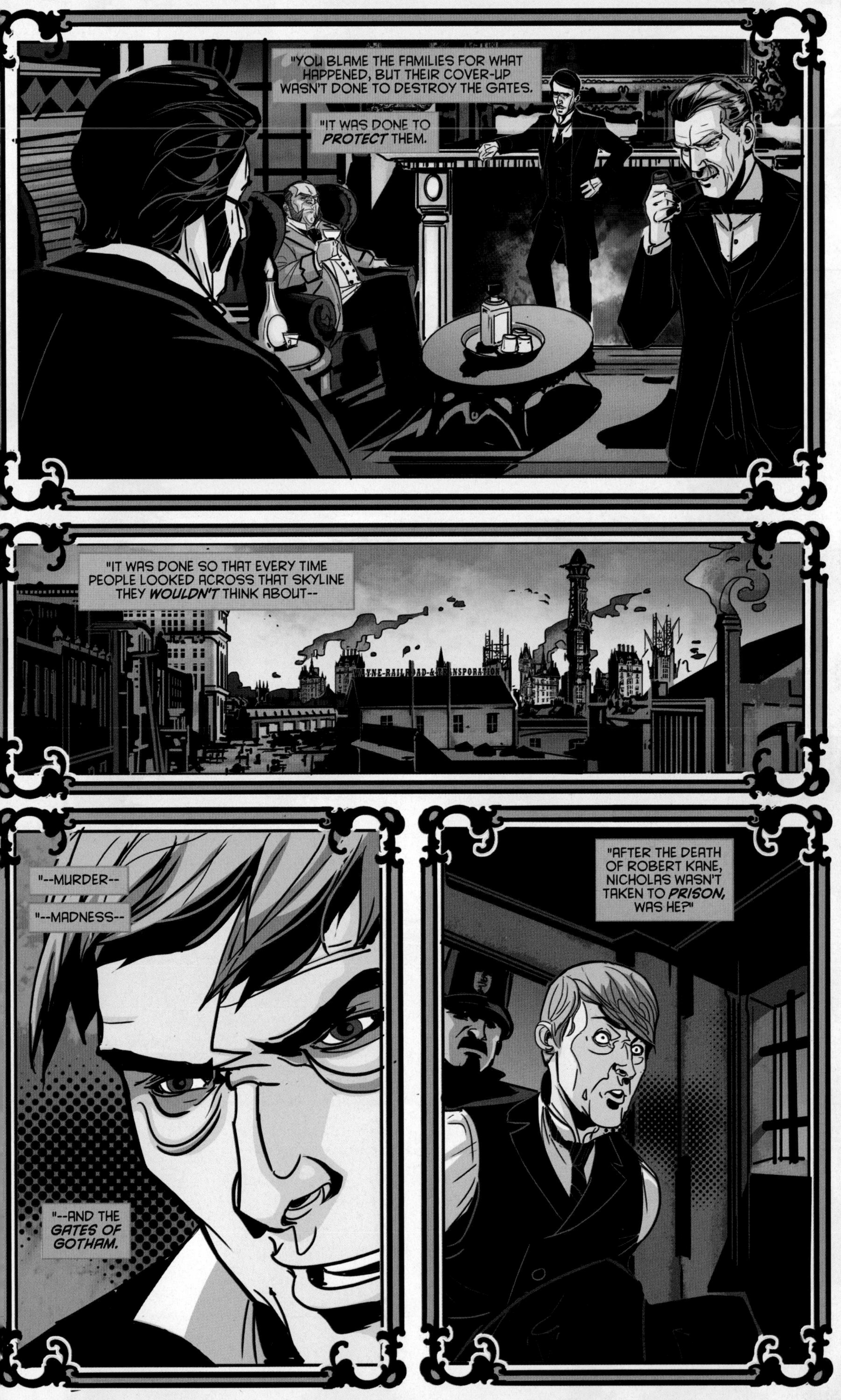
"YOU BLAME THE FAMILIES FOR WHAT HAPPENED, BUT THEIR COVER-UP WASN'T DONE TO DESTROY THE GATES.
"IT WAS DONE TO *PROTECT* THEM.
"IT WAS DONE SO THAT EVERY TIME PEOPLE LOOKED ACROSS THAT SKYLINE THEY *WOULDN'T* THINK ABOUT--
"--MURDER--
"--MADNESS--
"--AND THE *GATES OF GOTHAM.*
"AFTER THE DEATH OF ROBERT KANE, NICHOLAS WASN'T TAKEN TO *PRISON,* WAS HE?"

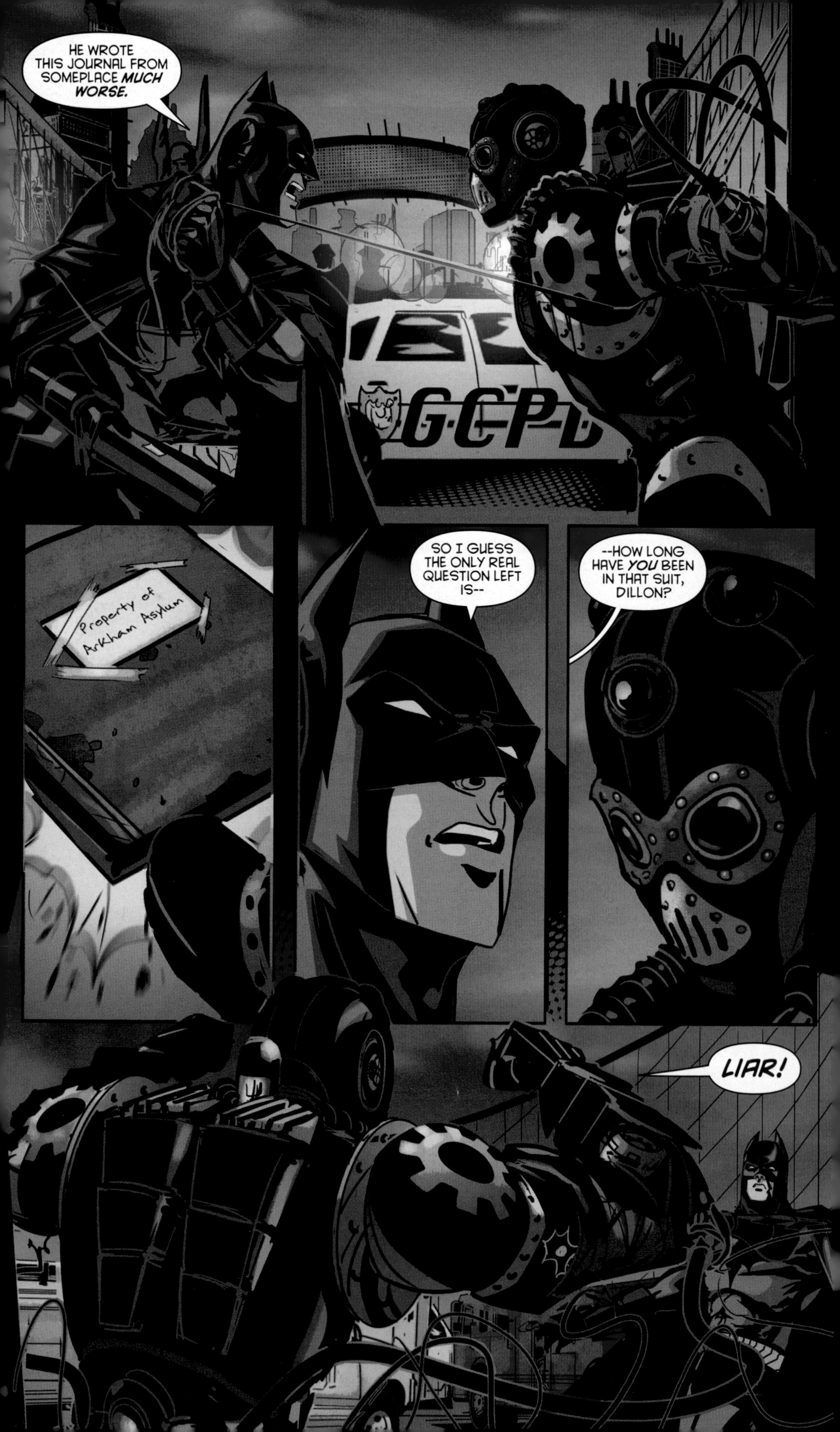
HE WROTE THIS JOURNAL FROM SOMEPLACE *MUCH WORSE.*
G·C·P·D
Property of Arkham Asylum
SO I GUESS THE ONLY REAL QUESTION LEFT IS--
--HOW LONG HAVE *YOU* BEEN IN THAT SUIT, DILLON?
LIAR!

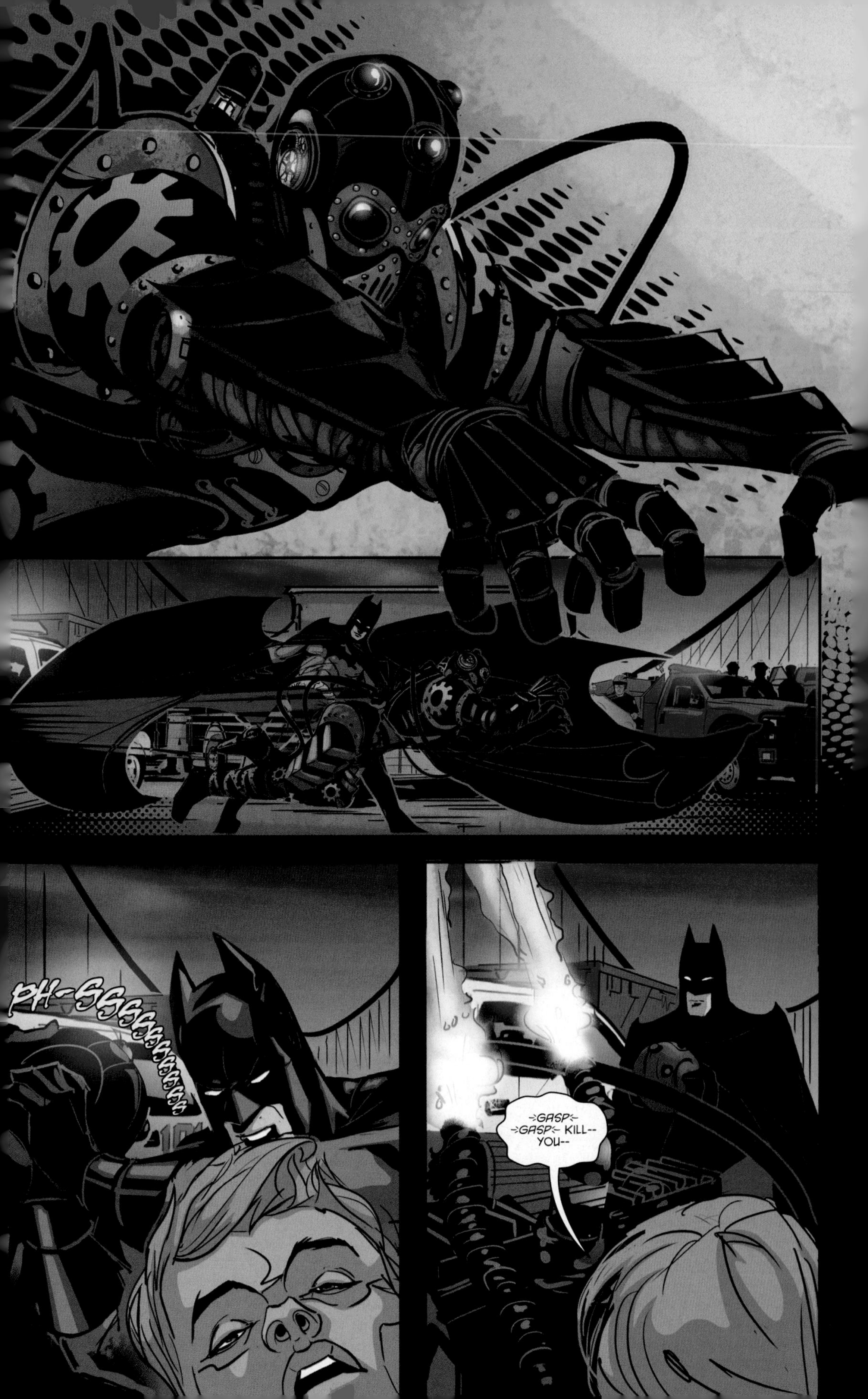
PH-SSSSSSSSSSSS
~GASP~
~GASP~ KILL--
YOU--

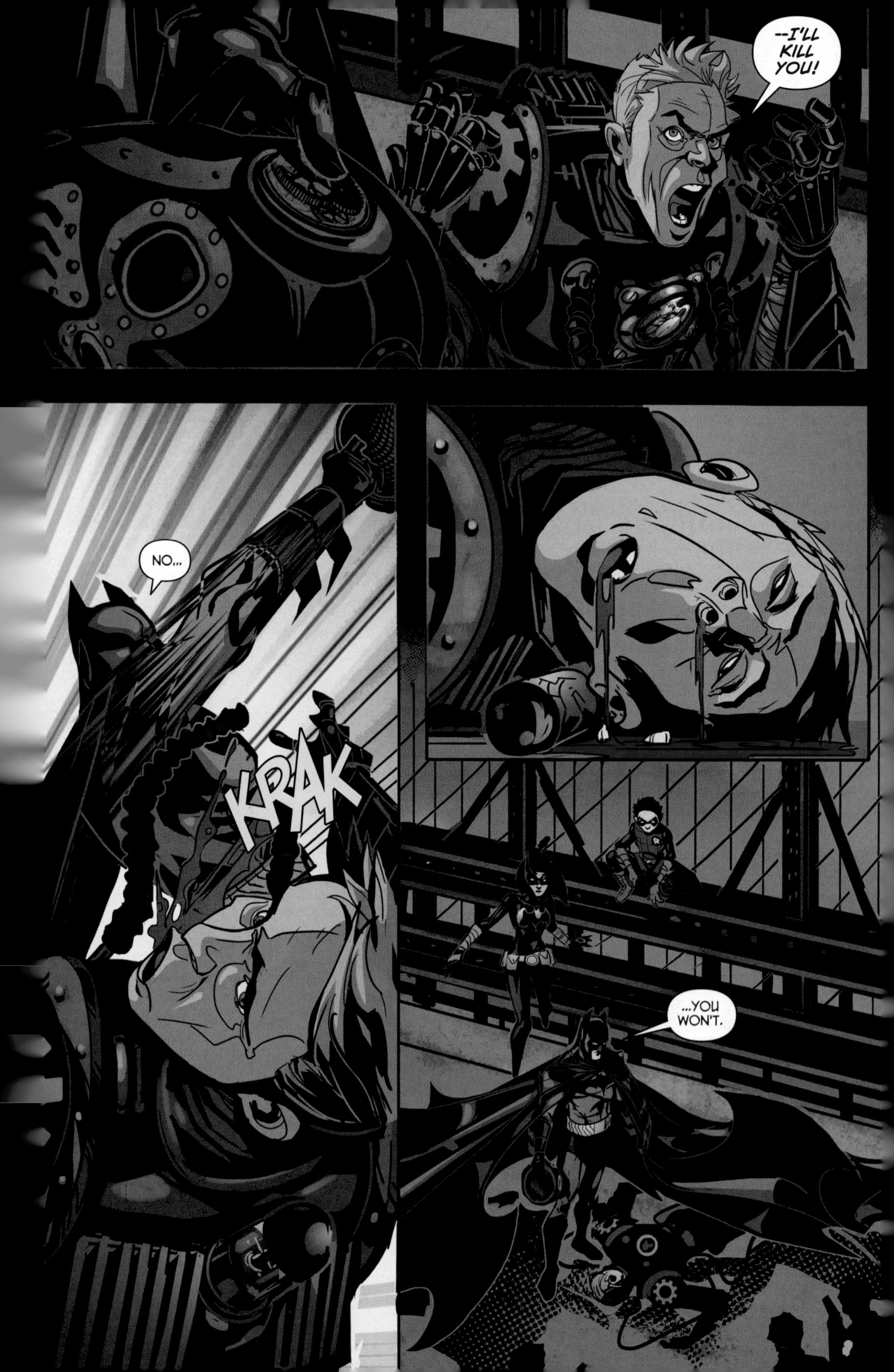
--I'LL KILL YOU!
NO...
KRAK
...YOU WON'T.

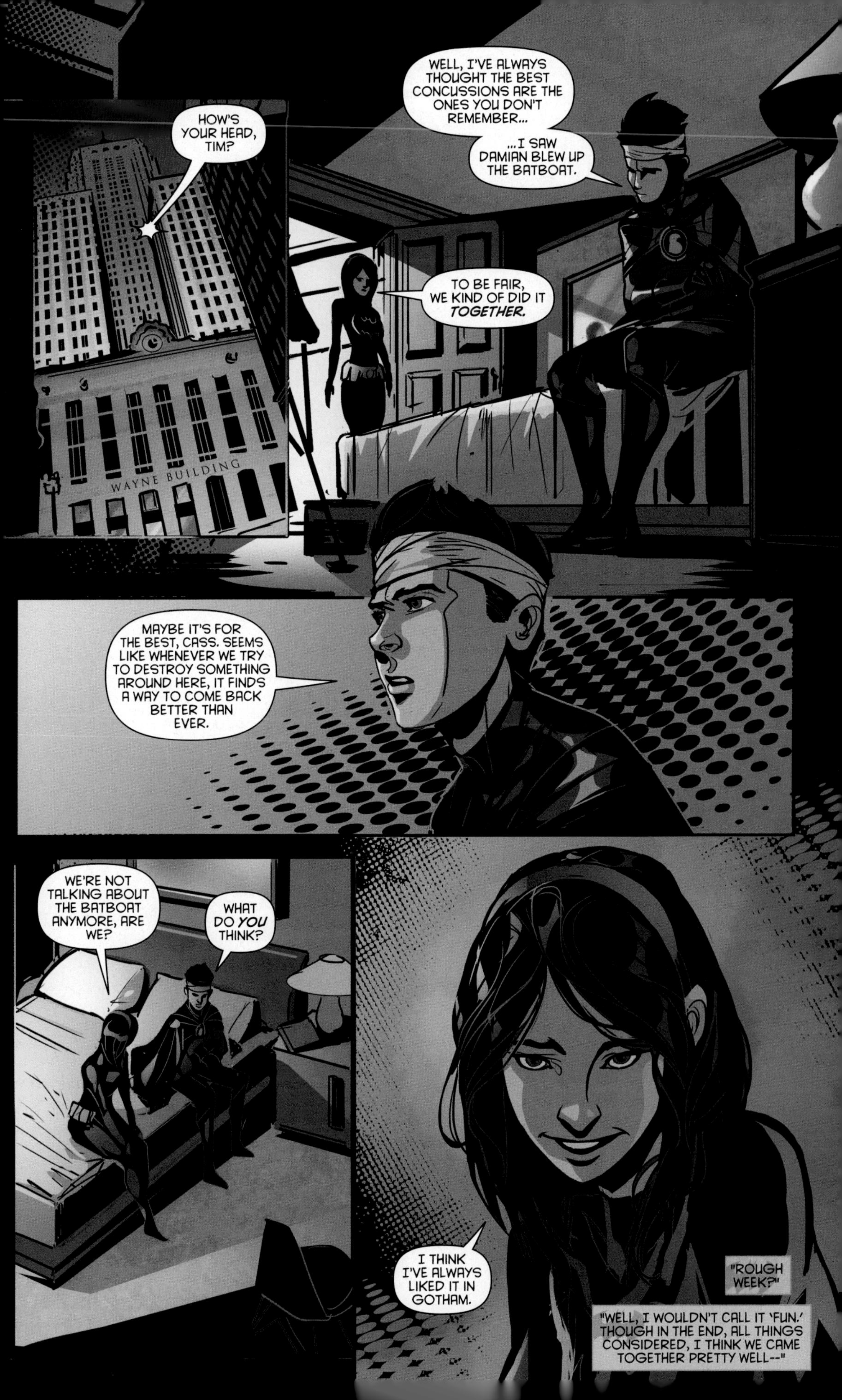
HOW'S YOUR HEAD, TIM?
WELL, I'VE ALWAYS THOUGHT THE BEST CONCUSSIONS ARE THE ONES YOU DON'T REMEMBER...
...I SAW DAMIAN BLEW UP THE BATBOAT.
TO BE FAIR, WE KIND OF DID IT *TOGETHER.*
WAYNE BUILDING
MAYBE IT'S FOR THE BEST, CASS. SEEMS LIKE WHENEVER WE TRY TO DESTROY SOMETHING AROUND HERE, IT FINDS A WAY TO COME BACK BETTER THAN EVER.
WE'RE NOT TALKING ABOUT THE BATBOAT ANYMORE, ARE WE?
WHAT DO *YOU* THINK?
I THINK I'VE ALWAYS LIKED IT IN GOTHAM.
"ROUGH WEEK?"
"WELL, I WOULDN'T CALL IT 'FUN.' THOUGH IN THE END, ALL THINGS CONSIDERED, I THINK WE CAME TOGETHER PRETTY WELL--"

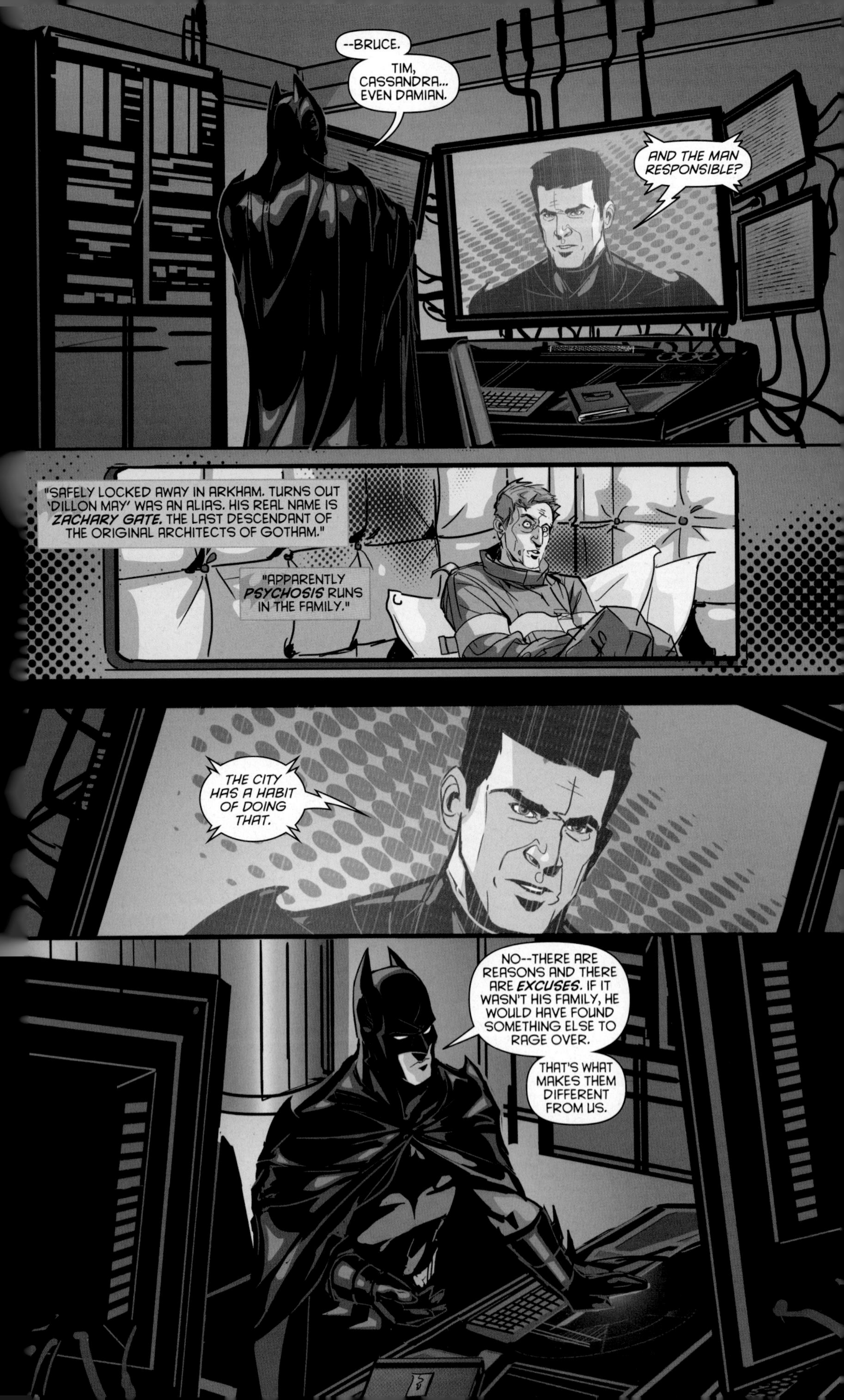
--BRUCE.
TIM, CASSANDRA... EVEN DAMIAN.
AND THE MAN RESPONSIBLE?
"SAFELY LOCKED AWAY IN ARKHAM. TURNS OUT 'DILLON MAY' WAS AN ALIAS. HIS REAL NAME IS ZACHARY GATE. THE LAST DESCENDANT OF THE ORIGINAL ARCHITECTS OF GOTHAM."
"APPARENTLY PSYCHOSIS RUNS IN THE FAMILY."
THE CITY HAS A HABIT OF DOING THAT.
NO--THERE ARE REASONS AND THERE ARE EXCUSES. IF IT WASN'T HIS FAMILY, HE WOULD HAVE FOUND SOMETHING ELSE TO RAGE OVER.
THAT'S WHAT MAKES THEM DIFFERENT FROM US.

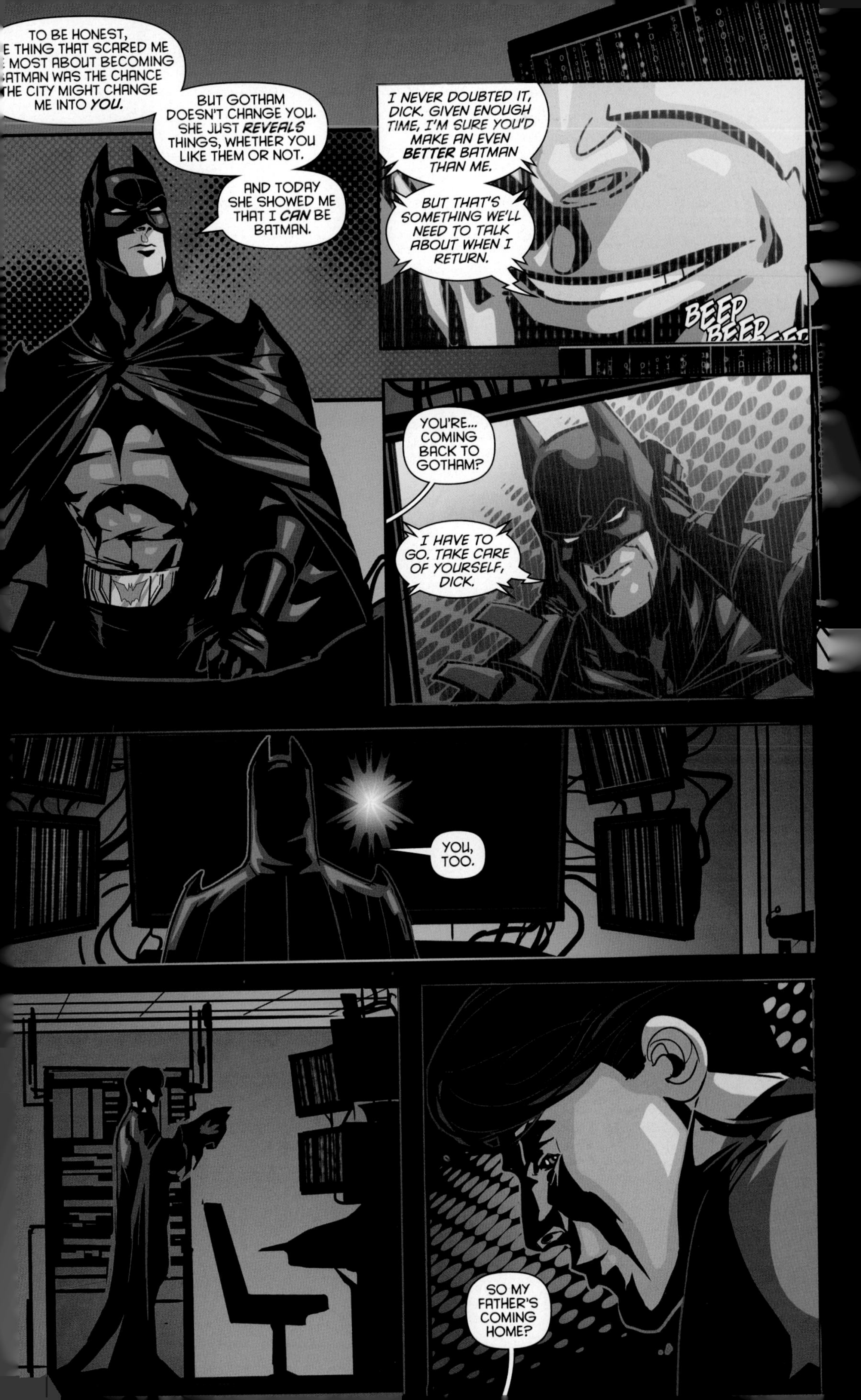
TO BE HONEST, E THING THAT SCARED ME E MOST ABOUT BECOMING ATMAN WAS THE CHANCE THE CITY MIGHT CHANGE ME INTO *YOU.*
BUT GOTHAM DOESN'T CHANGE YOU. SHE JUST ***REVEALS*** THINGS, WHETHER YOU LIKE THEM OR NOT.
AND TODAY SHE SHOWED ME THAT I ***CAN*** BE BATMAN.
I NEVER DOUBTED IT, DICK. GIVEN ENOUGH TIME, I'M SURE YOU'D MAKE AN EVEN ***BETTER*** *BATMAN THAN ME.*
BUT THAT'S SOMETHING WE'LL NEED TO TALK ABOUT WHEN I RETURN.
BEEP
YOU'RE... COMING BACK TO GOTHAM?
I HAVE TO GO. TAKE CARE OF YOURSELF, DICK.
YOU, TOO.
SO MY FATHER'S COMING HOME?

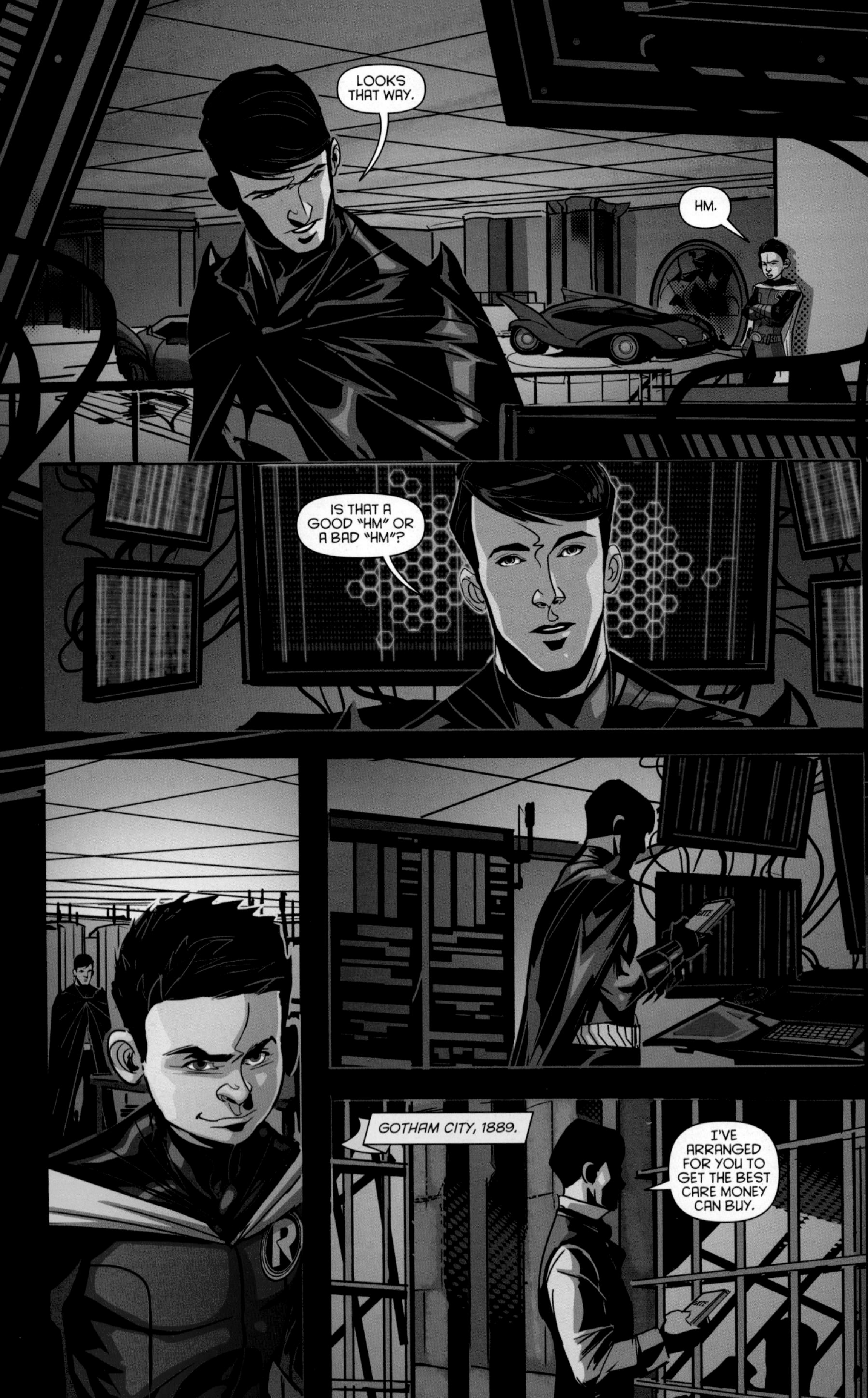
LOOKS THAT WAY.
HM.
IS THAT A GOOD "HM" OR A BAD "HM"?
GOTHAM CITY, 1889.
I'VE ARRANGED FOR YOU TO GET THE BEST CARE MONEY CAN BUY.

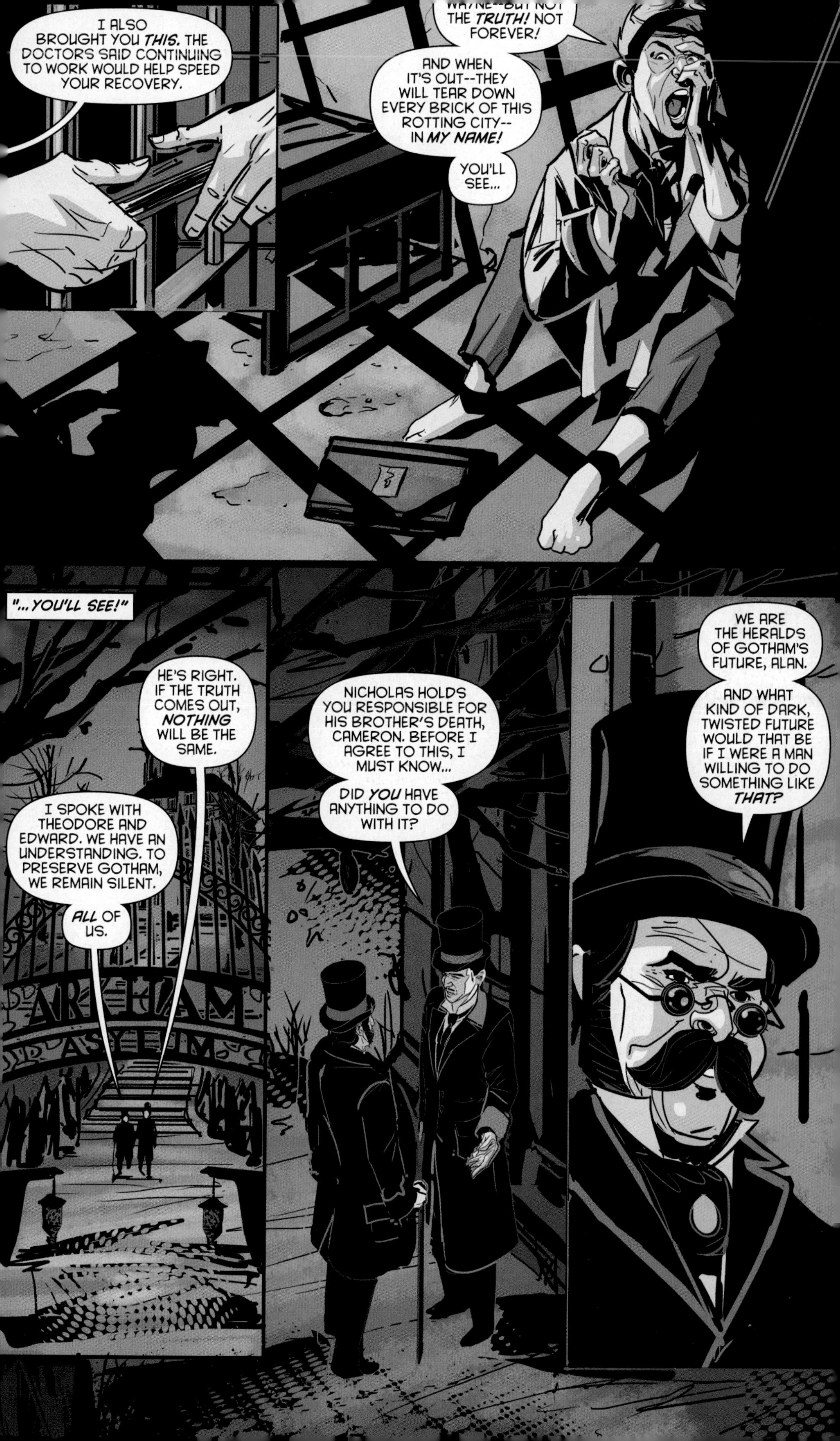
I ALSO BROUGHT YOU *THIS*. THE DOCTORS SAID CONTINUING TO WORK WOULD HELP SPEED YOUR RECOVERY.
THE *TRUTH!* NOT FOREVER!
AND WHEN IT'S OUT--THEY WILL TEAR DOWN EVERY BRICK OF THIS ROTTING CITY-- IN *MY NAME!*
YOU'LL SEE...
"...*YOU'LL SEE!*"
HE'S RIGHT. IF THE TRUTH COMES OUT, *NOTHING* WILL BE THE SAME.
I SPOKE WITH THEODORE AND EDWARD. WE HAVE AN UNDERSTANDING. TO PRESERVE GOTHAM, WE REMAIN SILENT.
ALL OF US.
ARKHAM ASYLUM
NICHOLAS HOLDS YOU RESPONSIBLE FOR HIS BROTHER'S DEATH, CAMERON. BEFORE I AGREE TO THIS, I MUST KNOW...
DID *YOU* HAVE ANYTHING TO DO WITH IT?
WE ARE THE HERALDS OF GOTHAM'S FUTURE, ALAN.
AND WHAT KIND OF DARK, TWISTED FUTURE WOULD THAT BE IF I WERE A MAN WILLING TO DO SOMETHING LIKE *THAT?*

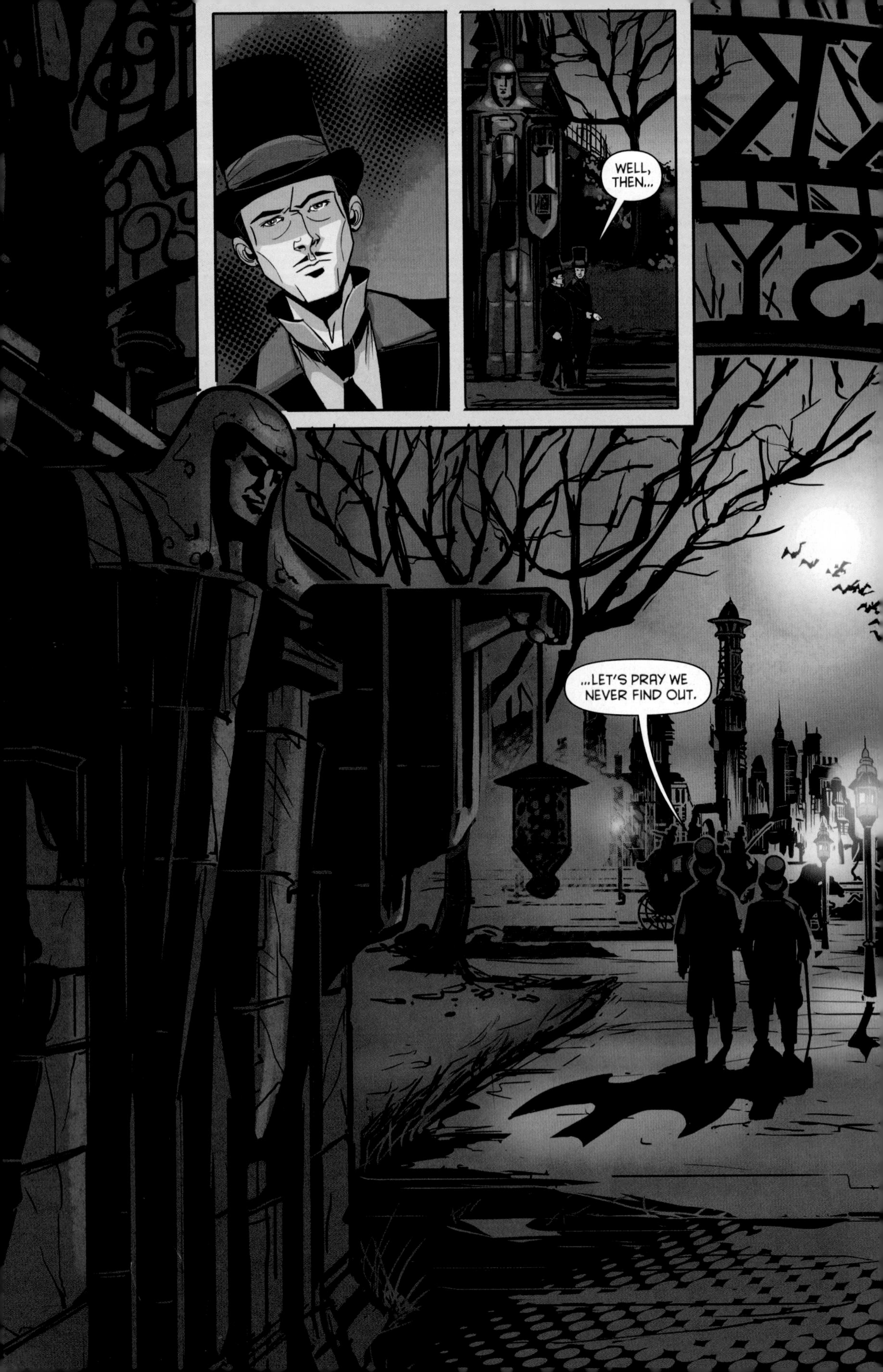
WELL, THEN...
...LET'S PRAY WE NEVER FIND OUT.

VARIANT COVER GALLERY

Variant covers by DUSTIN **NGUYEN**

BATMAN: **GATES OF GOTHAM 1**

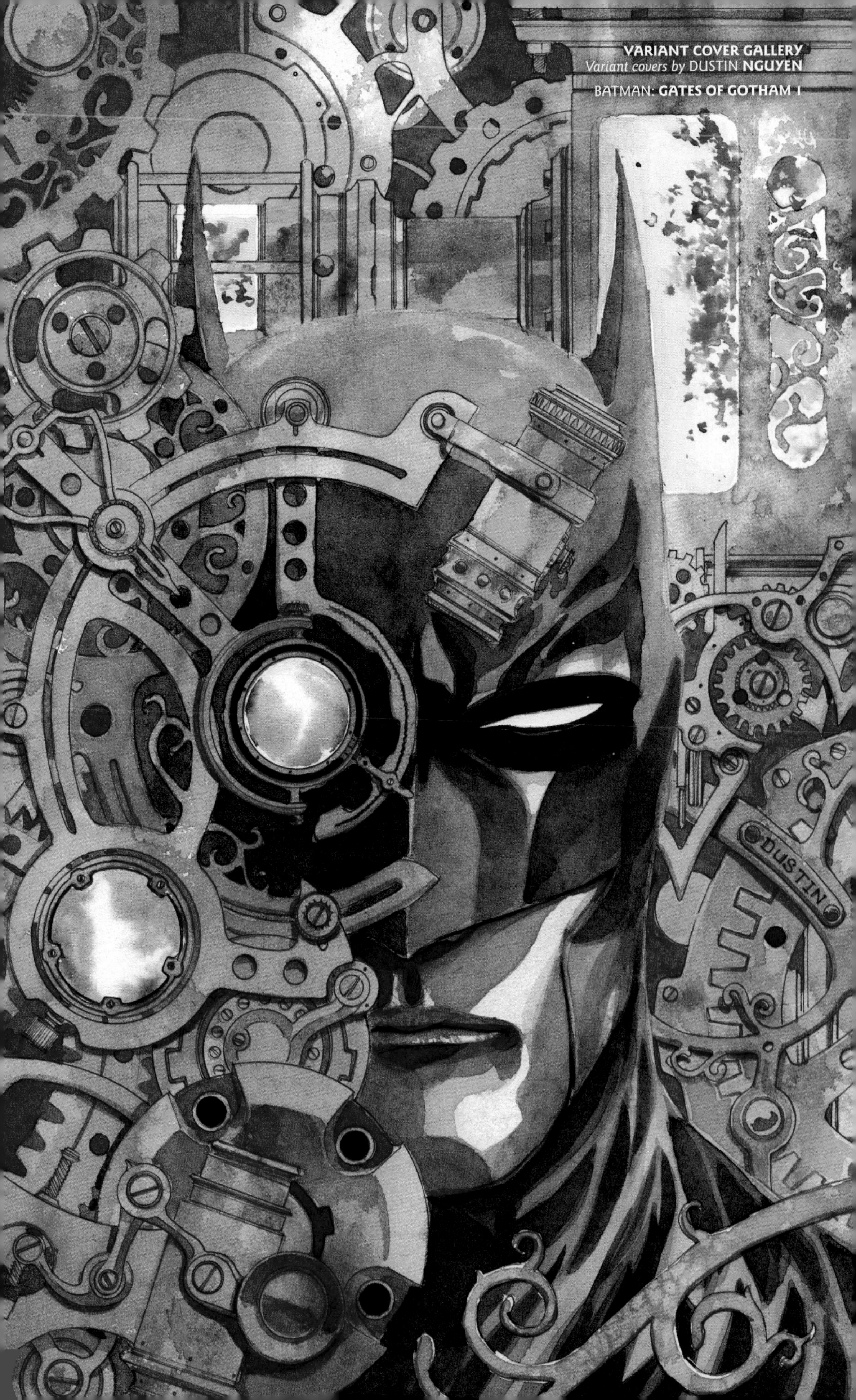
DUSTIN

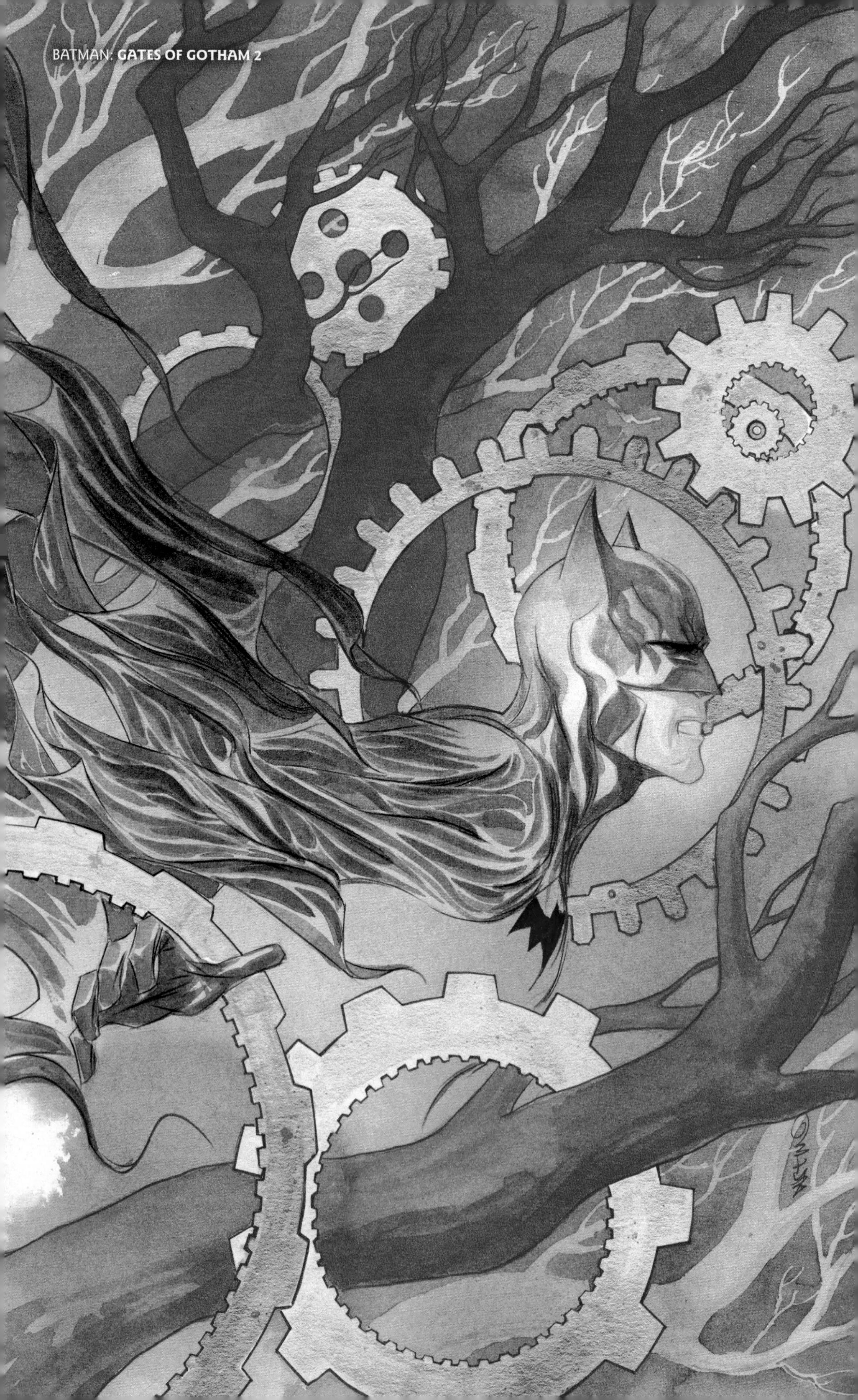

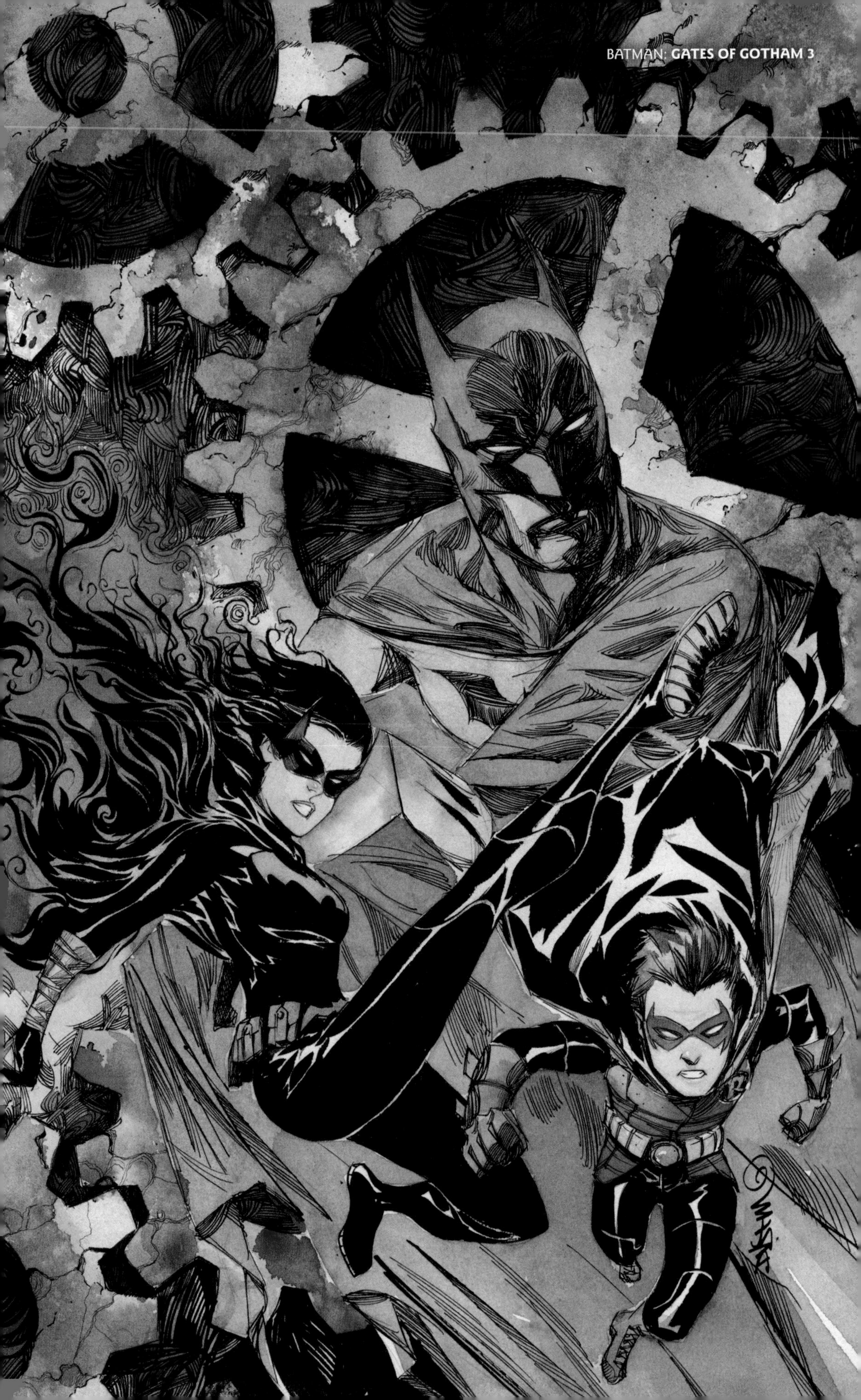

BATMAN: **GATES OF GOTHAM 4**

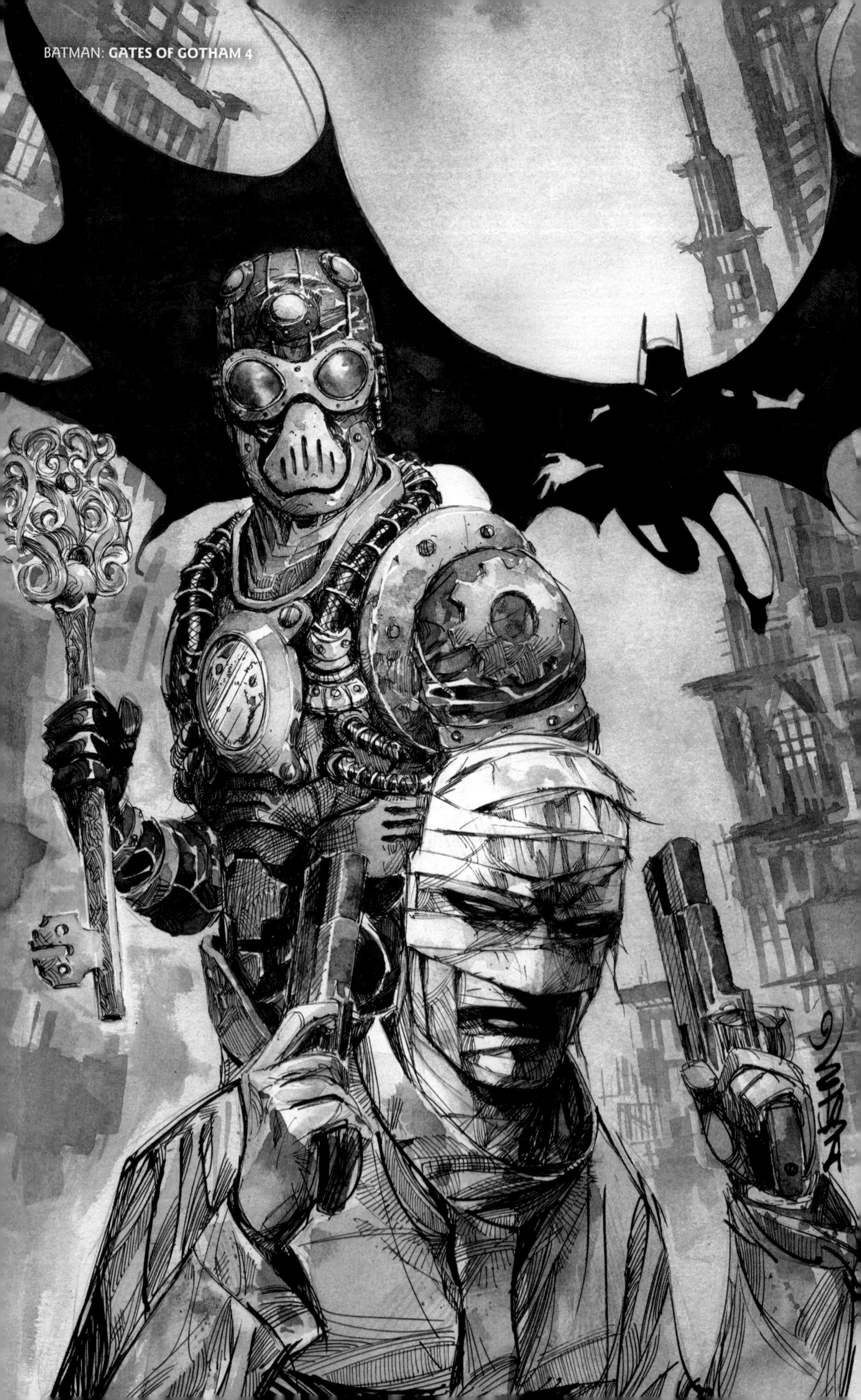

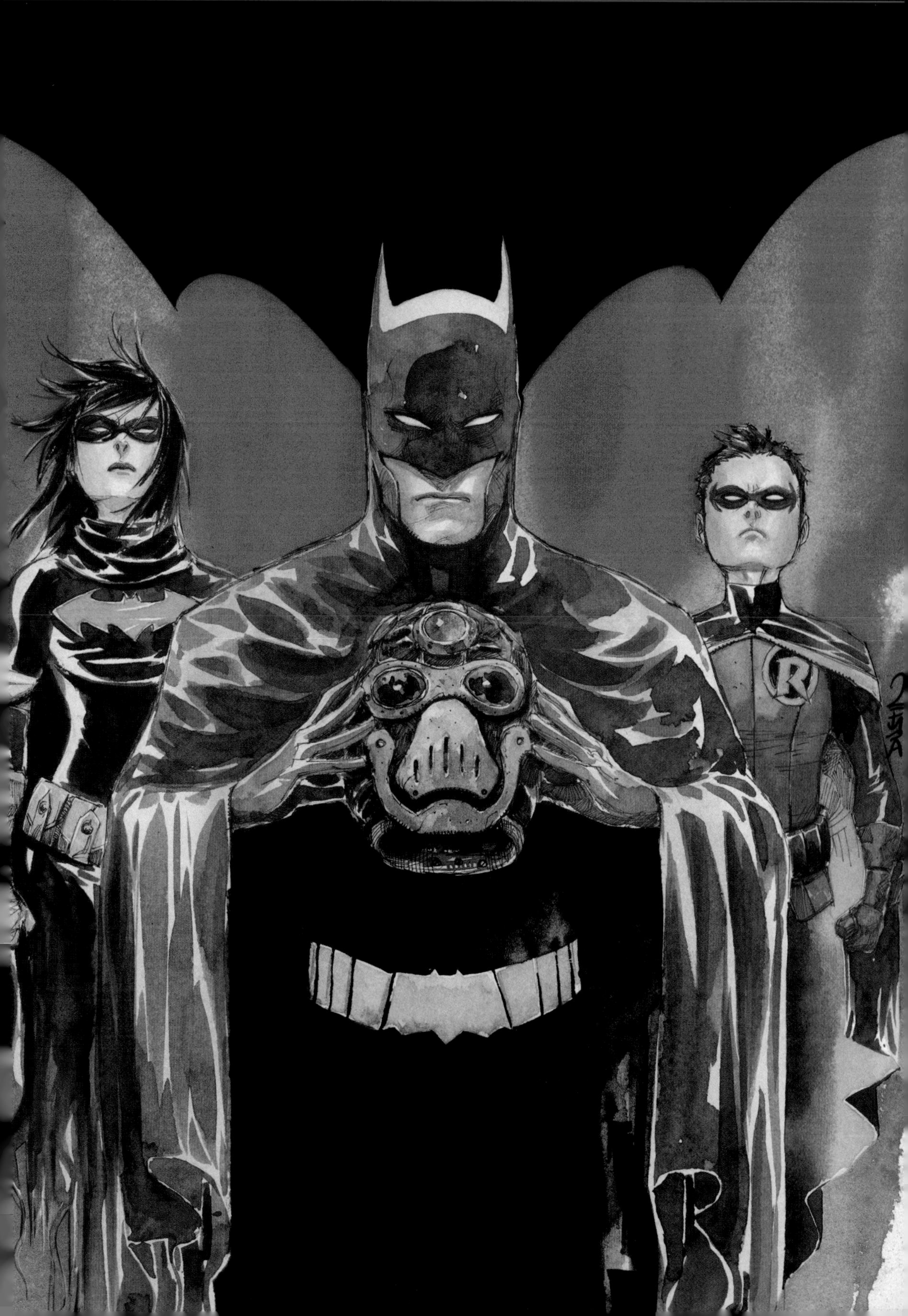

CHARACTER DESIGNS BY
Trevor McCarthy

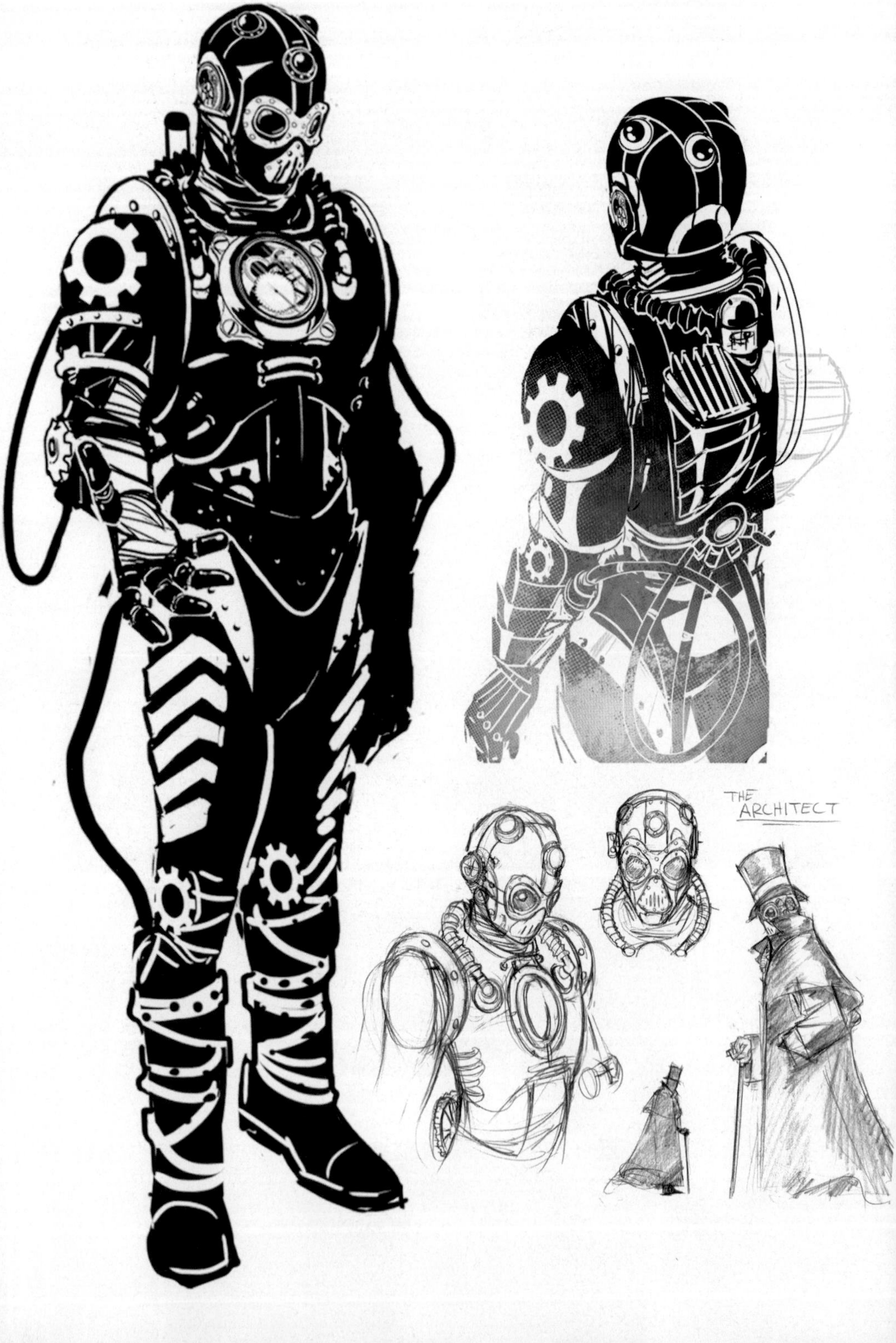
THE ARCHITECT

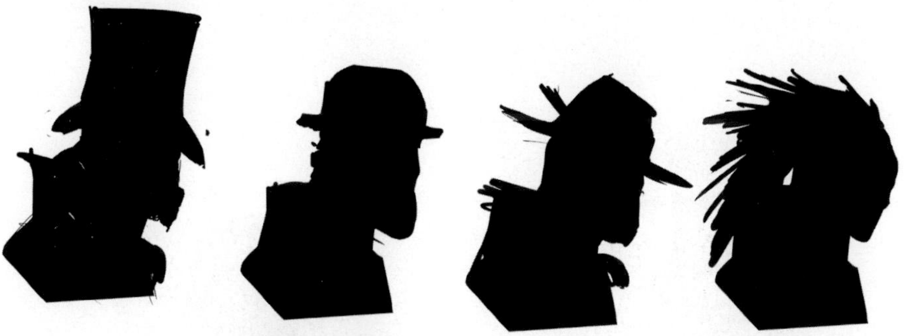

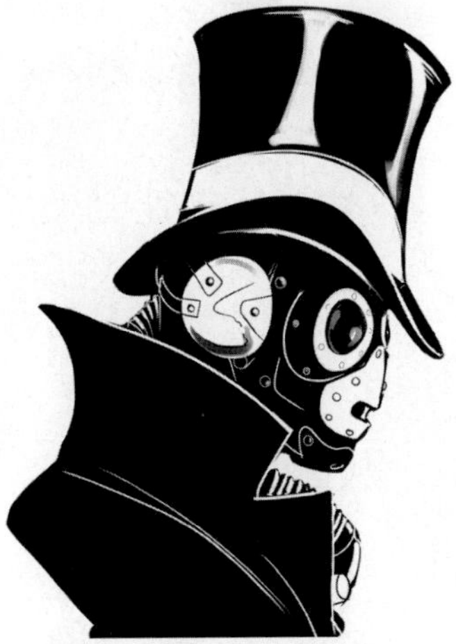

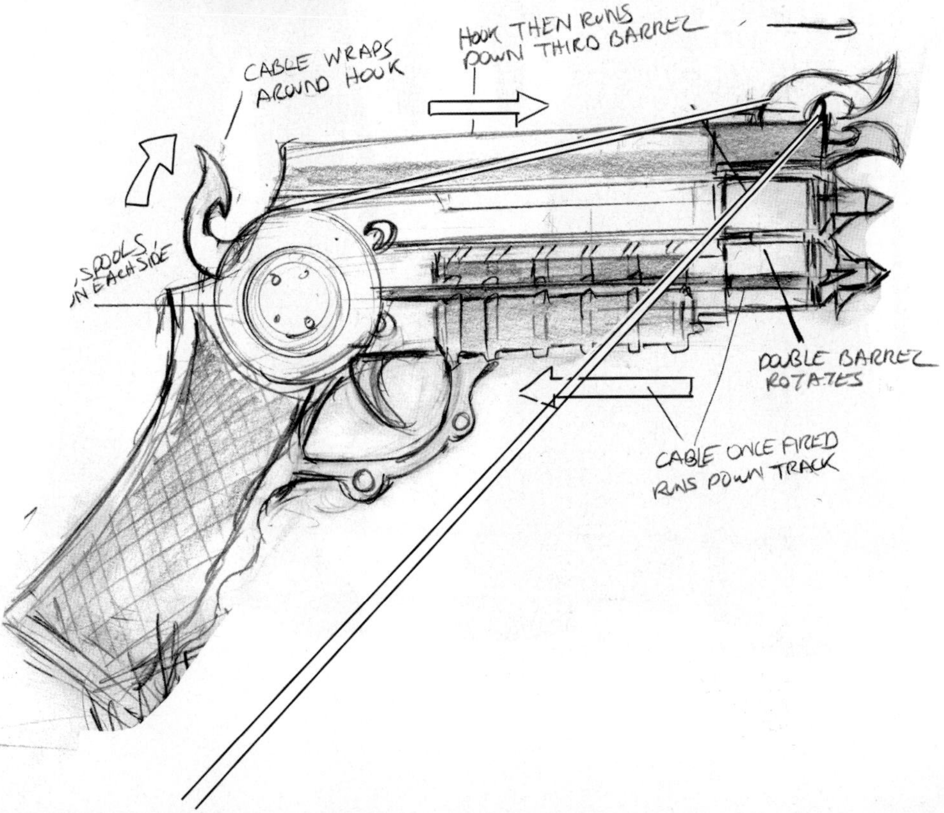
HOOK THEN RUNS
DOWN THIRD BARREL
CABLE WRAPS
AROUND HOOK
SPOOLS,
N EACH SIDE
DOUBLE BARREL
ROTATES
CABLE ONCE FIRED
RUNS DOWN TRACK

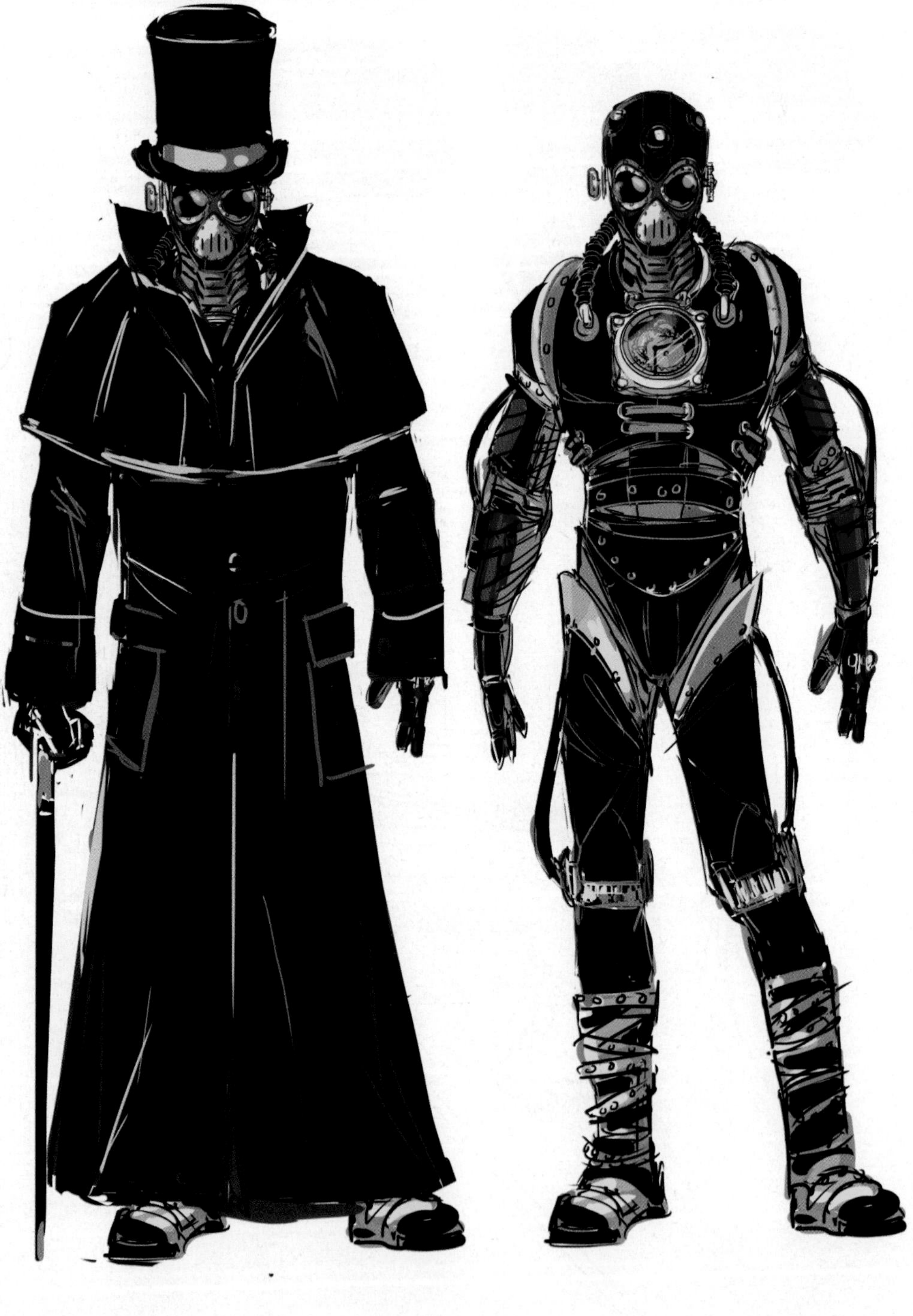

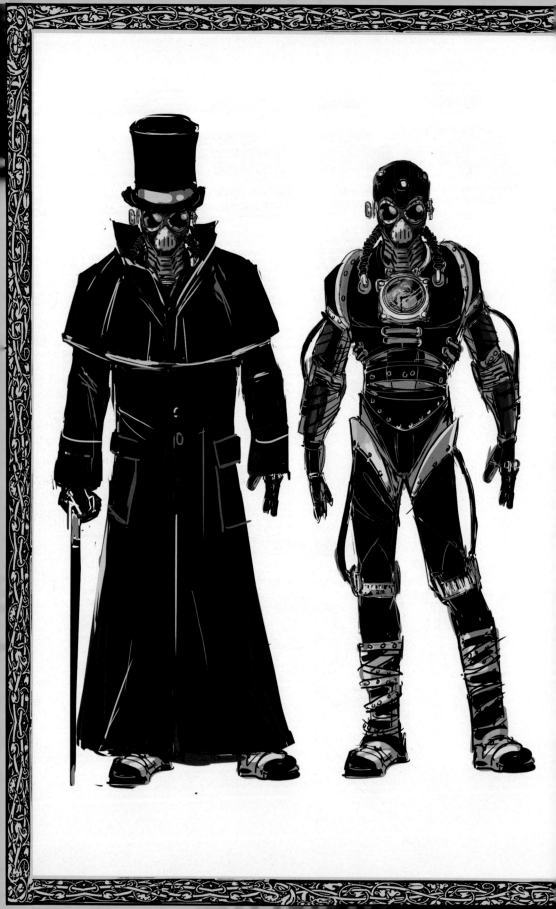

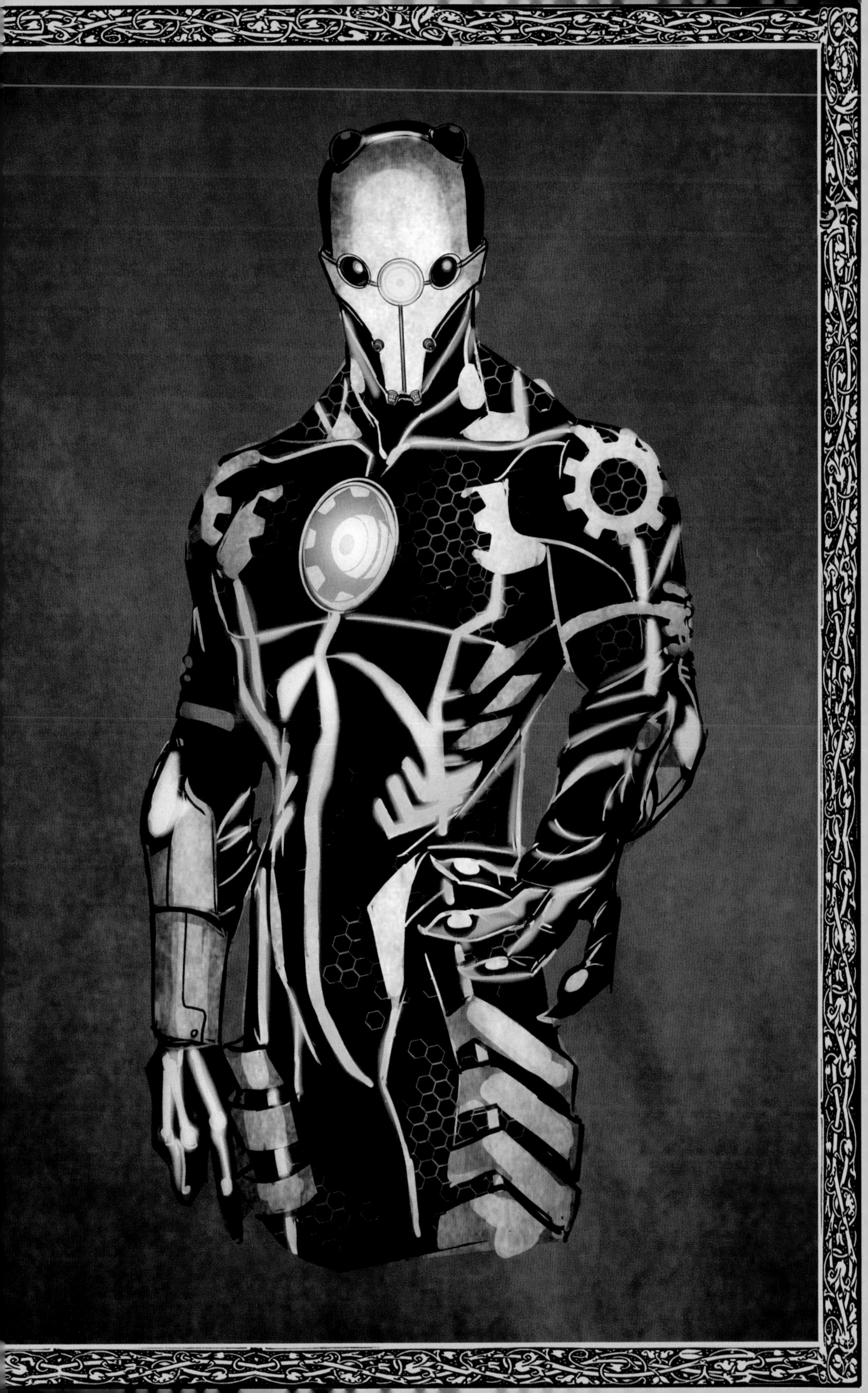

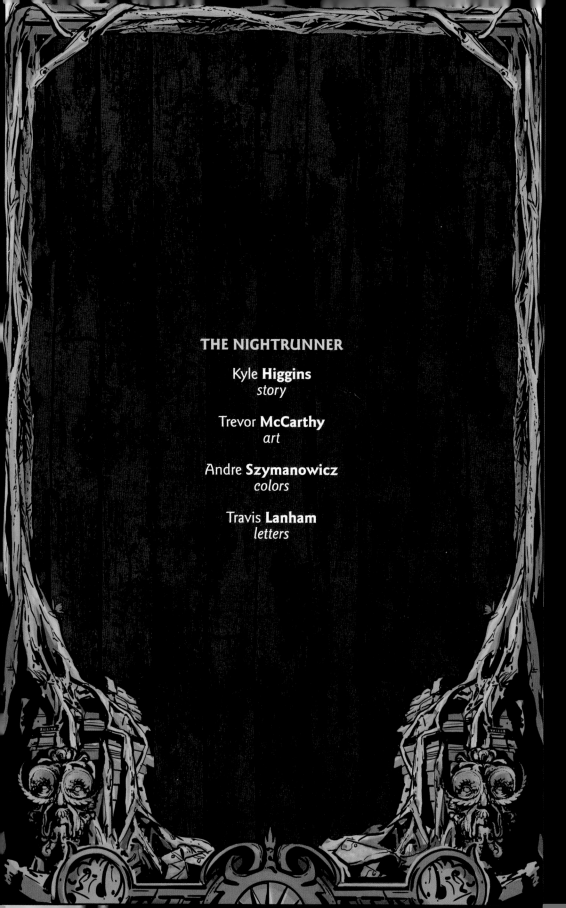

THE NIGHTRUNNER

Kyle **Higgins**
story

Trevor **McCarthy**
art

Andre **Szymanowicz**
colors

Travis **Lanham**
letters

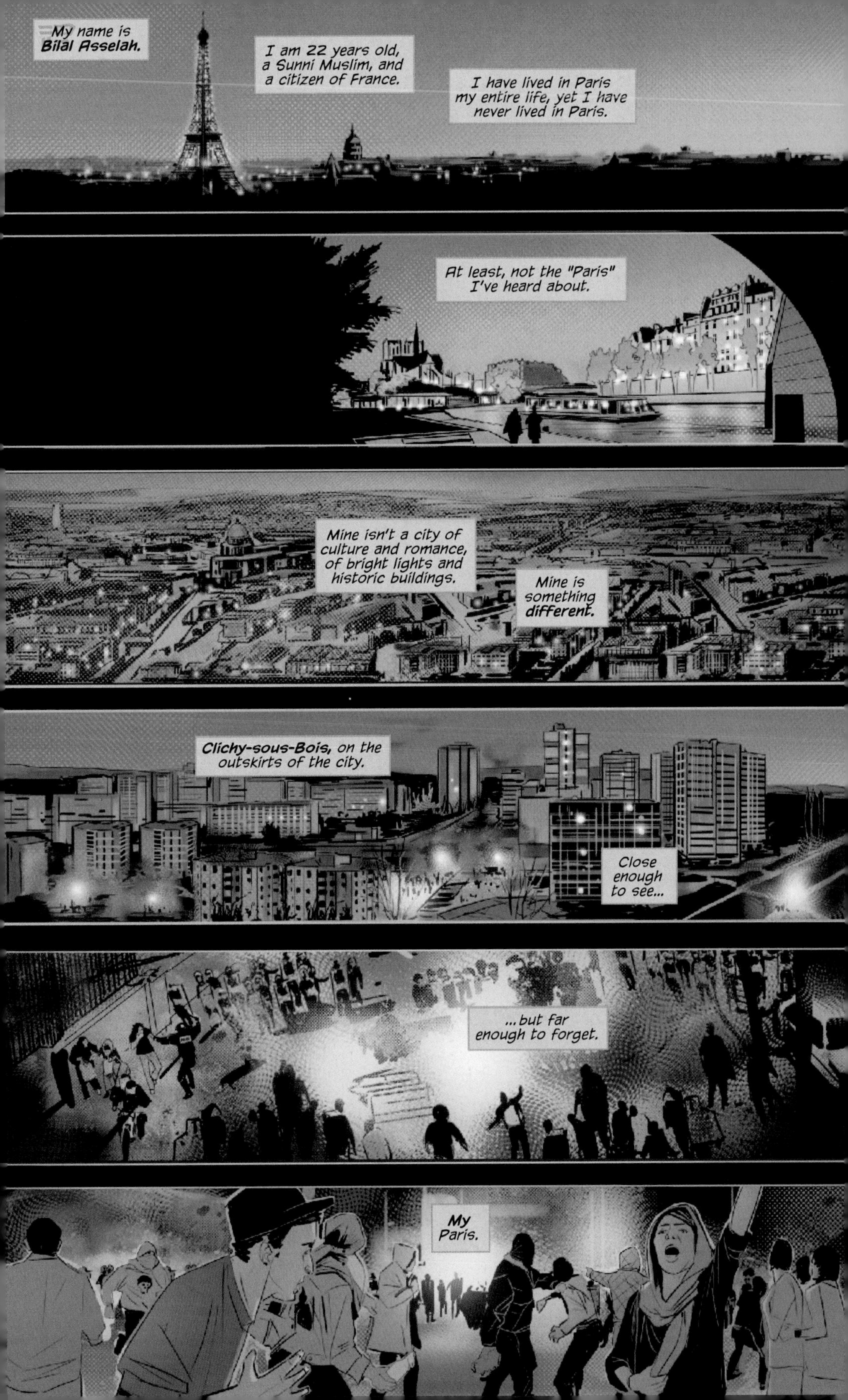
My name is Bilal Asselah.
I am 22 years old, a Sunni Muslim, and a citizen of France.
I have lived in Paris my entire life, yet I have never lived in Paris.
At least, not the "Paris" I've heard about.
Mine isn't a city of culture and romance, of bright lights and historic buildings.
Mine is something different.
Clichy-sous-Bois, on the outskirts of the city.
Close enough to see...
...but far enough to forget.
My Paris.

I was raised by my mother, in a one-bedroom apartment. We could barely afford a place in Clichy-sous-Bois, much less anywhere else.

So we never moved, even when the fighting started. This was our *home.* We weren't going to be run out of it.

I've been surrounded by the protests and riots for as long as I can remember.

...but *never* understood.

THEY'RE BLOCKING OFF GAGARINE BOULEVARD.

BILAL.

OKAY, OKAY...

THEY'VE STARTED THE FIRES.

They were always something I knew...

MOVE AWAY FROM THE EDGE, BILAL.

They were different from *us,* and *we* were different from *them.* That was never going to change.

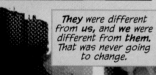

So why were we fighting?

My mother said it was because violence just led to more violence. That it was *"the cycle."*

But I didn't understand that, either.

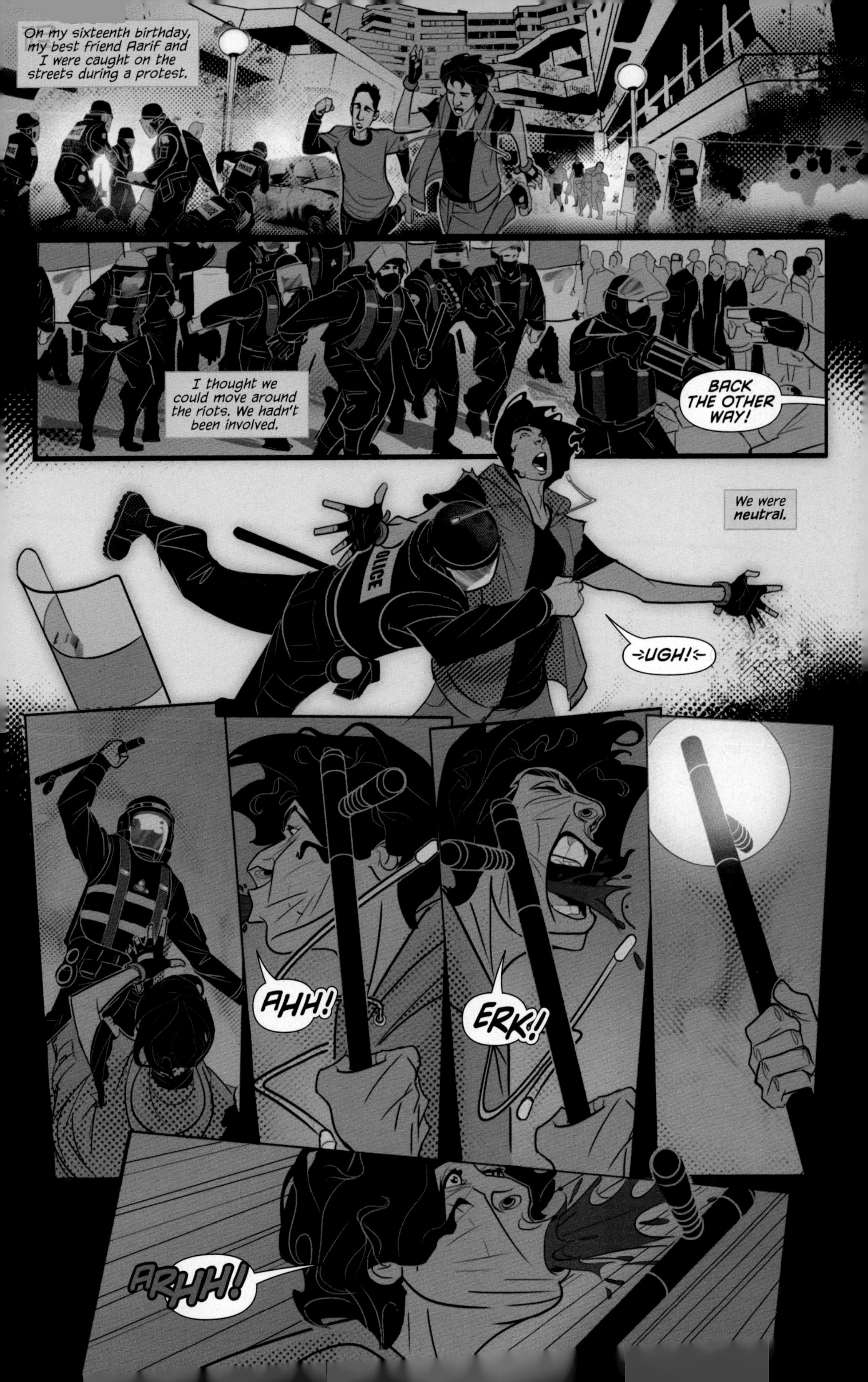

On my sixteenth birthday, my best friend Aarif and I were caught on the streets during a protest.
POLICE
I thought we could move around the riots. We hadn't been involved.
BACK THE OTHER WAY!
We were neutral.
OLICE
UGH!
AHH!
ERK!
ARHH!

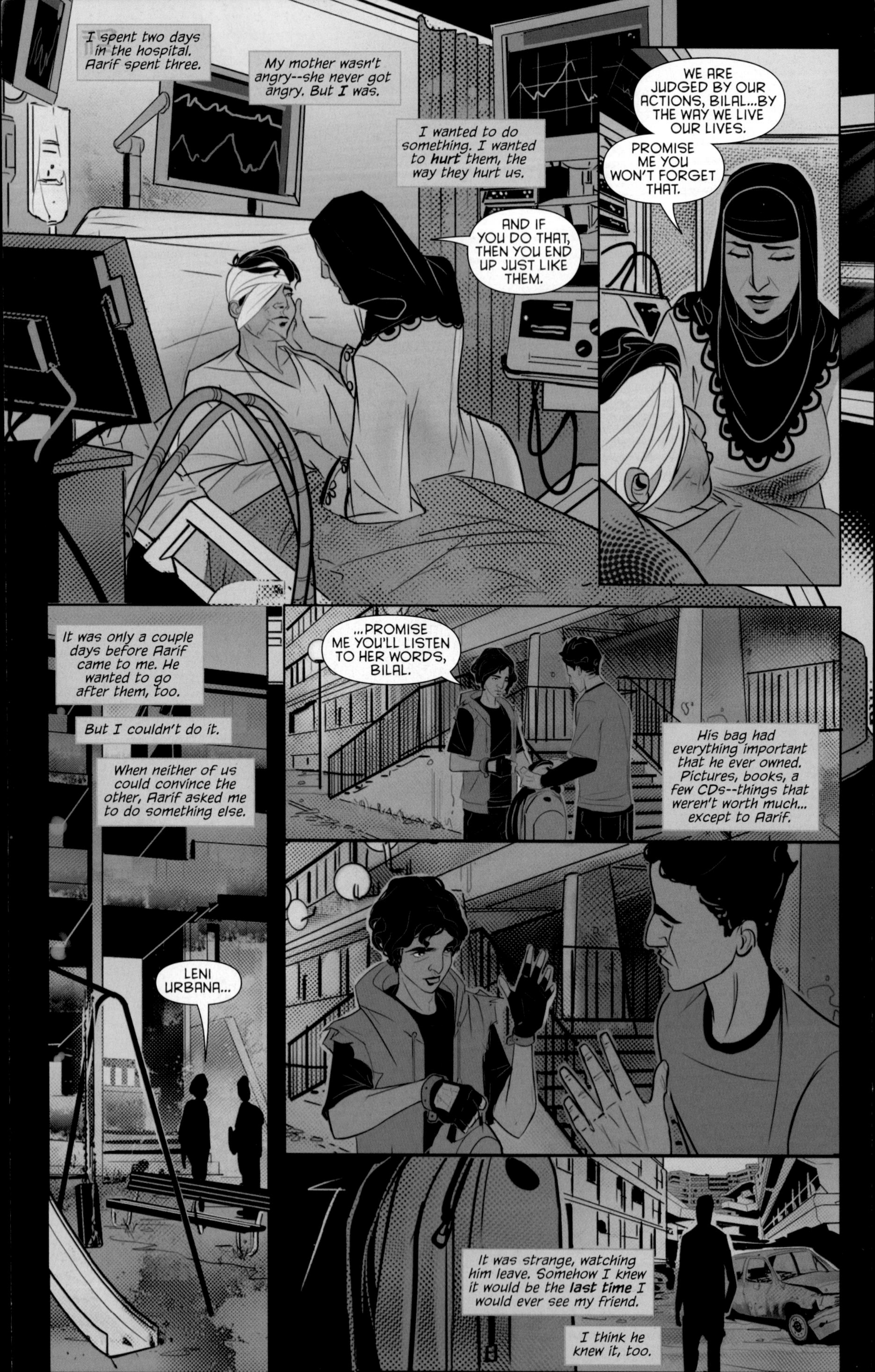
I spent two days in the hospital. Aarif spent three.
My mother wasn't angry--she never got angry. But I was.
I wanted to do something. I wanted to hurt them, the way they hurt us.
AND IF YOU DO THAT, THEN YOU END UP JUST LIKE THEM.
WE ARE JUDGED BY OUR ACTIONS, BILAL...BY THE WAY WE LIVE OUR LIVES.
PROMISE ME YOU WON'T FORGET THAT.
It was only a couple days before Aarif came to me. He wanted to go after them, too.
But I couldn't do it.
When neither of us could convince the other, Aarif asked me to do something else.
LENI URBANA...
...PROMISE ME YOU'LL LISTEN TO HER WORDS, BILAL.
His bag had everything important that he ever owned. Pictures, books, a few CDs--things that weren't worth much... except to Aarif.
It was strange, watching him leave. Somehow I knew it would be the last time I would ever see my friend.
I think he knew it, too.

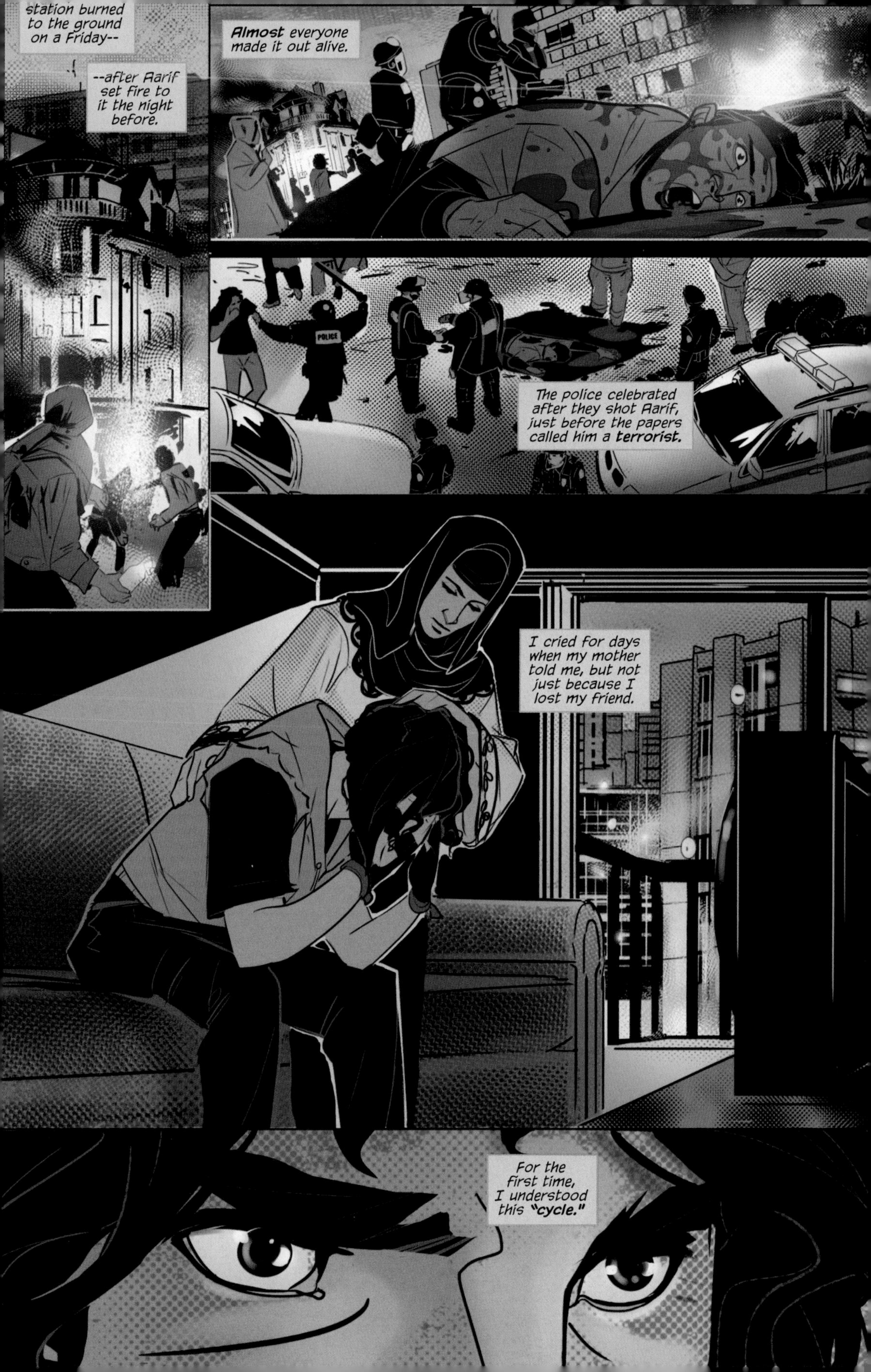
station burned
to the ground
on a Friday--
--after Aarif
set fire to
it the night
before.
Almost everyone
made it out alive.
POLICE
The police celebrated
after they shot Aarif,
just before the papers
called him a terrorist.
I cried for days
when my mother
told me, but not
just because I
lost my friend.
For the
first time,
I understood
this "cycle."

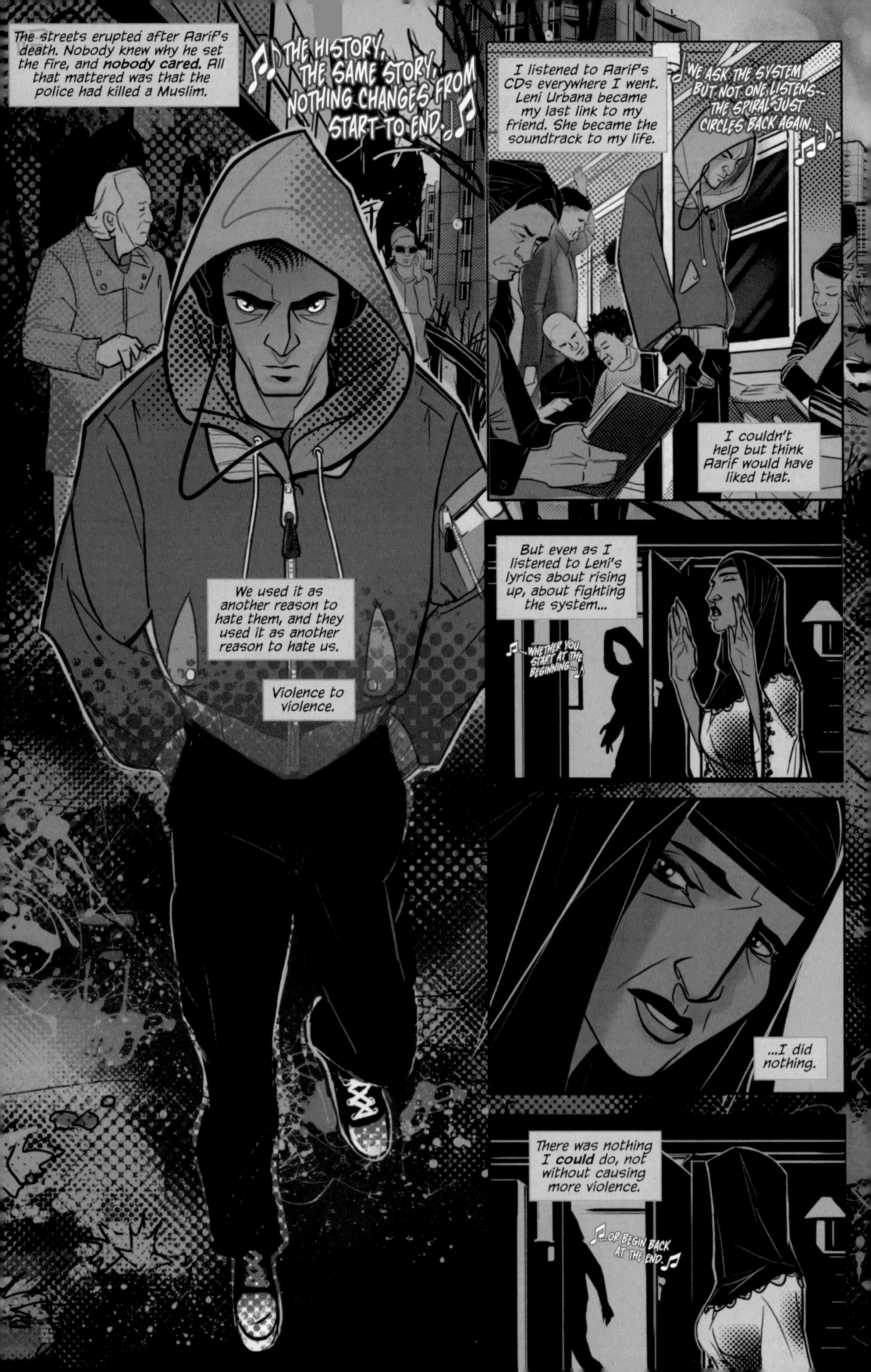

The streets erupted after Aarif's death. Nobody knew why he set the fire, and **nobody cared.** All that mattered was that the police had killed a Muslim.
THE HISTORY, THE SAME STORY, NOTHING CHANGES FROM START TO END.
We used it as another reason to hate them, and they used it as another reason to hate us.
Violence to violence.
I listened to Aarif's CDs everywhere I went. Leni Urbana became my last link to my friend. She became the soundtrack to my life.
WE ASK THE SYSTEM BUT NOT ONE LISTENS-- THE SPIRAL JUST CIRCLES BACK AGAIN...
I couldn't help but think Aarif would have liked that.
But even as I listened to Leni's lyrics about rising up, about fighting the system...
...WHETHER YOU START AT THE BEGINNING...
...I did nothing.
There was nothing I **could** do, not without causing more violence.
...OR BEGIN BACK AT THE END.

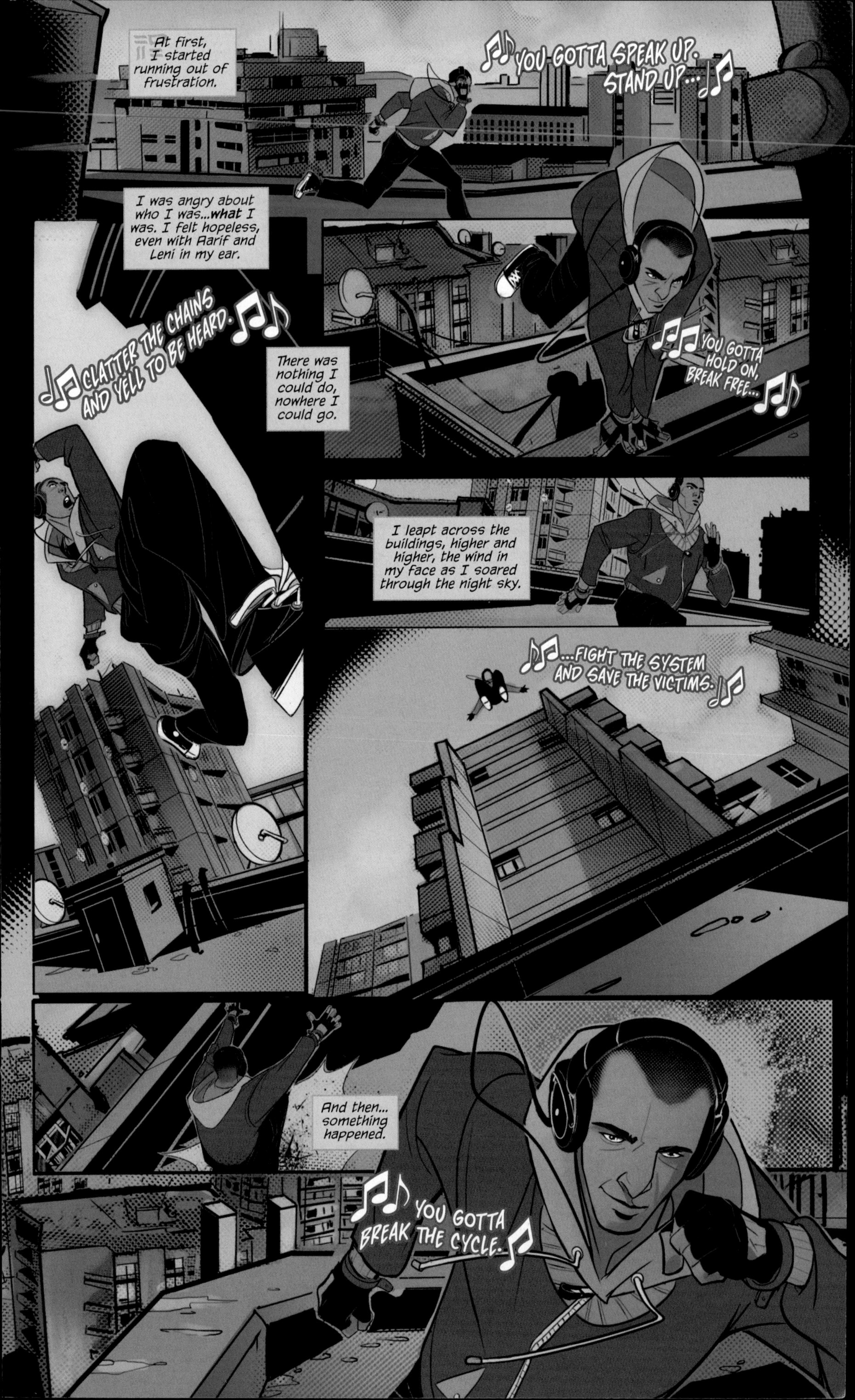
At first, I started running out of frustration.
♫♪ YOU GOTTA SPEAK UP. STAND UP... ♩♫
I was angry about who I was...**what** I was. I felt hopeless, even with Aarif and Leni in my ear.
♫♫ YOU GOTTA HOLD ON, BREAK FREE... ♫♪
♩♫ CLATTER THE CHAINS AND YELL TO BE HEARD. ♫♪
There was nothing I could do, nowhere I could go.
I leapt across the buildings, higher and higher, the wind in my face as I soared through the night sky.
♫♫ ...FIGHT THE SYSTEM AND SAVE THE VICTIMS. ♩♫
And then... something happened.
♫♪ YOU GOTTA BREAK THE CYCLE. ♫

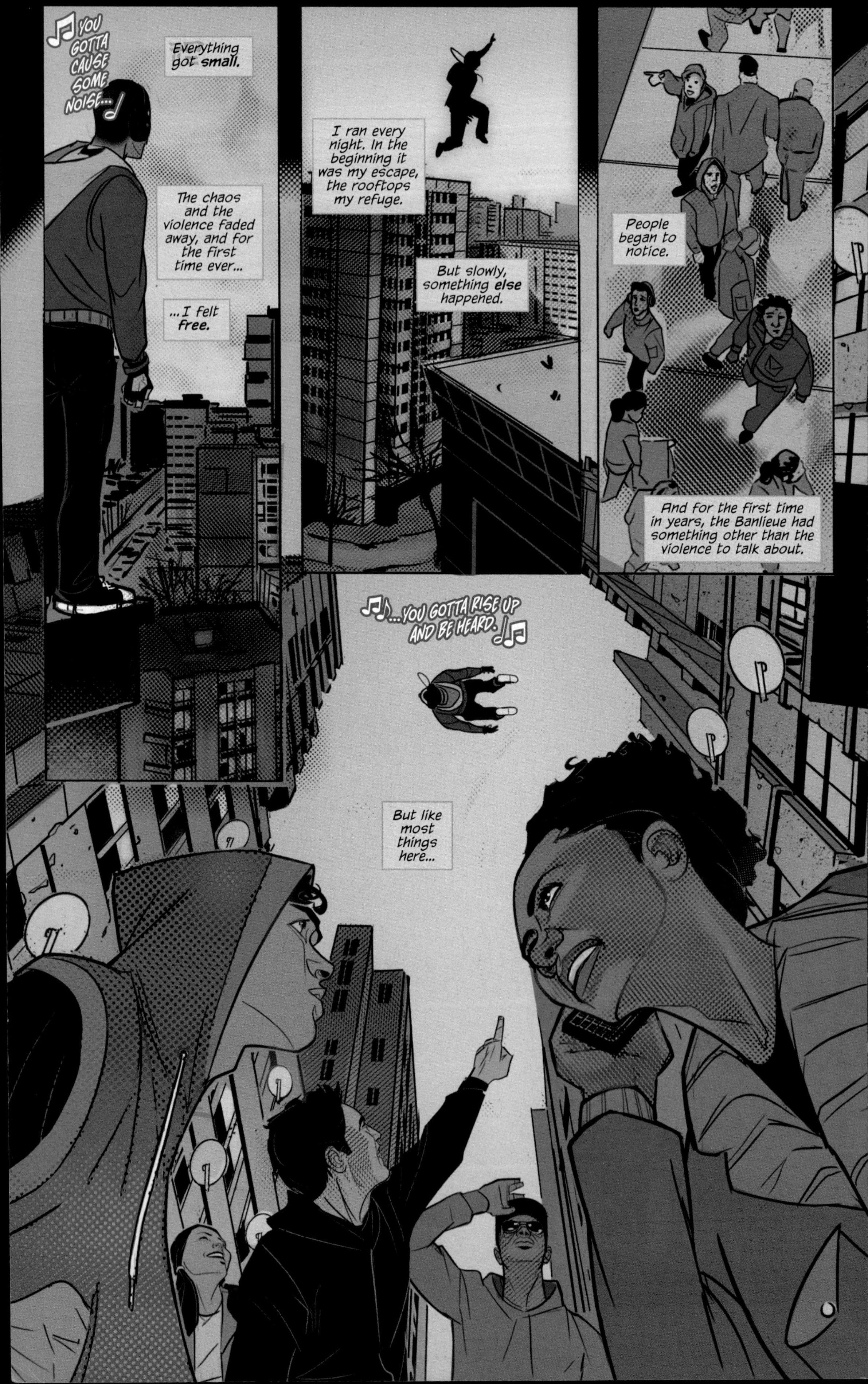
♫ YOU GOTTA CAUSE SOME NOISE... ♩
Everything got small.
The chaos and the violence faded away, and for the first time ever...
...I felt free.
I ran every night. In the beginning it was my escape, the rooftops my refuge.
But slowly, something else happened.
People began to notice.
And for the first time in years, the Banlieue had something other than the violence to talk about.
♫♪...YOU GOTTA RISE UP AND BE HEARD. ♩♫
But like most things here...

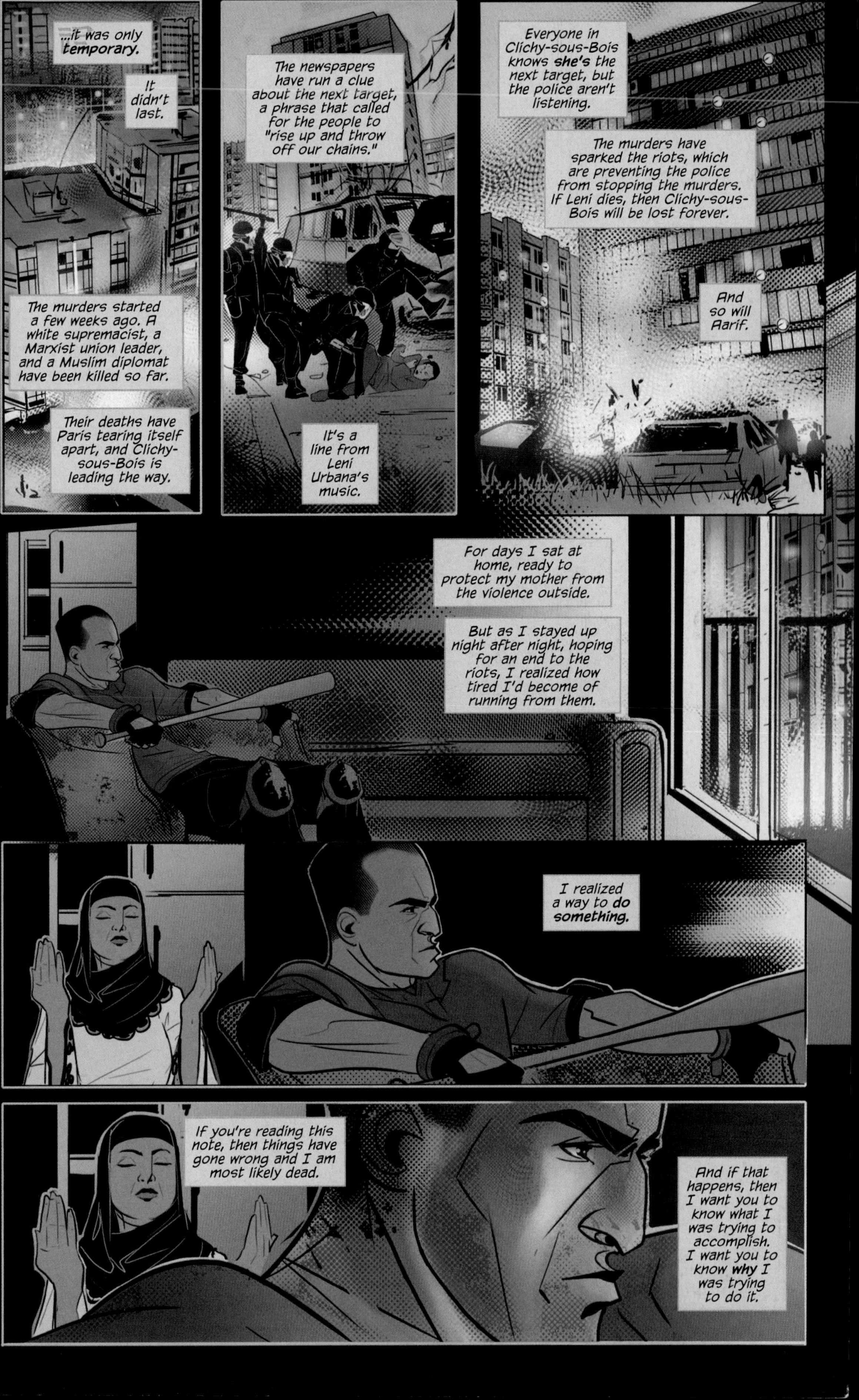

...it was only **temporary.**
It didn't last.
The murders started a few weeks ago. A white supremacist, a Marxist union leader, and a Muslim diplomat have been killed so far.
Their deaths have Paris tearing itself apart, and Clichy-sous-Bois is leading the way.
The newspapers have run a clue about the next target, a phrase that called for the people to "rise up and throw off our chains."
It's a line from Leni Urbana's music.
Everyone in Clichy-sous-Bois knows **she's** the next target, but the police aren't listening.
The murders have sparked the riots, which are preventing the police from stopping the murders. If Leni dies, then Clichy-sous-Bois will be lost forever.
And so will Aarif.
For days I sat at home, ready to protect my mother from the violence outside.
But as I stayed up night after night, hoping for an end to the riots, I realized how tired I'd become of running from them.
I realized a way to **do something.**
If you're reading this note, then things have gone wrong and I am most likely dead.
And if that happens, then I want you to know what I was trying to accomplish. I want you to know **why** I was trying to do it.

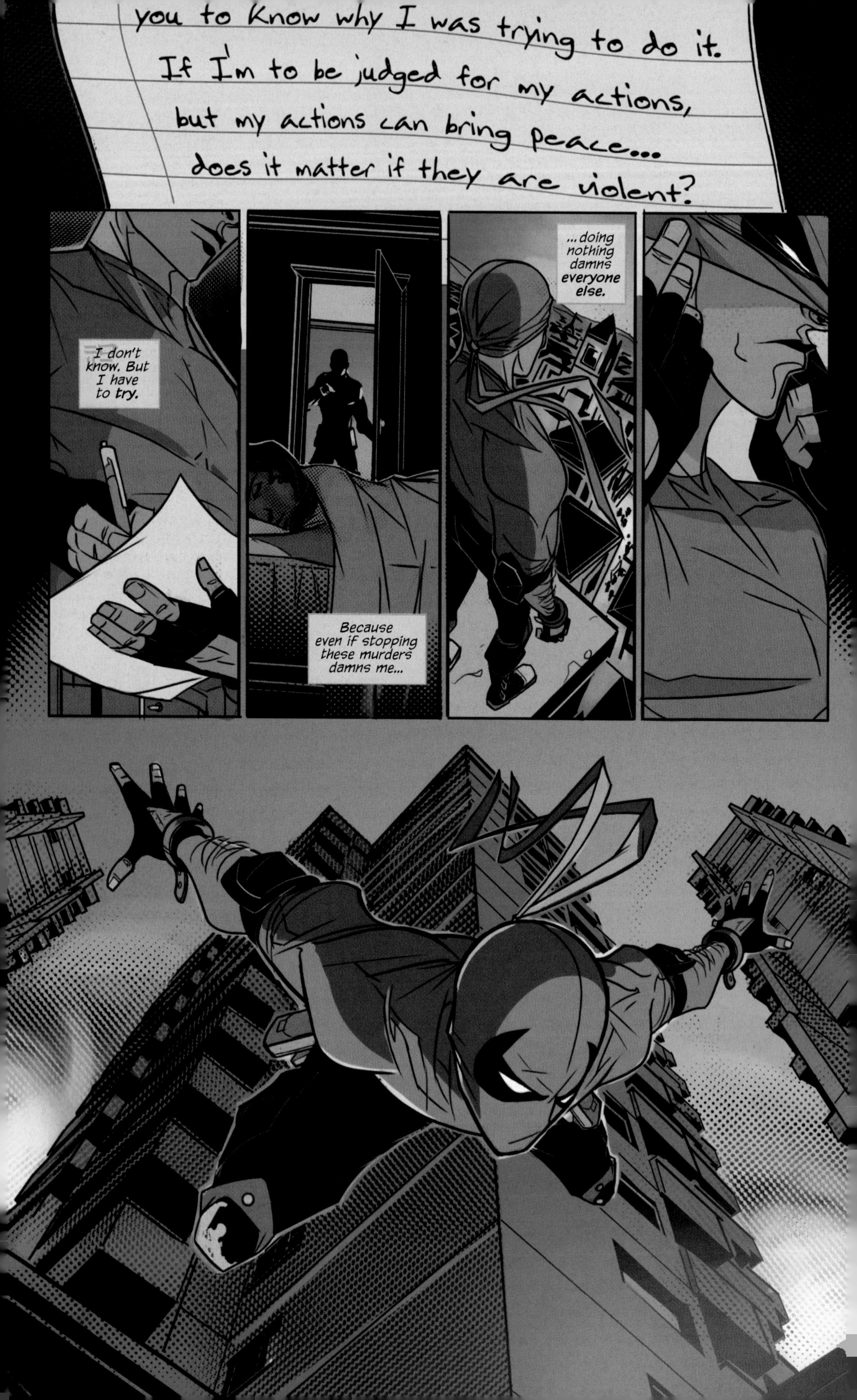
you to know why I was trying to do it.
If I'm to be judged for my actions,
but my actions can bring peace...
does it matter if they are violent?
I don't know. But I have to try.
Because even if stopping these murders damns me...
...doing nothing damns everyone else.

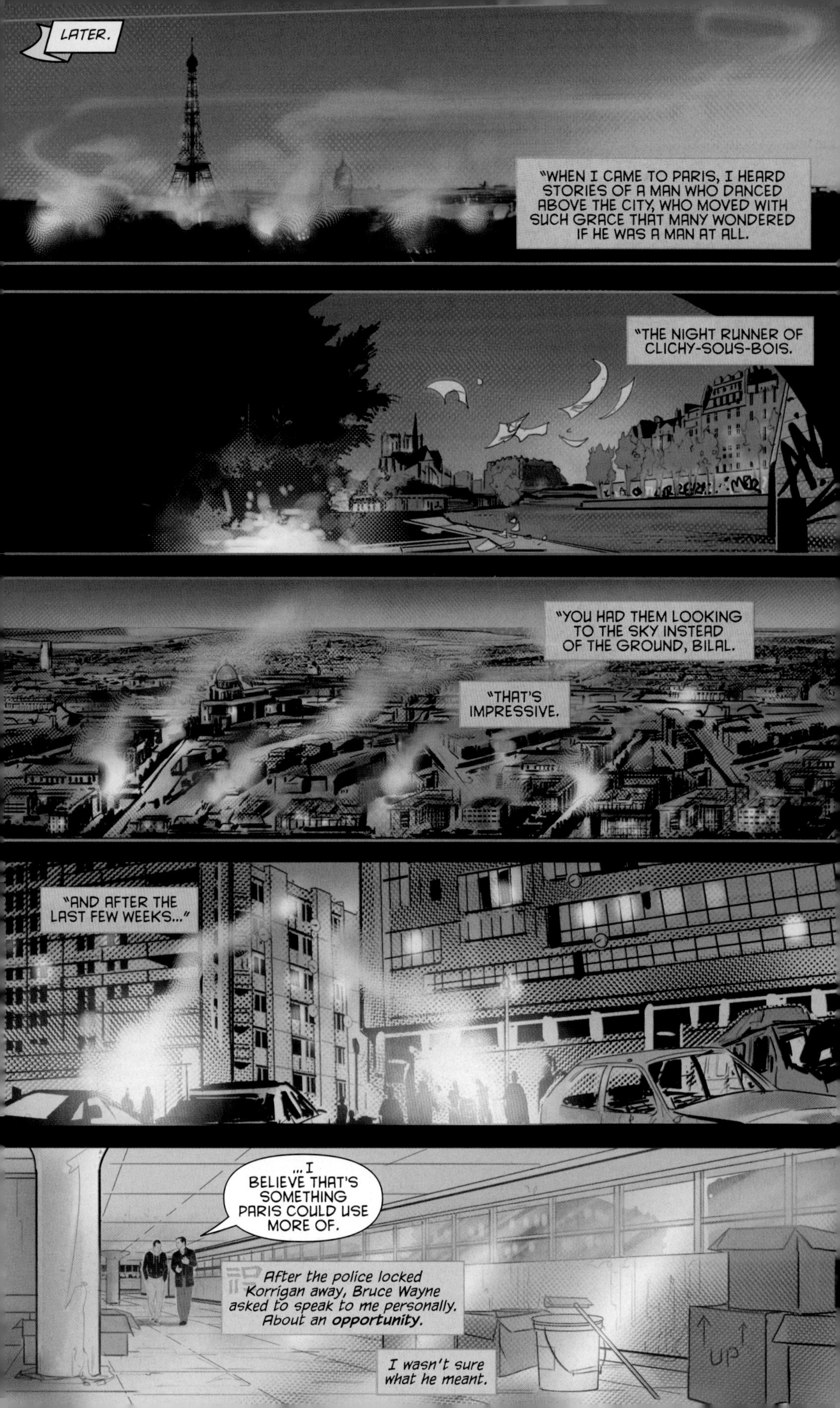
LATER.
"WHEN I CAME TO PARIS, I HEARD STORIES OF A MAN WHO DANCED ABOVE THE CITY, WHO MOVED WITH SUCH GRACE THAT MANY WONDERED IF HE WAS A MAN AT ALL.
"THE NIGHT RUNNER OF CLICHY-SOUS-BOIS.
"YOU HAD THEM LOOKING TO THE SKY INSTEAD OF THE GROUND, BILAL.
"THAT'S IMPRESSIVE.
"AND AFTER THE LAST FEW WEEKS..."
...I BELIEVE THAT'S SOMETHING PARIS COULD USE MORE OF.
After the police locked Korrigan away, Bruce Wayne asked to speak to me personally. About an **opportunity**.
I wasn't sure what he meant.
UP

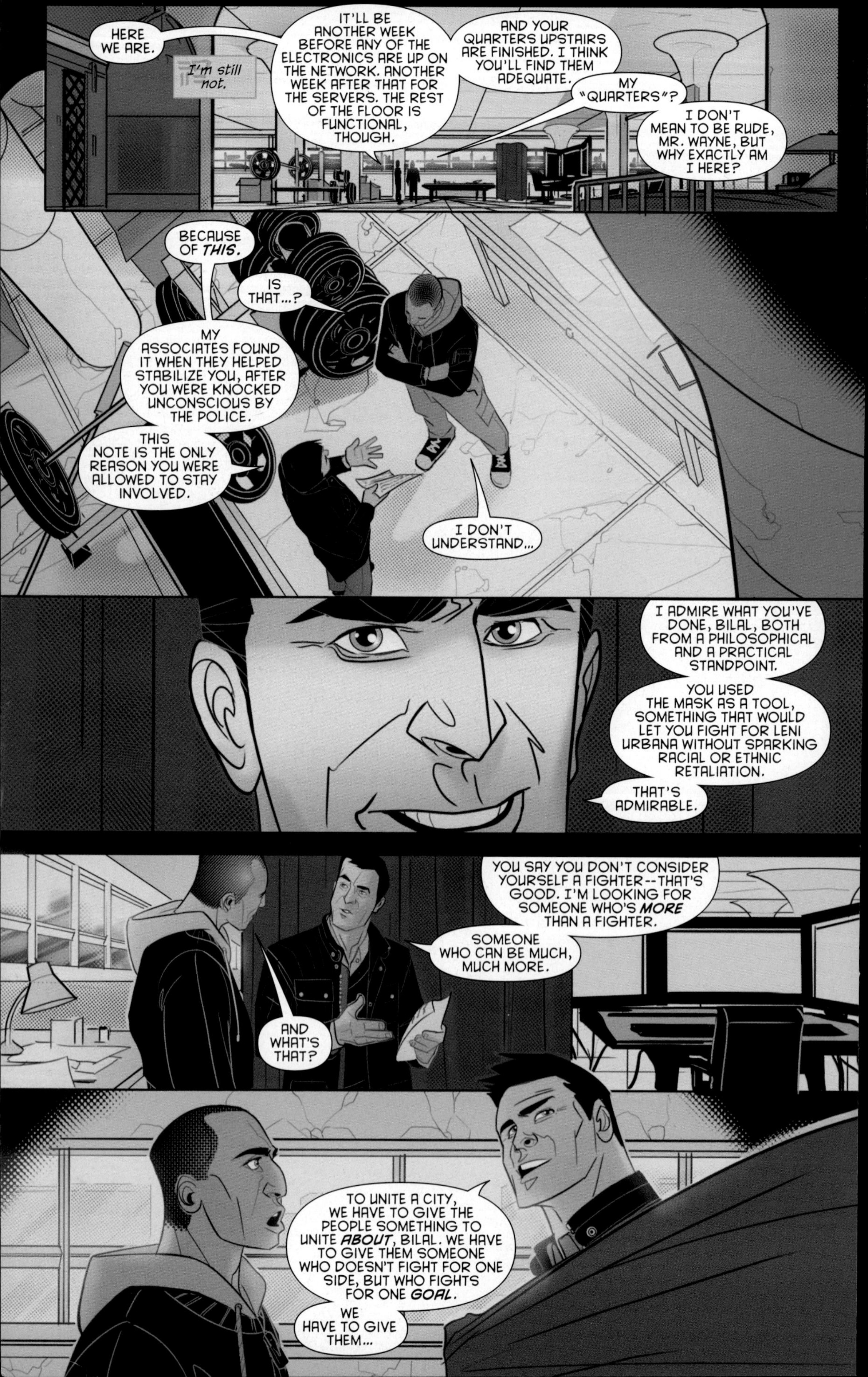
HERE WE ARE.
I'm still not.
IT'LL BE ANOTHER WEEK BEFORE ANY OF THE ELECTRONICS ARE UP ON THE NETWORK. ANOTHER WEEK AFTER THAT FOR THE SERVERS. THE REST OF THE FLOOR IS FUNCTIONAL, THOUGH.
AND YOUR QUARTERS UPSTAIRS ARE FINISHED. I THINK YOU'LL FIND THEM ADEQUATE.
MY "QUARTERS"?
I DON'T MEAN TO BE RUDE, MR. WAYNE, BUT WHY EXACTLY AM I HERE?
BECAUSE OF THIS.
IS THAT...?
MY ASSOCIATES FOUND IT WHEN THEY HELPED STABILIZE YOU, AFTER YOU WERE KNOCKED UNCONSCIOUS BY THE POLICE.
THIS NOTE IS THE ONLY REASON YOU WERE ALLOWED TO STAY INVOLVED.
I DON'T UNDERSTAND...
I ADMIRE WHAT YOU'VE DONE, BILAL, BOTH FROM A PHILOSOPHICAL AND A PRACTICAL STANDPOINT.
YOU USED THE MASK AS A TOOL, SOMETHING THAT WOULD LET YOU FIGHT FOR LENI URBANA WITHOUT SPARKING RACIAL OR ETHNIC RETALIATION.
THAT'S ADMIRABLE.
YOU SAY YOU DON'T CONSIDER YOURSELF A FIGHTER--THAT'S GOOD. I'M LOOKING FOR SOMEONE WHO'S MORE THAN A FIGHTER.
SOMEONE WHO CAN BE MUCH, MUCH MORE.
AND WHAT'S THAT?
TO UNITE A CITY, WE HAVE TO GIVE THE PEOPLE SOMETHING TO UNITE ABOUT, BILAL. WE HAVE TO GIVE THEM SOMEONE WHO DOESN'T FIGHT FOR ONE SIDE, BUT WHO FIGHTS FOR ONE GOAL.
WE HAVE TO GIVE THEM...

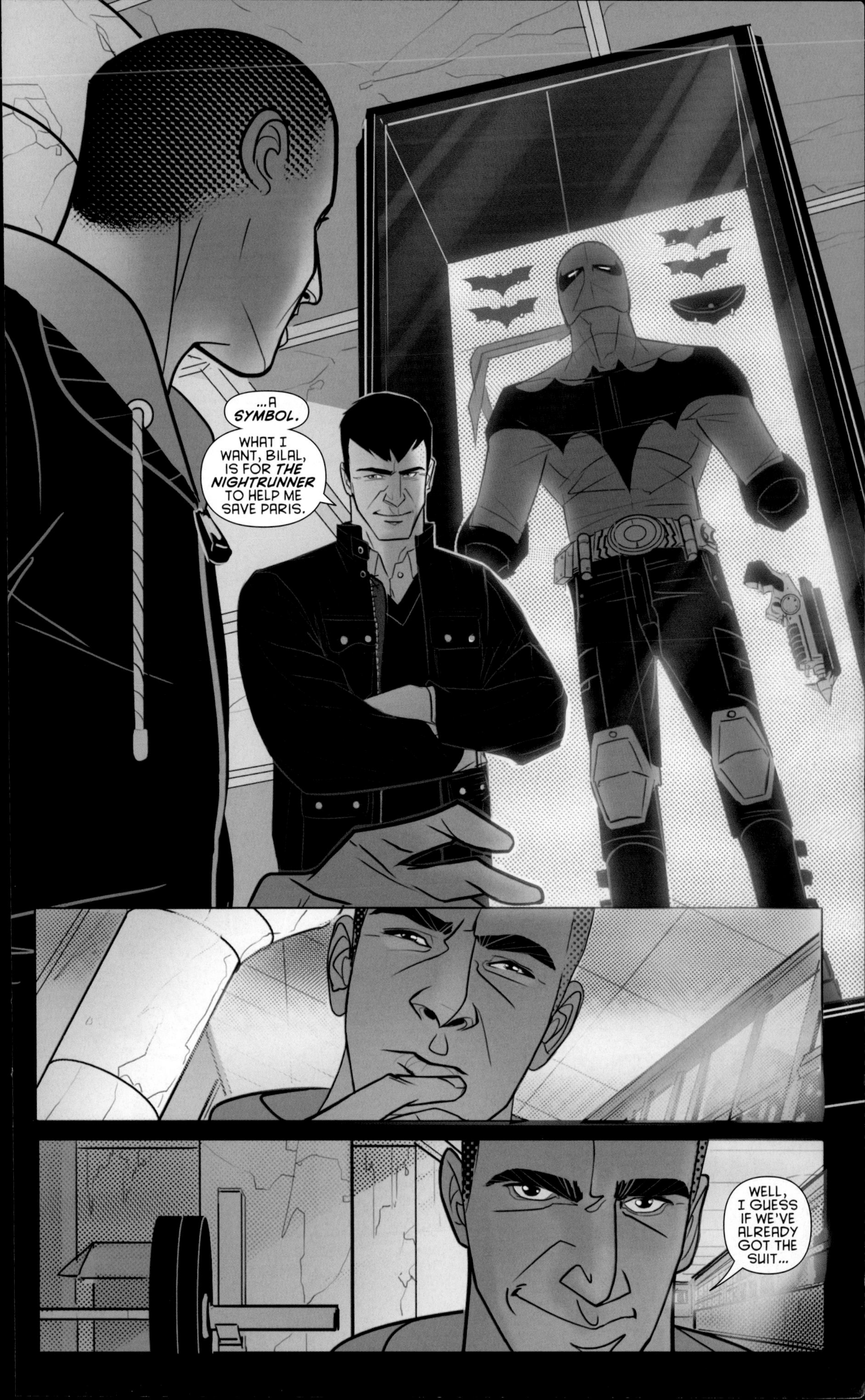
...A *SYMBOL.*
WHAT I WANT, BILAL, IS FOR *THE NIGHTRUNNER* TO HELP ME SAVE PARIS.
WELL, I GUESS IF WE'VE ALREADY GOT THE SUIT...

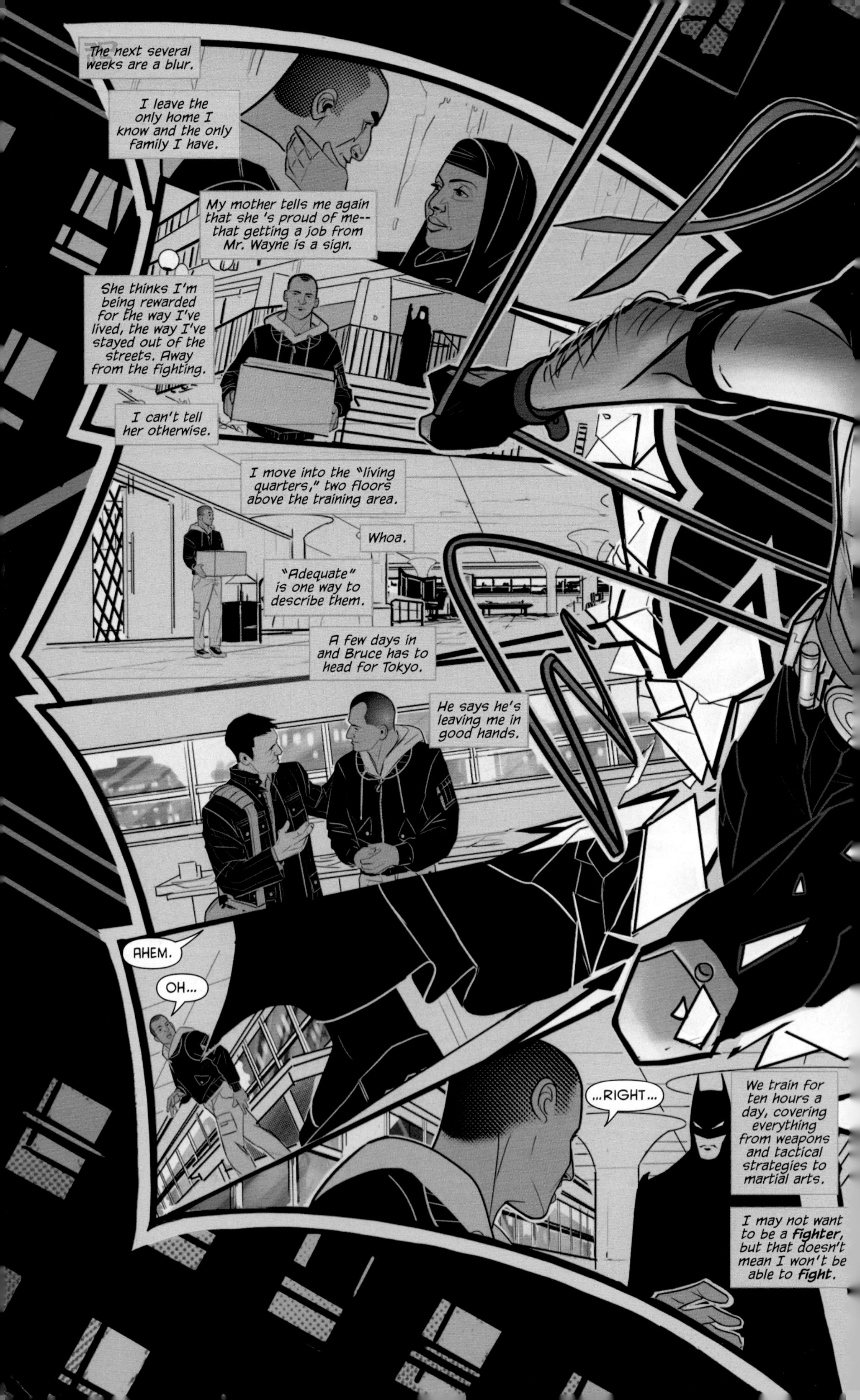
The next several weeks are a blur.
I leave the only home I know and the only family I have.
My mother tells me again that she 's proud of me--that getting a job from Mr. Wayne is a sign.
She thinks I'm being rewarded for the way I've lived, the way I've stayed out of the streets. Away from the fighting.
I can't tell her otherwise.
I move into the "living quarters," two floors above the training area.
Whoa.
"Adequate" is one way to describe them.
A few days in and Bruce has to head for Tokyo.
He says he's leaving me in good hands.
AHEM.
OH...
...RIGHT...
We train for ten hours a day, covering everything from weapons and tactical strategies to martial arts.
I may not want to be a **fighter**, but that doesn't mean I won't be able to **fight**.

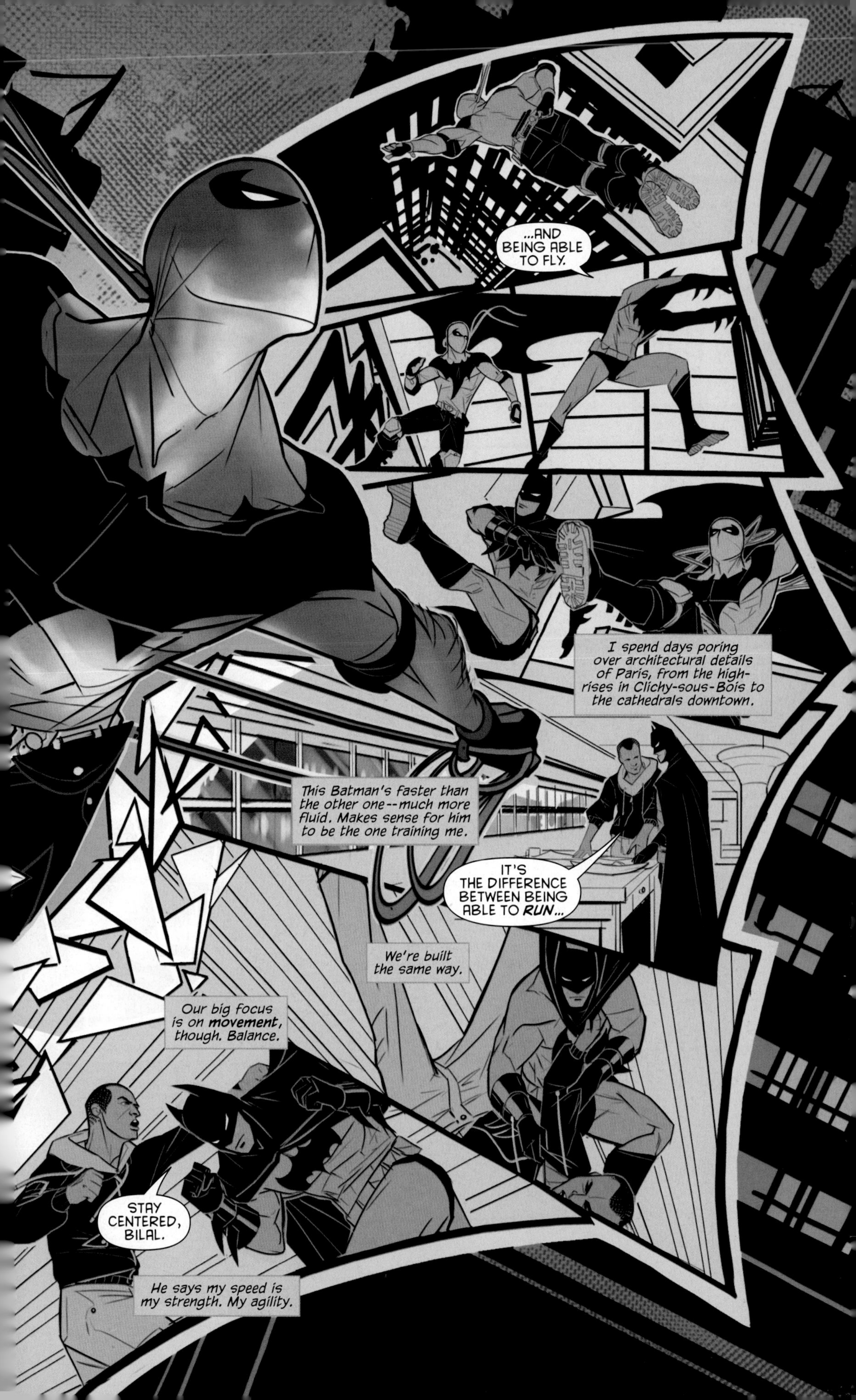

...AND BEING ABLE TO FLY.
I spend days poring over architectural details of Paris, from the high-rises in Clichy-sous-Bois to the cathedrals downtown.
This Batman's faster than the other one--much more fluid. Makes sense for him to be the one training me.
IT'S THE DIFFERENCE BETWEEN BEING ABLE TO RUN...
We're built the same way.
Our big focus is on movement, though. Balance.
STAY CENTERED, BILAL.
He says my speed is my strength. My agility.

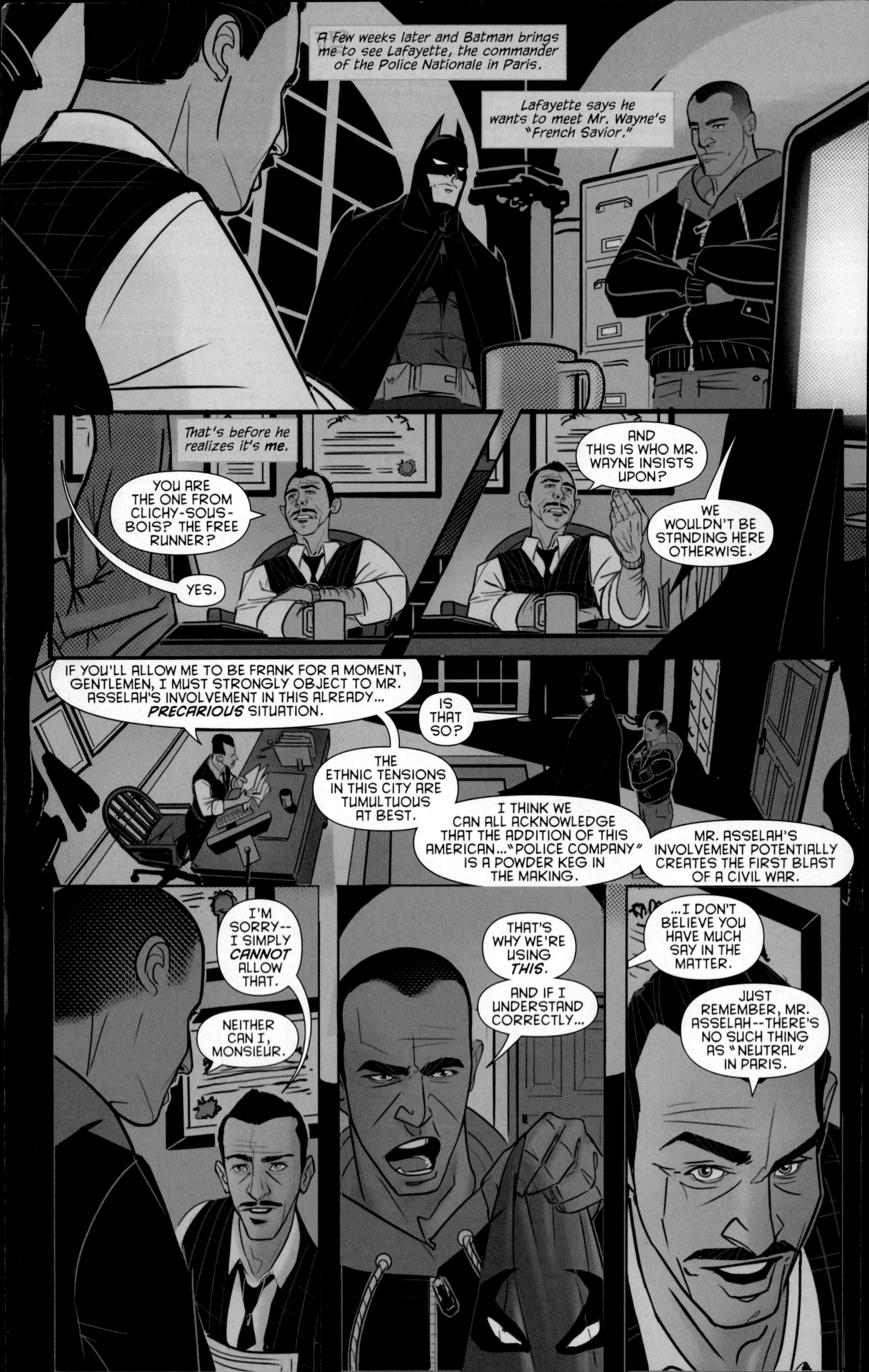
A few weeks later and Batman brings me to see Lafayette, the commander of the Police Nationale in Paris.
Lafayette says he wants to meet Mr. Wayne's "French Savior."
That's before he realizes it's me.
YOU ARE THE ONE FROM CLICHY-SOUS-BOIS? THE FREE RUNNER?
YES.
AND THIS IS WHO MR. WAYNE INSISTS UPON?
WE WOULDN'T BE STANDING HERE OTHERWISE.
IF YOU'LL ALLOW ME TO BE FRANK FOR A MOMENT, GENTLEMEN, I MUST STRONGLY OBJECT TO MR. ASSELAH'S INVOLVEMENT IN THIS ALREADY... PRECARIOUS SITUATION.
IS THAT SO?
THE ETHNIC TENSIONS IN THIS CITY ARE TUMULTUOUS AT BEST.
I THINK WE CAN ALL ACKNOWLEDGE THAT THE ADDITION OF THIS AMERICAN..."POLICE COMPANY" IS A POWDER KEG IN THE MAKING.
MR. ASSELAH'S INVOLVEMENT POTENTIALLY CREATES THE FIRST BLAST OF A CIVIL WAR.
I'M SORRY-- I SIMPLY CANNOT ALLOW THAT.
NEITHER CAN I, MONSIEUR.
THAT'S WHY WE'RE USING THIS.
AND IF I UNDERSTAND CORRECTLY...
...I DON'T BELIEVE YOU HAVE MUCH SAY IN THE MATTER.
JUST REMEMBER, MR. ASSELAH--THERE'S NO SUCH THING AS "NEUTRAL" IN PARIS.

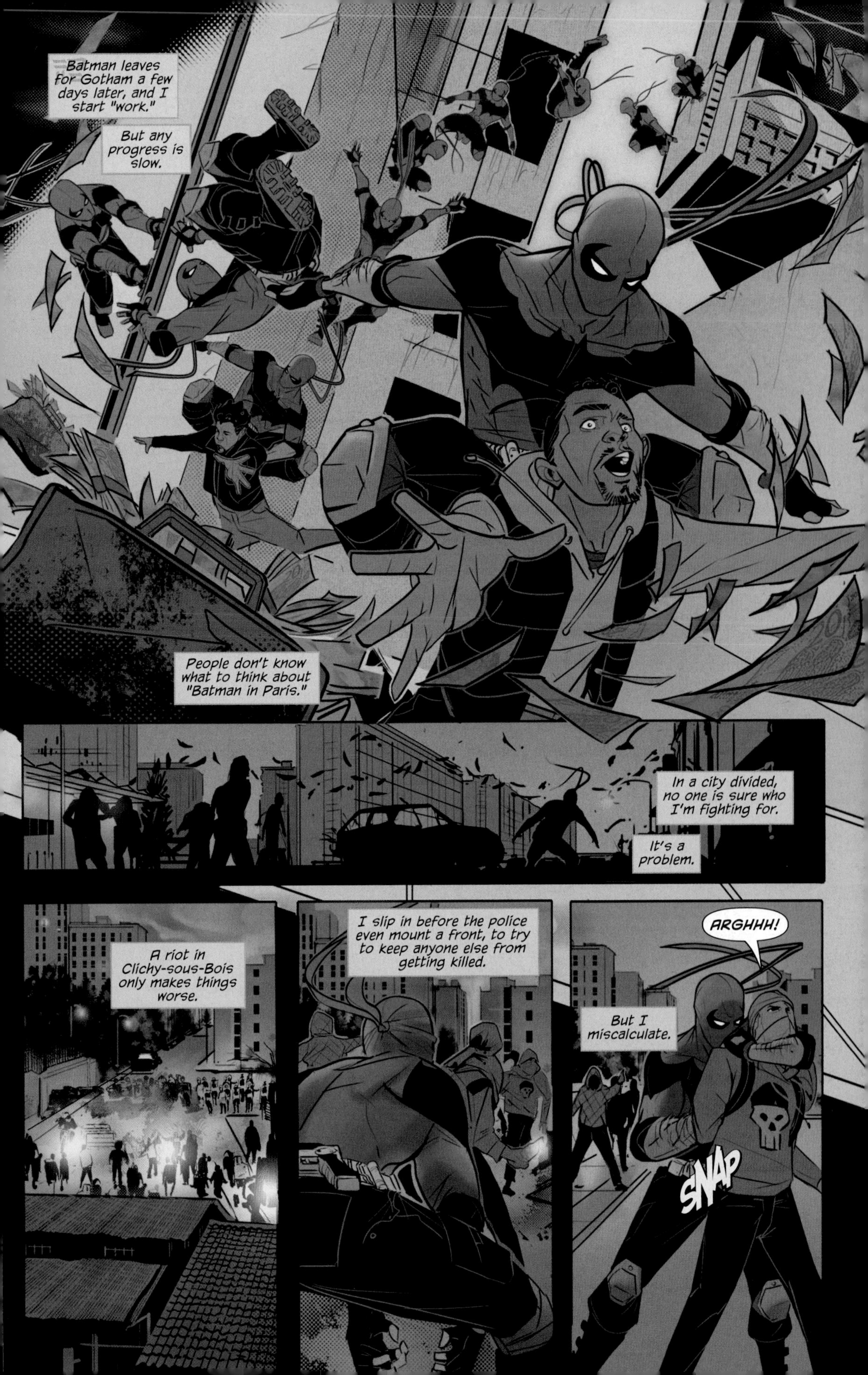

Batman leaves for Gotham a few days later, and I start "work."
But any progress is slow.
People don't know what to think about "Batman in Paris."
In a city divided, no one is sure who I'm fighting for.
It's a problem.
A riot in Clichy-sous-Bois only makes things worse.
I slip in before the police even mount a front, to try to keep anyone else from getting killed.
ARGHHH!
But I miscalculate.
SNAP

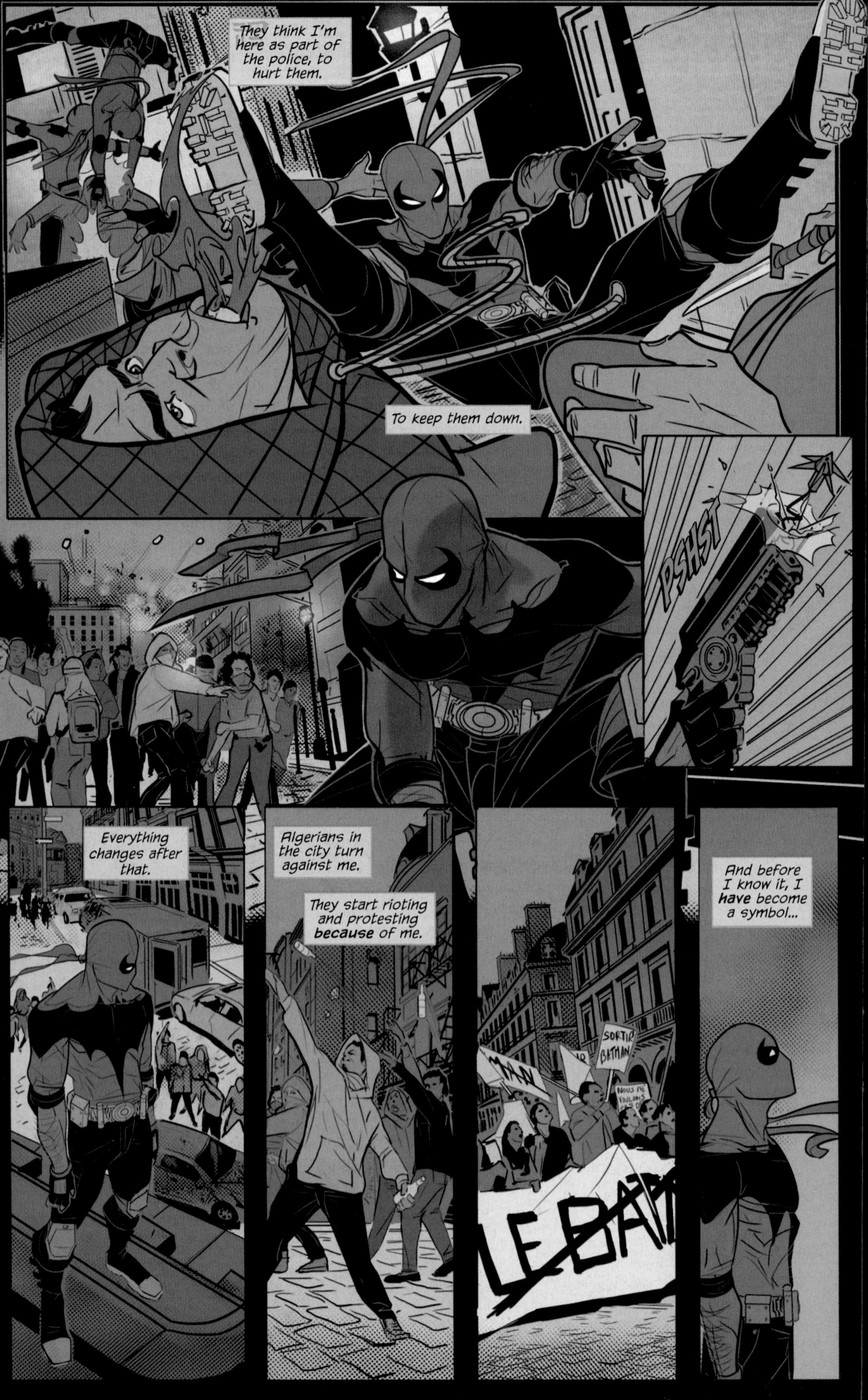
They think I'm here as part of the police, to hurt them.
To keep them down.
PSHST
Everything changes after that.
Algerians in the city turn against me.
They start rioting and protesting **because** of me.
SORTIR BATMAN
And before I know it, I **have** become a symbol...

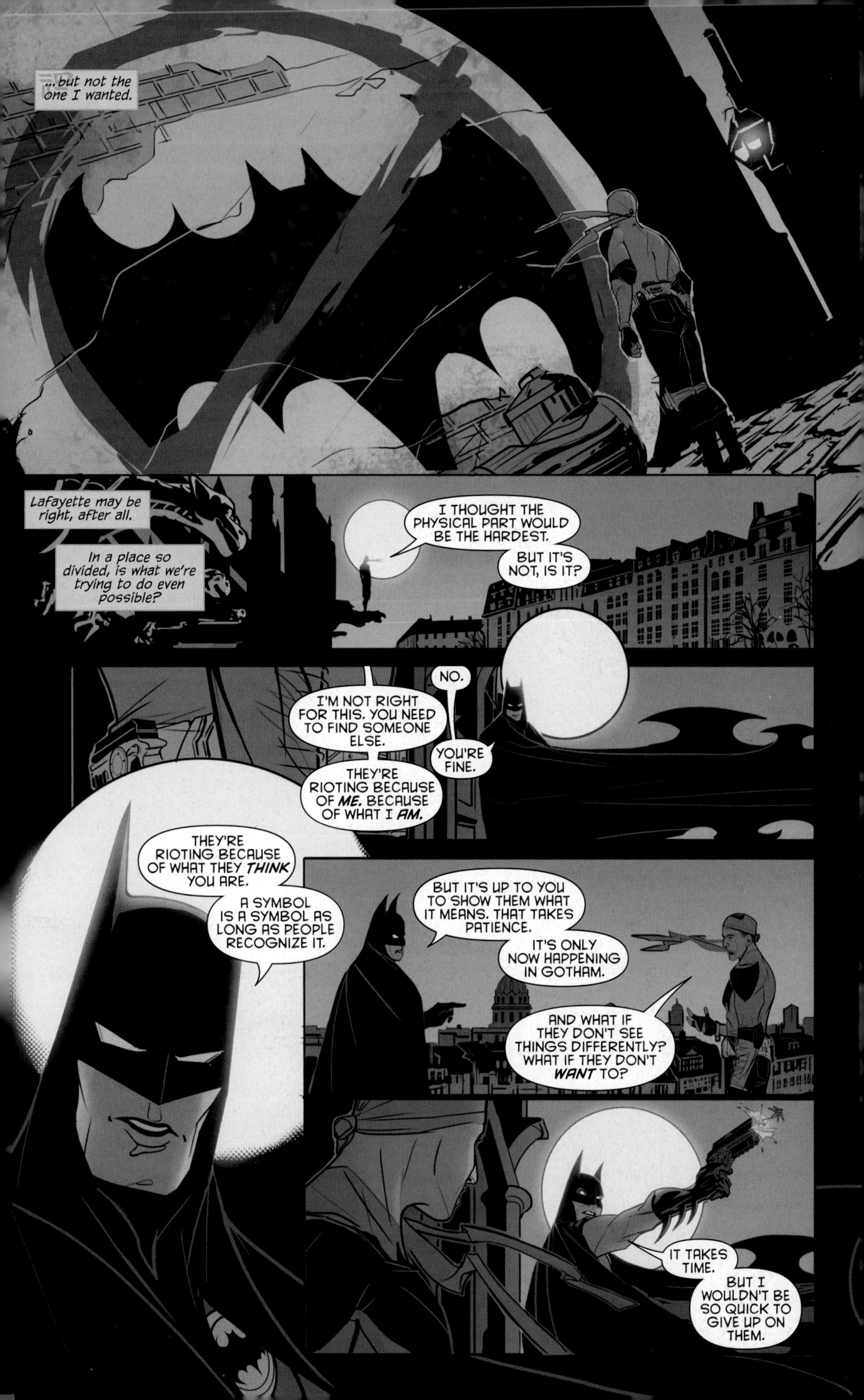
...but not the one I wanted.
Lafayette may be right, after all.
In a place so divided, is what we're trying to do even possible?
I THOUGHT THE PHYSICAL PART WOULD BE THE HARDEST.
BUT IT'S NOT, IS IT?
I'M NOT RIGHT FOR THIS. YOU NEED TO FIND SOMEONE ELSE.
THEY'RE RIOTING BECAUSE OF ME. BECAUSE OF WHAT I AM.
NO.
YOU'RE FINE.
THEY'RE RIOTING BECAUSE OF WHAT THEY THINK YOU ARE.
A SYMBOL IS A SYMBOL AS LONG AS PEOPLE RECOGNIZE IT.
BUT IT'S UP TO YOU TO SHOW THEM WHAT IT MEANS. THAT TAKES PATIENCE.
IT'S ONLY NOW HAPPENING IN GOTHAM.
AND WHAT IF THEY DON'T SEE THINGS DIFFERENTLY? WHAT IF THEY DON'T WANT TO?
IT TAKES TIME.
BUT I WOULDN'T BE SO QUICK TO GIVE UP ON THEM.

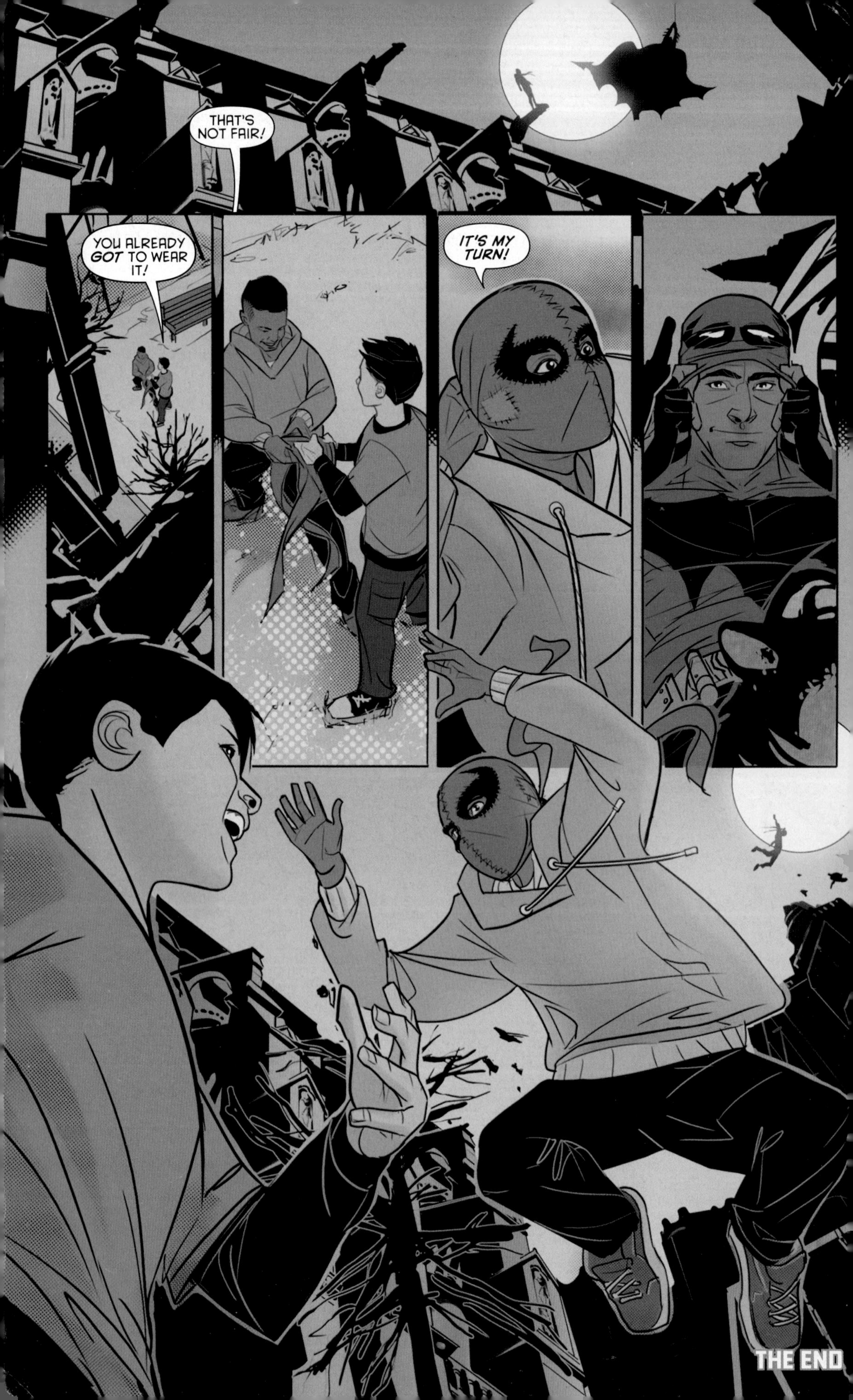
THAT'S NOT FAIR!
YOU ALREADY *GOT* TO WEAR IT!
IT'S MY TURN!
THE END